MODERN NOVELISTS

General Editor: Norman Page

MODERN NOVELISTS

Published titles

MARGARET ATWOOD   Coral Ann Howells
SAUL BELLOW   Peter Hyland
ALBERT CAMUS   Philip Thody
FYODOR DOSTOEVSKY   Peter Conradi
GEORGE ELIOT   Alan W. Bellringer
WILLIAM FAULKNER   David Dowling
GUSTAVE FLAUBERT   David Roe
E. M. FORSTER   Norman Page
ANDRÉ GIDE   David Walker
WILLIAM GOLDING   James Gindin
GRAHAM GREENE   Neil McEwan
ERNEST HEMINGWAY   Peter Messent
CHRISTOPHER ISHERWOOD   Stephen Wade
HENRY JAMES   Alan W. Bellringer
JAMES JOYCE   Richard Brown
D. H. LAWRENCE   G. M. Hyde
ROSAMOND LEHMANN   Judy Simons
DORIS LESSING   Ruth Whittaker
MALCOLM LOWRY   Tony Bareham
NORMAN MAILER   Michael K. Glenday
THOMAS MANN   Martin Travers
GABRIEL GARCÍA MÁRQUEZ   Michael Bell
TONI MORRISON   Linden Peach
IRIS MURDOCH   Hilda D. Spear
VLADIMIR NABOKOV   David Rampton
V. S. NAIPAUL   Bruce King
GEORGE ORWELL   Valerie Meyers
ANTHONY POWELL   Neil McEwan
MARCEL PROUST   Philip Thody
BARBARA PYM   Michael Costell
JEAN-PAUL SARTRE   Philip Thody
SIX WOMEN NOVELISTS   Merryn Williams
MURIEL SPARK   Norman Page
MARK TWAIN   Peter Messent
JOHN UPDIKE   Judie Newman
EVELYN WAUGH   Jacqueline McDonnell
H. G. WELLS   Michael Draper
PATRICK WHITE   Mark Williams
VIRGINIA WOOLF   Edward Bishop

Forthcoming titles

SIMONE DE BEAUVOIR   Terry Keefe
IVY COMPTON-BURNETT   Janet Godden
JOSEPH CONRAD   Owen Knowles
JOHN FOWLES   James Acheson
FRANZ KAFKA   Ronald Speirs and Beatrice Sandberg
SALMAN RUSHDIE   D. C. R. A. Goonetilleke
ALICE WALKER   Maria Lauret

MODERN NOVELISTS

MARGARET ATWOOD

Coral Ann Howells

St. Martin's Press   New York

MARGARET ATWOOD

St. Martin's Press, Scholarly and Reference Division,
175 Fifth Avenue, New York, N. Y. 10010

First published in the United States of America in 1995
ISBN 0–312–12891–6
Printed in Great Britain

Published in Great Britain by Macmillan Press
ISBN 0–333–51915–9 hardcover
ISBN 0–333–51916–7 paperback

Library of Congress Cataloging-in-Publication Data
Howells, Coral Ann.
Margaret Atwood / Coral Ann Howells.
p. cm. — (Modern novelists)
Includes bibliographical references and index.
ISBN 0–312–12891–6
1. Atwood, Margaret Eleanor, 1939– —Criticism and interpretation.
2. Women and literature—Canada—History—20th century. 3.
Canada–
–In literature. I. Title. II. Series.
PR9199.3.A8Z695 1996
818'.5409—dc20   95–24442
                                          CIP

First edition 1995
10 9 8 7 6 5 4 3 2

For Robin, Phoebe and Miranda

Contents

Acknowledgements

This book is the product of my sustained attention to Margaret Atwood's fiction since the early 1980s and of my attempts to understand the dynamics which underlie all her writing. During that period I have given many lectures and conference papers and have written many essays on her work, with the result that several of the chapters in this book are, inevitably, the reworkings of earlier versions (some published, some unpublished) where I hope I have clarified my understanding of crucial issues. My admiration for Atwood's total achievement has continued to grow, together with my urgent curiosity to know what she will write next. This experience of 'growing into an Atwood reader' is one that I know is shared by an increasing number both in Canada and internationally, and it is for such readers that I have written this book.

To keep the record straight, my thanks are due to the following: to the *British Journal of Canadian Studies* and to Anansi Press for permission to include materials on the theme of 'Wilderness' that appear in different versions in *British Journal of Canadian Studies*, vol. 9:2 (1994) and in *Various Atwoods* (1995); to Longman York Press for allowing me to incorporate some of the material in my York Notes on *The Handmaid's Tale* (1993); to Macmillan for permission to reproduce with slight modifications my essay on *Cat's Eye* which appeared in *Margaret Atwood: Writing and Subjectivity* (1994). I am particularly grateful to Margaret Atwood for permission to quote from her manuscript materials in the Margaret Atwood Papers, Fisher Rare Book Library, University of Toronto, and to the library staff there who were extraordinarily helpful to me. I am also grateful to the Foundation for Canadian Studies in the United Kingdom and to the University of Reading Research Board for travel assistance on my frequent visits to Canada, and to the Department of English at Reading for an alleviated term's teaching so that I could complete the writing of a substantial part of this book.

Many friends and colleagues have encouraged and listened to me and have offered invaluable critical advice. My special thanks are due to members of the Literature Group of the British Association for Canadian Studies, in particular Lynette Hunter and Shirley Chew, and to Colin Nicholson, John Thieme, Annis May Timpson, W. J. Keith and Jay Macpherson. I would also like to thank the students in my undergraduate classes on Canadian women's writing at the University of Reading, and also at the Magistero, University of Messina in Sicily and at SNDT Women's University in Bombay. For generous hospitality in Canada once again I thank Paula Bourne in Toronto and Linda Marshall in Guelph. I am also very grateful to Maisie Collard who typed this book so impeccably from my almost indecipherable script; to Vivien Hughes, Michael Regan and Elizabeth Richie of the Canadian High Commission in London for their assistance in selecting the cover picture; and to Margaret Bartley my editor, for her enthusiasm and patience. Finally, my best thanks as always to my husband and daughters, Robin, Phoebe and Miranda.

The author and publishers wish to thank the following for permission to use copyright-material:

Random House UK Ltd, McClelland and Stewart, Toronto, and Phoebe Larmore on behalf of the author, for the extracts from Margaret Atwood, *The Handmaid's Tale* (Jonathan Cape, 1983) and Margaret Atwood, *Bodily Harm* (Jonathan Cape, 1982);

Times Newspapers Ltd, for the extracts from a review by Philip Howard, *The Times*, 14 March 1980; copyright © Times Supplements Ltd, 1980;

Virago Press Ltd and Phoebe Larmore on behalf of the author, for the extracts from Earl E. Ingersoll (ed.), *Margaret Atwood: Conversations* (1992).

Every effort has been made to trace all the copyright-holders, but if any have been inadvertently overlooked the publishers will be pleased to make the necessary arrangement at the first opportunity.

General Editor's Preface

The death of the novel has often been announced, and part of the secret of its obstinate vitality must be its capacity for growth, adaptation, self-renewal and self-transformation: like some vigorous organism in a speeded-up Darwinian ecosystem, it adapts itself quickly to a changing world. War and revolution, economic crisis and social change, radically new ideologies such as Marxism and Freudianism, have made this century unprecedented in human history in the speed and extent of change, but the novel has shown an extraordinary capacity to find new forms and techniques and to accommodate new ideas and conceptions of human nature and human experience, and even to take up new positions on the nature of fiction itself.

In the generations immediately preceding and following 1914, the novel underwent a radical redefinition of its nature and possibilities. The present series of monographs is devoted to the novelists who created the modern novel and to those who, in their turn, either continued and extended, or reacted against and rejected, the traditions established during that period of intense exploration and experiment. It includes a number of those who lived and wrote in the nineteenth century but whose innovative contribution to the art of fiction makes it impossible to ignore them in any account of the origins of the modern novel; it also includes the so-called 'modernists' and those who in the mid- and late twentieth century have emerged as outstanding practitioners of this genre. The scope is, inevitably, international; not only, in the migratory and exile-haunted world of our century, do writers, refuse to heed national frontiers – 'English' literature lays claim to Conrad the Pole, Henry James the American, and Joyce the Irishman – but geniuses such as Flaubert, Dostoevsky and Kafka have had an influence on the fiction of many nations.

Each volume in the series is intended to provide an introduction to the fiction of the writer concerned, both for those approaching him or her for the first time and for those who are already familiar with some parts of the achievement in question and now wish to place it in the context of the total *œuvre*. Although essential information relating to the writer's life and times is given, usually in an opening chapter, the approach is primarily critical and the emphasis is not upon 'background' or generalisations but upon close examination of important texts. Where an author is notably prolific, major texts have been made to convey, more summarily, a sense of the nature and quality of the author's work as a whole. Those who want to read further will find suggestions in the select bibliography included in each volume. Many novelists are, of course, not only novelists but also poets, essayists, biographers, dramatists, travel writers and so forth; many have practised shorter forms of fiction; and many have written letters or kept diaries that constitute a significant part of their literary output. A brief study cannot hope to deal with all these in detail, but where the shorter fiction and the non-fictional writings, public and private, have an important relationship to the novels, some space has been devoted to them.

NORMAN PAGE

1
Fact File and Significant Characteristics

Margaret Atwood's first novel *The Edible Woman* appeared late in 1969, and during 1970 readers in Canada, the United States and Britain were beginning to ask, 'Margaret *who?*' Atwood was known if at all as a young poet who had won an important Canadian literary prize, the Governor General's Award, for *The Circle Game* in 1966. By 1985, when *The Handmaid's Tale* appeared, the reviewer in the *London Review of Books* could claim that Margaret Atwood was 'the most distinguished novelist under fifty currently writing in English',[1] and now twenty five years on from *The Edible Woman* she is an international literary celebrity whose work has been translated into more than twenty languages and published in twenty-five countries. A versatile and prolific writer, Atwood has produced eight novels, ten books of poetry, three short story collections, in addition to an important book of literary criticism and numerous essays and reviews. She has also written two children's books, compiled and illustrated *The Can Lit Food Book*, and is the editor of the *Oxford Book of Canadian Verse in English* and co-editor of the *Oxford Book of Canadian Short Stories in English*. She has not, however, written a biography or an autobiography, and as she said in an interview, deliberately distancing her private self from her public image, 'Don't know that I ever will.'[2]

So what is the secret of Atwood's appeal? An important clue might be found in the comment made by *The Times* reviewer of *Life Before Man* in 1980:

> In spite of the triple handicap of being a token 'feminist' author, a Canadian, and a poet, Margaret Atwood manages to be a true novelist. She opens our eyes to ways in which we think and behave,

irrespectiveof sex and nationality. Life among the dinosaurs may
have been simpler .... But it cannot have been anything like as
interesting.[3]

Life Before Man was the novel that brought international recognition
for Atwood, and *The Times* comment is interesting for a number of
reasons – not least because of its negative qualifications which show
the obstacles Atwood has had to overcome in her literary career.
Ironically, that 'triple handicap' now spells out the distinctive marks
of her fiction. Her writing is grounded in a strong sense of her own
cultural identity as white, English-speaking, Canadian and female;
but she also challenges the limits of such categories, questioning
stereotypes of nationality and gender, exposing cultural fictions and
the artificial limits they impose on our understanding of ourselves
and others as human beings. As she wrote in 1982:

> If writing novels – and reading them – have any redeeming social
> value, it's probably that they force you to imagine what it's like to
> be somebody else.
> Which, increasingly, is something we all need to know.[4]

This leads us back to *The Times* comment on Atwood's being a 'true
novelist' and via the dinosaur reference to the wider parameters of
Atwood's search to find an adequate definition of what it means to
be 'human'. In *Life Before Man* she engages with questions of human
behaviour in relation to history and prehistory, as well as with the
implied threat of human extinction, for 'You aren't and can't be
apart from nature. We're all part of the biological universe: men as
well as women' (*Conversations*, p. 120). The dinosaurs signal an
important fantasy dimension, for alongside her realistic representations of modern Toronto life there exist other imagined worlds
which belong to romance, fairy tale or to her characters' obsessional
private agendas. These may be worlds of escape, but they may also be
fantasies which exist alongside everyday life and which absorb the
neuroses of contemporary Western society. As Atwood remarked,
'Ways of going crazy are culturally determined' (*Conversations*,
p. 114). The social dimensions of Atwood's fiction are always under-
pinned and sometimes undermined by representations of individual
behaviour, for if there is a single distinguishing Atwoodian marker, it
is her insistently ironic vision which challenges her readers' compla-
cent acceptance of easy definitions about anything. As a novelist who
was first and still is a poet with a poet's fascination for the endless

possibilities of language, she also shows the same speculative interest in the possibilities of narrative which she views as fictional space to be opened up beyond the constraints of traditional genre conventions. With their combination of empirical and speculative intelligence, her novels challenge her readers to see more by seeing differently. As the female artist in *Cat's Eye* realises when confronted by her brother's scientific perspective on the world, 'There are, apparently, a great many more dimensions than four.'

Atwood, now in her early fifties, was born in 1939 in Ottawa, Canada. She spent her early childhood moving around in the forests and small settlements of Northern Ontario and Quebec with her parents and her elder brother (her younger sister was born in 1951), for her father was a field entomologist. It was not until after the end of the Second World War that her family settled in Toronto, where her father became a university professor. Atwood went to school there and then on to Victoria College, University of Toronto, where she took an Arts degree with honours in English. During that time she was busy writing and reviewing for her college magazine and designing programmes for the drama society. This visual dimension has remained an important feature of Atwood's work, where 'vision' is often elaborated to include insight and hallucination as well as merely seeing. In 1961, her graduation year, she had her first book of poems published, a collection called *Double Persephone*. But Atwood never felt at home in the city; she says she has always suffered from 'culture shock' after her bush childhood (*Conversations*, p. 121). Her first experience of the United States came when she went on a graduate fellowship to Radcliffe College, Harvard, where she studied Victorian and American literature and began her PhD thesis on 'The English Metaphysical Romance'. It was there that she had another culture shock when she realised that to the Americans Canada was invisible:

> It's not that the Americans I met had any odd or 'upsetting' attitudes toward Canada. They simply didn't have any attitudes at all. They had a vague idea that such a place existed – it was that blank area north of the map where the bad weather came from. (*Conversations*, p. 78)

Atwood's was the common colonial experience of moving to a metropolitan culture where people know nothing and care nothing

about one's home place. Here might be located the roots of
Atwood's Canadian nationalism which developed in the late 1960s
and frequently defined itself against the United States, a position
which she scrutinises in her early 1970s work, *Surfacing* and *Survival.*
Atwood moved back to Canada without finishing her doctorate and
spent the next ten years, her 'Rooming House' years as she describes
them,[5] teaching in university English departments across Canada,
from Vancouver to Montreal and Toronto, making her first trip to
Europe, getting married for the first time, and writing the draft of
her first novel. By 1970 she had won two more poetry prizes: the
Centennial Commission Poetry Competition for *The Animals in That
Country* (1967) and the Union Poetry Prize for five poems from
Procedures for Underground (1969).

   During the 1970s Atwood was extremely productive, publishing
three novels, a book of short stories, five books of poetry, a book of
literary criticism, and a children's book. This was the period when
her national and international reputation was made, and the stages
of her rise to fame make an interesting chronicle, coinciding as they
did with the rise of feminism and a resurgence of cultural nationalism centred on Canada's Centennial Year 1967.[6] *The Edible Woman*
had been welcomed as the best first novel of 1969, where, according
to *The Times* critic in London, 'it stuck out above the rest like a sugar
plum fairy on top of a Christmas cake'.[7] However, Atwood was still
seen as a poet, also as a colonial writer and a feminist. It was really
with the double production in autumn 1972 of her second novel
Surfacing and her literary history *Survival: A Thematic Guide to
Canadian Literature* that she made her first serious claim for critical
attention, though as she recalls, responses varied according to the
different ideological perspectives of her reviewers. While in the
United States, *Surfacing* was reviewed 'almost exclusively as a feminist
or ecological treatise, in Canada it was reviewed almost exclusively as
a nationalistic one' (*Conversations*, p. 117). In Britain where the novel
was published early in 1973, these political implications were of less
importance than its theme of psychological quest, and *The Sunday
Times* reviewer praised it for what has come to be recognised as
Atwood's characteristic doubleness of vision, 'the balance between
the narrator's interior vision and sharp observation of the real world
outside her head'.[8] Her third novel, *Lady Oracle* (1976), 'extravagant,
macabre, and melodramatic', marked the shift to Atwood's decisive
identification as a novelist, and it was welcomed in *Newsweek* as 'the
kind of novel that makes reviewers send out fresh green sprouts'.[9]
Life Before Man (1979) received enthusiastic reviews in the United

States, most notably one by Marilyn French on the front page of the *New York Times Book Review*,[10] and in Britain in *The Times* and *The Times Literary Supplement*.[11] In Canada Atwood was becoming a prominent figure in cultural politics, where she was a founder member of the Writers' Union of Canada, on the editorial board of the newly established Anansi Press in Toronto, and a member of Amnesty International. As she remarked, her involvement with 'political' issues was

> not separate from writing. When you begin to write, you deal with your immediate surroundings; as you grow, your immediate surroundings become larger. There's no contradiction.[12]

She has maintained an active engagement with cultural politics and human rights issues not only in Canada but on the international scene:

> [American interviewer, 1983]: Seemingly, then, you feel a great sense of responsibility as a writer.
> Atwood: No, not as a writer, as a human being.
> (*Conversations,*   p. 163)

As her literary reputation grew she began travelling extensively, reading and lecturing in Britain, Italy, Australia and Afghanistan in the late 1970s. During this period, Atwood, now divorced, met the Ontario novelist Graeme Gibson; their daughter was born in 1976.

In 1980 Atwood moved with her family to Toronto, which has been their permanent home ever since. That combination of high literary productivity, Toronto home life and international travel has continued, with brief periods in the United States as Professor of Creative Writing at several university campuses, and two longish spells living away from Canada – first in England (1983–4) and then in France (1991–2). Her output as novelist, poet, critic and essayist has been prodigious, often at the rate of more than one book per year: in 1981 *True Stories* (poems) and *Bodily Harm* (novel), in 1982 *Second Words: Selected Critical Prose*; in 1983 *Murder in the Dark* (prose poems) and *Bluebeard's Egg* (short stories); in 1984 *Interlunar* (poems); in 1985 *The Handmaid's Tale*; in 1986 *Selected Poems II*; in 1987 *The Can Lit Food Book*, compiled and illustrated by Atwood in aid of PEN International; in 1988 *Cat's Eye* (novel); in 1990 *Margaret Atwood: Conversations*; in 1991 *Wilderness Tips* (short stories); in 1992 *Good Bones* (short fictions); in 1993 *The Robber Bride* (novel); and in 1995 *Morning in the Burned House* (poems). At the time *The Handmaid's*

Tale was published, Atwood was described in Britain as 'Canada's most renowned writer and one of its most profitable exports'.[13] In Britain that novel was shortlisted for the Booker Prize; in Canada it won Atwood her second Governor General's Award; in the States it won the Arthur C. Clarke Science Fiction Prize and the *Los Angeles Times* fiction prize. In 1989 *Cat's Eye* was again a nominee for the Booker Prize and Atwood continues to gather literary prizes, academic honours and an ever-widening readership. She is the most written-about Canadian writer ever, and there is an enormous amount of academic criticism on her work produced not only in North America but also in Britain, and increasingly in Europe, Australia and India. As Atwood remarked in 1986, 'The truth is that I am a literary writer who has acquired, Lord knows how, a larger than usual audience for such things' (*Conversations*, p. 219).

As a writer in mid-career, Atwood has become in her own words 'a sort of eminent fixture' not only in Canada but also internationally – 'A public face, a face worth defacing. This is an accomplishment', as her woman artist wryly remarks in *Cat's Eye*.[14] Atwood is an extremely versatile writer, and in every novel she takes up the conventions of a different narrative form – Gothic romance, fairy tale, spy thriller, science fiction or history – working within those conventions and reshaping them. Her writing insistently challenges the limits of traditional genres, yet this experimentalism is balanced against a strong continuity of interests which are both aesthetic and social: 'I do see the novel as a vehicle for looking at society – an interface between language and what we choose to call reality, although even that is a very malleable substance' (*Conversations*, p. 246). Atwood has always believed in the social function of art and in the writer's responsibility to her readers:

> If you think of a book as an experience, as almost the equivalent of having the experience, you're going to feel some sense of responsibility as to what kinds of experiences you're going to put people through. You're not going to put them through a lot of blood and gore for nothing; at least I'm not.   (*Conversations*, p. 151)

From *The Edible Woman* onwards, her novels have focused on contemporary social and political issues. 'And what do we mean by "political"?' she asks in an interview after *The Handmaid's Tale*: 'What we mean is how people relate to a power structure and vice versa' (*Conversations*, p. 185). This wide definition of politics accommodates Atwood's abiding thematic concerns: her scrutiny of relations between men and women, which she has always construed as a form of power politics; her engagement with the question of Canadian national identity together with the associated narratives of Canada's relationship with the United States and issues of postcolonialism; her ecological interests and increasingly urgent warnings about global pollution; her wider humanitarian concerns with basic human rights and their infringement by institutional oppression.

It is in order to reflect these continuities that I have adopted a chapter arrangement which is not strictly chronological. Instead, it arches over and doubles back across Atwood's career to indicate significant refigurations of the same topics beneath the shifts of emphasis from one novel to the next. Chapter 2 highlights Atwood's treatment of the wilderness as Canada's emblematic geographical space and as cultural myth, where I trace the shifts of emphasis in her representations of wilderness over the 20 year period from *Surfacing* and *Survival* in the early 1970s to *Wilderness Tips* in 1992. These changes have social and political implications, for they reflect changes in Canadian narratives of national identity at the same time as they indicate Atwood's increasingly urgent engagement with environmental issues related to ecology and pollution. Chapter 3 focuses on Atwood's feminism through a discussion of representations of the female body in two texts written over 20 years apart and in different genres. Whereas *The Edible Woman* is a comic novel written at the very beginning of the Women's Liberation movement, 'The Female Body', written in early 1990s is a savagely feminist fable about sexual power politics. Chapter 4 is concerned with the pervasiveness of Gothic throughout Atwood's career, while the remaining chapters each centre on the close reading of one particular novel in the Atwood canon, following the order of publication. I also refer to other related texts and manuscript materials, for the manuscripts provide valuable amplification on Atwood's working methods, while the other texts offer a commentary on Atwood's fictional techniques and the multiple perspectives from which similar topics might be treated in different forms.

Of course thematics are important but so too are questions of textuality, and with Atwood our attention is always directed back to the words on the page, for she is what *The Times* reviewer called 'a true novelist':

A novel, in order to be successful, has first to hold the attention of the reader; second, it has to function on the level of the language in which it's composed. If the use of the language is terrible you're going to have a poor novel regardless of the consciousness it's reflecting or focusing. The same is true for women's work. (*Conversations*, p. 111)

Incidentally, Atwood has made one of the most sensible comments that one is likely to see on the best way to read novels. When asked how she envisaged her ideal reader, she replied:

> The Ideal Reader for me is somebody who reads the book on the first read-through to see what happens ... I read books to see what happens to the people in them. And after that I can sit back and admire how well it was done and what great skill was brought to bear. But the first time through I want to read the book. (*Conversations*, p. 168)

Her close attention to people and relationships in a particular historical and social location gives her novels the appeal of traditional realistic fiction, even when she is presenting a futuristic vision like *The Handmaid's Tale*. Any one of her novels shows how Atwood challenges the conventions of realism while working within them for she never pretends that words and stories offer an unproblematic access to the real world. Instead, there are always gaps to be negotiated, by the characters in the novels and also by the reader. The Canadian critic Linda Hutcheon gives a precise description of Atwood's fictional method in her analysis of the way that postmodern novelists

> use and abuse the conventions of the realist novel. They ask us to rethink those conventions, this time *as conventions*, but also as ideological strategies. Such novelists destabilize things we used to think we could take for granted when we read novels.[15]

Atwood's fiction draws attention not only to the ways in which stories may be told but also to the function of language itself: the slipperiness of words and double operation of language as symbolic representation and as agent for changing our modes of perception. As Atwood pointed out in an interview:

> The word *woman* already has changed because of the different constellations [of meaning] that have been made around it. Language changes within our lifetime. As a writer you're part of that process – using an old language, but making new patterns with it. Your choices are numerous. (*Conversations*, p. 112)

That comment focuses the political dimensions of the question, what does 'writing like a woman' mean, when language itself codes in such ideological shifts? The greatest challenge for a woman writer is how to position herself in her response to changing cultural definitions of 'woman' and its 'constellations' like 'feminine' and 'feminist'. Atwood has continuously engaged with that challenge in a concerted attempt to widen the dimensions of the debate.

Many critics have commented on Atwood's revision of traditional fictional genres as she draws attention to the cultural myths they embody and to the multiple inherited scripts through which our perceptions of ourselves and the world are structured. What does 'revision' mean in this context? Perhaps the most quoted definition is the American poet Adrienne Rich's in 'When We Dead Awaken: Writing as Re-Vision'. Rich writes in a specifically feminist context, whereas for Atwood the definition needs to be widened to include her Canadian postcolonial context as well:

> Re-Vision – the act of looking back, of seeing with fresh eyes, of entering an old text from a new critical direction – is for women more than a chapter in cultural history; it is an act of survival ... We need to know the writing of the past and to know it differently ... not to pass on a tradition but to break its hold over us.[16]

In other words, revision involves a critical response to the traditional narratives of a culture and then a reinterpretation of them from a new perspective, which offers a critique of the value structures and power relations (the 'ideological implications') coded into texts. Revision does not break with tradition, though it aims to 'break its hold over us'. As early as 1976 Atwood was explaining the relation between her poetry and popular art in such revisionist terms: 'In *Power Politics* I was using myths such as Bluebeard, Dracula, and horror comic material, to project certain images of men and women, and to examine them' (*Conversations*, p. 42).

Atwood's fictions are criss-crossed with allusions to other texts, signalling her literary inheritance while at the same time marking significant differences from her predecessors. To illustrate the way this challenge to tradition operates, we might glance briefly at two different versions of Gothic romance in *Lady Oracle* and *Bodily Harm*. *Lady Oracle* is a very funny parody of the popular genre of women's 'bodice rippers', but at the same time as it exposes the artifice of Gothic conventions with their female victim fantasies and their double dealing, it also attempts to analyse the insidious appeal of

Gothic for women readers. In *Bodily Harm* witty comedy changes to
something far more threatening where female dread of male violence spills over from fiction into real life, first via pornographic
fantasy and sexual crime in Toronto, and then through the account
of a military coup in a newly independent Caribbean republic. Here
the shifts between Gothic romance and realism operate as ironic critique of both modes, exemplifying Atwood's narrative method which
induces double vision in her readers. While our attention is directed
to reassuringly familiar plots and character stereotypes, we are also
forced to acknowledge the limits of such conventions when borders
blur between fiction and real life. One by one her female protagonists are forced to confront the gap between traditional narratives of
female helplessness and a far more complex reality which forces
women to revise their life stories. It is the female narrator's process
of growth into an awareness of personal moral responsibility which is
repeatedly figured in all Atwood's novels.

   Obviously revisionist perspectives have narrative consequences not
only for narrators but also for readers, turning our attention towards
processes of deconstruction and reconstruction while emphasising
the provisionality of any narrative structure. Atwood's novels are
characterised by their refusals to invoke any final authority as their
open endings resist conclusiveness, offering instead hesitation,
absence or silence while hovering on the verge of new possibilities.
Their indeterminacy is a challenge to readers, for one of the problems we have to confront is how to find a critical language to
describe Atwood's 'borderline fiction'[17] with its ironic mixture of
realism and fantasy, fictive artifice and moral engagement.

I wish to return to the other two elements of Atwood's 'triple handicap': her Canadianness and her feminism. A Canadian by birth and
upbringing (born of parents from Nova Scotia where family traditions go back to the Empire Loyalists who left Massachusetts after
the American Declaration of Independence), Atwood has done
much through her writing and interviews to make Canadian culture
visible outside her country. She began however by spelling out traditions to Canadians themselves with her literary history *Survival* and
her novel *Surfacing,* both published in 1972. For an international
readership her project has been that of 'translating Canada',
mapping its geography, its history of European exploration and set-
tlement, its literary and artistic heritage, and its cultural myths. Her

representation of Canada is a combination of documentary realism and imaginative interpretation from her own perspective as a white anglophone Canadian woman living in Ontario. She is not an immigrant or a Native Person, nor from Western Canada or Quebec, any of which would make a difference to her representation of Canadianness. Though several of her novels move outside Canada to the United States, the Caribbean, or to Europe, yet her fiction is based on a strong sense of local identity, for as she says,

> To me an effective writer is one who can make what he or she is writing about understandable and moving to someone who has never been there ... It doesn't mean becoming something called 'international'. There is no such thing. (*Conversations*, p. 143)

This sense of location is the basis of Atwood's realism. She writes about Canadian cities and small towns, about the Canadian wilderness with its forests and lakes, and sometimes about the Arctic North. In her novels she continues to give updated versions of the city of Toronto from the mid-1940s to the 1990s, and it is not difficult for a reader to chart that city's post-war history from *The Edible Woman* to *The Robber Bride*. *Cat's Eye* features a woman painter brought up in Toronto in the 1950s and 1960s who returns 30 years later as a minor celebrity, only to find the place defamiliarised by time:

> I've been walking for hours it seems, down the hill to the downtown, where the streetcars no longer run. It's evening, one of those grey watercolour washes, like liquid dust, the city comes up with in fall. The weather at any rate is still familiar.
>
> Now I've reached the place where we used to get off the streetcar, stepping into the curbside mounds of January slush, into the grating wind that cut up from the lake between the flat-roofed dowdy buildings that were for us the closest thing to urbanity. But this part of the city is no longer flat, dowdy, shabby-genteel. Tubular neon in cursive script decorates the restored brick façades, and there's a lot of brass trim, a lot of real estate, a lot of money. Up ahead there are huge oblong towers, all of glass, lit up, like enormous gravestones of cold light. Frozen assets.
>
> I don't look much at the towers though, or the people passing me in their fashionable get-ups, imports, handcrafted leather, suede, whatever. Instead I look down at the sidewalk, like a tracker. (*Cat's Eye*, pp. 8–9)

That imaginative reconstruction of place and the narrator's attempt to orientate herself in a wilderness of signs will be familiar to any Atwood reader. In Chapter 2 I shall discuss Atwood's treatment of wilderness landscape, which I believe to be the cornerstone in her representations of Canadianness. However, I wish to comment here on Atwood's position within the anglophone Canadian literary tradition and on her significance as a writer who is highly sensitive to the evolving Canadian narrative of national identity. Any nation's identity is an ideological construction by which it defines its difference from its neighbours and from the rest of the international community, an increasingly difficult thing to do in the late modern world of global communications and transnational economic relations. Canada's image as a bilingual multicultural nation contains within it the narratives of a New World history as well as contemporary narratives of cultural difference within the country itself. Historically, Canada has been defined in relation to its two European 'mother countries', Britain and France, and its southern neighbour the United States of America. This is an 'emergent nation' story which follows patterns characteristic of the shift from colonial status to postcolonial nationhood. In Canada's case the story is complicated by the pluralities within its own political discourse where debates between anglophone and francophone communities are amplified by diverse voices representing different regions, different ethnic and immigrant groups, and the voices of Native peoples, all of which have implications for an evolving narrative of national identity.[18] In her fiction over almost 25 years Atwood has closely charted Canada's story with its political crises and shifts of ideological emphasis, as a novelist engaged in an ongoing project of cultural representation and critique. To encounter the nation as it is written by Atwood is to follow a history of shifting and often contradictory representations which range from 1970s English-centred cultural nationalism to more complex articulations of Canadian multicultural differences in the late 1980s and 1990s. Atwood's latest fiction shows popular national myths to be in urgent need of revision, in order to take account not only of changing demographic patterns but also changing ideologies of nationhood. National boundaries begin to blur as Atwood responds to her widening international readership, arguing for a shared recognition of complicity in a globalised scenario which threatens human survival.

Although as Atwood has said repeatedly, she had no reason in the late 1950s to believe that she would ever be able to make her living as a writer in Canada, she did in fact belong to a new generation who were 'busy discovering the fact of our existence as Canadians', 'searching for an indigenous mode of expression as well as indigenous subject matter', and 'heavily involved in developing our own publishing houses' (*Conversations*, p. 135). She was also one of the first generation of students who were taught that there was a Canadian literary tradition in poetry if not in fiction. It was presented as dominantly anglophone, representing the voices of the majority culture to which Atwood herself belonged.[19] As an undergraduate in Toronto she was taught by the late Professor Northrop Frye and the poet Jay Macpherson, whose influence as role model Atwood gratefully acknowledges: 'It's all very well to have Elizabeth Barrett Browning and Charlotte Brontë kicking around in the nineteenth century, but to actually be able to look at someone and say, that person has published a book! You can't imagine how important that was to a Canadian living at that time' (*Conversations*, p. 112). It was in Macpherson's private library that Atwood read her way into the Canadian poetic tradition, while she was also influenced by Frye's myth-centred criticism and his efforts to translate European myths into a new Canadian cultural context. She began her writing career with advantages that no earlier generation of Canadians had possessed. Given the context, it is not surprising that she would have begun by writing poetry, nor that her first critical work, *Survival*, should have been an attempt to map a parallel Canadian tradition in fiction. Since the 1970s Atwood has maintained her active engagement with Canadian literary and cultural politics, though she is now so well known internationally that readers tend to forget where she comes from. Atwood herself never forgets this, and her fictions are pervaded by Canadian cultural codes. At the same time the meanings of her novels cannot be restricted to a Canadian frame of reference, for stories are fabrications made out of language and they use narrative conventions which transcend self-conscious political ideologies:

I write for people who like to read books. They don't have to be Canadian readers. They don't have to be American readers. They don't have to be Indian readers, although some of them are. I'm translated into fourteen languages by now [1982; now the figure is at least twenty], and I'm sure that some of the people reading those books don't get all the references in them, because they're not familiar with the setting. I don't get all the references in William Faulkner either. That doesn't mean I don't enjoy the books, or can't understand them. You can pick up a lot of things from context. (*Conversations*, p. 144)

It is a similarly non-exclusive attitude which characterises Atwood's relation to feminism: 'Some people *choose* to define themselves as feminist writers. I would not deny the adjective, but I don't consider it inclusive' (*Conversations*, p. 139). Atwood is now probably the best known feminist novelist writing in English, though that statement made in 1979 still accurately describes her position. I believe there are two main reasons for this: first, because Atwood sees sexual politics as only one of the areas in which power relations are the crucial issue, and secondly, because as a novelist she insists on her aesthetic freedom to write from her 'sense of the enormous complexity, not only of the relationships between Man and Woman, but also of those between those other abstract intangibles, Art and Life, Form and Content, Writer and Critic, etcetera'.[20] Her novels might best be characterised as 'experiments' (to adopt her own scientific vocabulary and method of inquiry), always testing the limits of theory and exceeding ideological definitions. Her fiction canvasses such a comprehensive range of social issues and from such a variety of perspectives that it eludes the simplicity of any single 'feminist' position. That being said, it remains true that growing up in the late 1950s and early 1960s in Toronto and then going as a graduate student to Harvard, Atwood's formative years coincided with the emergence of 'second wave' North American feminism and her fiction reflects the changing climate when Women's Liberation was becoming a political issue. Ever since *The Edible Woman,* which Atwood described as 'protofeminist', her novels have provided a chronicle and critique of the changing fashions within feminist politics over the past 30 years.

The early 1960s signal the beginnings of a new politically self-conscious phase of feminist awareness in North America at grass-roots and institutional levels. A great deal has been written about the emergence of the Women's Liberation Movement in the States, which was energised by the political radicalism of the American Civil Rights Movement. There was in fact a parallel, feminist movement developing in Canada though the distinctive outlines of the Canadian women's movement are only now being extensively documented by collectives of women scholars in Ottawa and Toronto.[21] 1960 was the year that the Voice of Women, the first Canadian national women's organisation, was founded as a group to lobby federal and provincial governments on women's issues and peace issues, and in 1967 the first Canadian Royal Commission on the Status of Women was set up. From the beginning Canadian women's groups worked more closely within legal and governmental structures than their sisters in the States. Although women's struggle centred on resistance to traditional concepts of male dominance, its distinctively 'political' feature was the shift away from private experience to the recognition of the relatedness between domestic and social structures as women were encouraged to reflect on their position in post war North American society. As Betty Friedan phrased it in her polemical treatise, *The Feminine Mystique* (1963), in a first chapter entitled 'The Problem That Has No Name':

> The problem lay buried unspoken for many years in the minds of American women. It was a strange stirring, a sense of dissatisfaction, a yearning that women suffered in the middle of the twentieth century.[22]

Friedan's book signalled the shift from individual women's discontents to a collective gender consciousness which came to characterise 'second wave' feminism.[23] Friedan, following in the footsteps of Simone de Beauvoir's *The Second Sex* (1949; translated into English in 1953), mounted the first popular critique of North American cultural myths of femininity, reminding women how much they had lost by allowing their lives to be restricted to the suburbs in the 1950s following the return to civilian life after the war. Atwood refers to *The Second Sex* and *The Feminine Mystique* as the two most significant influences on her thinking as a young woman in early 1960s.[24] In the States Friedan founded her radical political group NOW (National Organization of Women) in 1966; in Canada the Royal Commission's report on women was published in 1970. Meantime, in London in 1966 Juliet Mitchell's New Left-inspired study *Women: The Longest Revolution* was published, and in 1969 Mitchell began teaching the first women's studies course in Britain. In 1970 Robin Morgan's *Sisterhood Is Powerful: An Anthology of Writings from the Women's Liberation Movement* was published in New York, the same year as Germaine Greer's *The Female Eunuch* in London. Feminist newspapers and periodicals began to appear and the number of reformist women's groups grew remarkably during the 1970s. It is within this historical context of women's dissent that *The Edible Woman* assumes its proper significance for us, and, as I shall argue in Chapter 3, *The Feminine Mystique* provides a powerful lens through which Atwood's first novel may be read. Both texts focus on the predicament of young university-educated women trapped in social myths of femininity, though *The Edible Woman* is a novelist's imaginative response cast as comic social satire in vividly metaphorical language. This is sociology translated into the private idiom of one fictive female character where unconscious resistance to her social destiny takes the form of a hysterical eating disorder. Written in 1965 and published in 1969, Atwood's novel represents an imaginative response to a current social malaise. It is parallel to, though not a product of the new Women's Movement although that Movement created the conditions for its popular reception. Atwood has always been seen as a feminist icon, albeit a resistant and at times an inconvenient one.

During the 1970s there was a flood of feminist writing in North America, England and France as women sought to define their positions on social and political issues within every discipline (literary criticism and the media, history, psychoanalysis, anthropology, science, theology). The most startling innovation was in the explicit treatment of female sexuality and desire, for suddenly those hitherto unspoken territories were mapped and written about: Shulamith Firestone's *The Dialectic of Sex* (1970), the Boston Women's Book Collective's *Our Bodies Our Selves* (1971), and Hilda Bruch's study of anorexia nervosa *The Golden Cage* (1975) focused on women's bodies; while feminist revisions of Freudian theories of femininity appeared in Phyllis Chesler's *Women and Madness* (1972) and Juliet Mitchell's *Psychoanalysis and Feminism* (1974). Adrienne Rich's *Of Woman Born* (1976) and Nancy Chodorow's *The Reproduction of Mothering* (1978) scrutinised women's experiences of motherhood (Atwood reviewed Rich's *Of Woman Born*, in the *Toronto Globe and Mail*, 11 November 1976); while the darker areas of male violence against women began to be explored by Susan Brownmiller in *Against Our Will: Men, Women and Rape* (1975). Laura Mulvey's study of the male gaze in *Visual Pleasure and Narrative Cinema* (1975) analysed the politics of male dominance within the media, which in turn is related to the analysis of male fantasies of aggression and violence in Andrea Dworkin's *Pornography: Men Possessing Women* (1981). In the field of literary criticism, the most significant innovations were the theorising of a feminist writing practice and the establishment of a female literary tradition such as we find in Ellen Moers's *Literary Women* (1976) and Elaine Showalter's *A Literature of Their Own* (1977) both of which were supplemented by Tillie Olsen's study of the great unwritten tradition of women's creativity in *Silences* (1978).

These innovative texts provide an historical framework within which to read Atwood's fiction of the 1970s and a similar pattern of dialogue may be traced through the 1980s and 1990s. 'Context is all', as the Handmaid asserted. A complex web of interrelatedness is developed as the novelist responds to her changing cultural climate and to the writings produced by the most significant social movement of the past 30 years. All the representative feminist as well as many of the anti-feminist positions could be illustrated with examples from Atwood's novels, which have insistently challenged traditional male power structures while giving readers some of their funniest and most trenchant models for a feminist critique. Just as feminist theory has developed strong historical and cultural dimensions through its investigation of the institutions of marriage and motherhood, so Atwood has explored similar territory in her representations of 'female, feminine and feminist' positions. On the question of women's relation to language and literary conventions Atwood has been continuously engaged in the revision of traditional genres, opening up spaces for women as subjects speaking and writing about their own experience, though still forced to acknowledge what Linda Hutcheon calls 'the power of the (male "universal") space in which it [women's writing] cannot avoid, to some extent, operating'.[25]

However readers of Atwood need to be as discriminating as Atwood herself when describing her as a feminist writer, for her fiction is a combination of engagement, analysis and critique of the changing fashions within feminism. As she declared in an interview following publication of *The Handmaid's Tale*: 'In any monolithic regime I would be shot. They *always* do that to the artists. Why? Because the artists are messy. They don't fit' (*Conversations*, p. 183). In there from the beginning, Atwood realised very clearly the implications of the early 1970s feminist slogan 'The Personal is Political', and she has been exploring this interdependence ever since. Feminism cannot be reduced to parodic slogans like 'the oppression of women by men' or 'women are always right.' Certainly, feminism has always insisted that women have rights, in the sense of individual human rights (which immediately relates the woman question to wider political issues) but feminism also means looking at the ways in which women use the powers traditionally granted to them and how they have attempted to enlarge the scope of their influence; it also means looking at the effects on women of not having legitimised power. That lack can turn them into victims or manipulators, or it can launch them into guerrilla warfare, all of which are positions explored in Atwood's fiction. At every stage Atwood has speculated beyond the issues addressed by the feminist movement with her awkward and daring questions, not only about relations between women and men, but about relations between women and women. She has explored the relations between mothers and daughters or between little girls or adult female friends, and most recently the challenge posed by a flambuoyantly sexy woman who is a *femme fatale* to members of both sexes. With every novel Atwood lights out into new and dangerous territory, exposing the limits and blind spots of feminist ideologies when faced with the slipperiness and variety of individual women:

> As for Woman, capital W, we got stuck with that for centuries. Eternal Woman. But really, 'Woman' is the sum total of women. It doesn't exist apart from that, except as an abstracted idea. (*Conversations*, p. 201)

In *The Handmaid's Tale* and *The Robber Bride* Atwood has taken an historical view of the North American feminist movement, charting some of the ways in which feminism has changed from Women's Liberation to the more theorised and subtly politicised feminism of the late 1980s and 1990s. Her analysis is a cultural one which traces patterns of social interaction and consequences, for just as feminism has contributed to shifts in social ideology so has feminism itself been transformed. In a way analogous to changes in the word 'feminine', feminism has rejected notions of essentialism and become pluralised into 'feminisms' in order to include the different agendas of other formerly marginalised groups of women: black women in America, Third World women, and lesbians whose interests are closer to Gay Rights than to traditionally liberal feminist agendas. In Toronto, which is Atwood's 'home ground', though it sometimes looks to her protagonists like 'foreign territory', the first generation inspired by Friedan and De Beauvoir are now middle-aged women in positions of power, like Atwood herself who writes about middle-aged successful women artists (such as Elaine Risley in *Cat's Eye*) or businesswomen and university professors (such as Roz and Tony in *The Robber Bride*), well aware that the idiom of feminism in the 1990s has changed and that there are eddying cross-currents which signal the 'post feminist' era: 'Most women don't want to read about other women who achieve. It makes them feel unsuccessful' (*The Robber Bride*, p. 370). It is symptomatic of her double vision that with one eye on the present Atwood is also aware of the long history of exceptional women's achievements in the past, and *The Robber Bride* ends by tracking back through history to celebrate the name of a medieval French female military commander, Dame Giraude, who defended her fortified castle to the death in 1211, then even further back to recall the figure of Jezebel whose story is told in both the Old and the New Testaments – no doubt to remind readers not to fall into any blinkered attitude of presentism.

Atwood's resistance to generalisations about 'Woman' is a crucial feature in her feminist understanding of the importance of history and culture in shaping women's lives. In her interviews (rather than in her fiction where her protagonists are all English-speaking and white) she insists on specificity of context as a prerequisite for definitions of feminism:

> *Feminist* is now one of the all-purpose words. It really can mean anything from people who think men should be pushed off cliffs to people who think it's O.K. for women to read and write. All those could be called feminist positions. Thinking that it's O.K. for women to read and write would be a radically feminist position in Afghanistan. So what do you mean?   (*Conversations*, p. 140)

Readers will be reminded here of that wickedly funny parody of the newspaper interview in *Cat's Eye* when a middle-aged woman artist refuses to accept easy feminist labels:

> 'Well, what about, you know, feminism?' she says. 'A lot of people call you a feminist painter.'
> 'What indeed,' I say, 'I hate party lines, I hate ghettoes. Anyway, I'm too old to have invented it and you're too young to understand it, so what's the point of discussing it at all?'
> 'So it's not a meaningful classification for you?' she says.
> 'I like it that women like my work. Why shouldn't I?'   (p. 90)

In Atwood's fiction there are no essentialist definitions of 'woman' or 'feminism' or even 'Canadian', but instead representations of the endless complexity and quirkiness of human behaviour which exceeds ideological labels and the explanatory power of theory. As a 'feminist' and a 'nationalist', Atwood is a 'political' writer in the widest sense, for she is interested in an analysis of the dialectics of power and in shifting structures of ideology. What is more, as a 'true novelist' she is interested in the dynamic powers of language and story:

> There is no single, simple, static 'women's point of view.' Let's just say that good writing of any kind by anyone is surprising, intricate, strong, sinuous.   (*Conversations*, p. 242)

2

Atwood's Canadian Signature: From *Surfacing* and *Survival* to *Wilderness Tips*

As far as I'm concerned, life begins with geology, and with geography ... look at a map of Canada.

(*Conversations*, p. 131)

'Canadian signature' is a phrase that Atwood used in *Survival* back in 1972; and since then readers have been alerted by the French critic Jacques Derrida to the peculiar properties of a signature as the symbolic representation of an absent person, a signifier of presence which inevitably draws attention to absence and to the gap between real life and writing.[1] It is precisely that gap with its verbal slippages and imaginative possibilities which is the space occupied by fiction. Yet a signature is also an individual mark, and my emphasis here is on the distinctive ways in which Canada and Canadianness are figured within the textual spaces of Atwood's fiction, literary criticism and poetry. Writers are rooted in a particular place, and Atwood's place is Canada:

> You come out of something, and you can then branch out in all kinds of different directions, but that doesn't mean cutting yourself off from your roots and from your earth. (*Conversations*, p. 143)

This organic image of the tree and the emphasis on location points directly towards the most significant element in Atwood's construc-

20

tion of Canadian identity, the concept of wilderness. Wilderness has multiple functions – as geographical location marker, as spatial metaphor, and as Canada's most popular cultural myth. In its endless refigurings in her work, we may trace the ongoing narrative of Atwood's responses to shifts in Canadian social attitudes and ideology. In the 1970s with *The Journals of Susanna Moodie, Surfacing* and *Survival,* Atwood began by representing wilderness to Canadians as their own distinctive national space; in the 1990s with the short story collection *Wilderness Tips* the emphasis has shifted to a much bleaker reading where wilderness as geographical place is under threat from pollution and the spread of urbanisation, while as cultural myth of national identity it stands in need of revision. The new Canadian ideology of multiculturalism, the Separatist Movement in Quebec, and significant Native voices talking about land rights and First Nations culture have made a difference to perceptions about Canada both nationally and internationally. An interesting shift of emphasis in concepts of Canadianness can be located in this major wilderness image in Atwood's writing, and there are clear signs of her awareness of a growing international readership in her urgent warnings against the environmental dangers of global pollution.

Geographically, wilderness is defined as wild uncultivated land, which in Canada includes vast tracts of forest with innumerable lakes and also the Arctic North. The important question for any narrative of Canadian identity is the way in which, and by whom, these unexplored spaces have been appropriated as popular cultural myth. The myth of wilderness as empty space is of course a white myth, for the wilderness was not really empty; it was only indecipherable to Europeans, who came to the New World as explorers, traders, soldiers, missionaries and settlers. Within colonial discourse wilderness was presented as a space outside civilised social order and Christian moral laws, the place of mysterious and threatening otherness. In this sense only could it be construed as blank, for of course there were traces all through the forests of the indigenous inhabitants and the tracks of wild animals. Inevitably this construction of wilderness produced contradictory responses: on the one hand, it was construed by most Europeans as a place where one could get lost or killed; while on the other, it would be seen as the space of freedom from social constraints. Atwood's double vision entertains both these possibilities, while recognising the third possibility that wilderness might be interpreted very differently from a Native perspective. The discourse of wilderness is now under revision, thanks to the increasing intervention of voices from the First Nations during the 1980s and 1990s which intermesh with contemporary environmental awareness. There are hints of this alternative vision in *Surfacing* and these are elaborated in the *Wilderness Tips* stories.

For Atwood wilderness was already a cultural myth when she inherited it in the 1940s, and her fiction is full of references to the Canadian literary tradition of explorers' narratives, animal stories, woodcraft and survival manuals which she read as a child and to representations of wilderness in the Canadian paintings of the Group of Seven. Atwood spent a great deal of her childhood in the forests of northern Ontario and Quebec, and then attended summer camps as a teenager in the 1950s; this is the territory to which she keeps returning in her fiction. There is a vivid representation of the wilderness in her ghost story 'Death by Landscape' done in the pictorial idiom of the Group of Seven, where the forest is presented as silent territory empty of any human figures, though their traces are there:

> They are pictures of convoluted tree trunks on an island of pink wave-smoothed stone, with more islands behind; of a lake with rough, bright, sparsely wooded cliffs; of a vivid river shore with a tangle of bush and two beached canoes, one red, one grey; of a yellow autumn woods with the ice-blue gleam of a pond half-seen through the interlaced branches.[2]

Out of the dual context of lived experience and cultural tradition Atwood has constructed her changing versions of wilderness as she writes and rewrites her distinctively Canadian signature.

Atwood's first complete figuring of wilderness occurs in the early poetic sequence *The Journals of Susanna Moodie* (1970), which represents a nineteenth-century Englishwoman's response to the landscape of eastern Canada.[3] Moodie had published her own autobiographical story *Roughing It in the Bush* (1852), and these poems reinvent that pioneer woman through whom Atwood articulates the 'inescapable doubleness of vision' which she sees as a peculiar historical characteristic of the Canadian psyche:

> We are all immigrants to this place, even if we were born here: the country is too big for anyone to inhabit completely, and in the parts unknown to us we move in fear, exiles and invaders.[4]

Initially wilderness is presented as alien landscape which threatens to erase Susanna Moodie's sense of her identity as a Victorian lady, yet as the sequence develops it becomes the place of mysterious transformations. 'Crept in upon by green', Moodie begins to perceive her surroundings in a new way, no longer as threat but as harmonious natural order. In this process of shifting subjective perceptions Atwood sketches a feminised reading of wilderness in the relation between woman and the natural world, so that although Susanna Moodie leaves the bush before she learns its secret language, a hundred years later her ghost appears as a witness to the presence of the past in 1960s Toronto:

> Turn, look down:
> There is no city;
> This is the centre of a forest
> Your place is empty.
>   ('A Bus along St Clair: December', p. 61)

As Atwood comments, 'Susanna Moodie has finally turned herself inside out, and has become the spirit of the land she once hated,' (p. 64) and it is the city which has become the unexplored threatening wilderness. With characteristic doubleness Atwood reinvents white English-Canadian constructions of identity, charting a distinctive New World positioning in relation to history, geography and culture suggestive of a continuity between immigration narratives and a contemporary awareness of psychic dislocation. This paradoxical position is emblematised in *Surfacing* by the narrator's comment: 'Now we're on my home ground, foreign territory'[5] as borders blur between 'home' and 'exile' in a wilderness place which may be buried under the city pavements of Toronto, but is still there in memory and myth.

Atwood uses this wilderness sign of distinctive national heritage when she addresses Canadian readers in *Surfacing* and *Survival*, both products of early 1970s cultural nationalism. Those texts arguably exist in a symbiotic relationship, for although the novel was written first it was through writing it that Atwood realised certain common themes that her fiction shared with other Canadian writing, and so she set out to write her literary history. Beginning with the question, 'What is distinctive about Canadian literature?' her project is clearly related to raising her readers' cultural self-consciousness. In *Survival* she describes key patterns of plot, theme and imagery which are 'like the field-markings in bird-books: they will help you to distinguish this species from all others, Canadian literature from the other literatures [English and American] with which it often compared or confused'.[6] Significantly, her definition of Canadianness hinges on

concepts of wilderness and survival in the tradition of woodcraft
manuals:

> We need such a map desperately, we need to know about here,
> because here is where we live. For members of a country or a
> culture, shared knowledge of their place, their here, is not a luxury
> but a necessity. Without that knowledge we will not survive.   (p. 19)

Having traced a Canadian literary tradition which is dominantly
anglophone from the early nineteenth century to the 1970s, Atwood
moves at the end of her account beyond literary history to wider
questions of cultural politics, urging her fellow Canadians to rehabilitate themselves in a postcolonial context, resisting both their
European 'mother countries' and the United States by taking
control of their own country:

> control our own space, physical as well as cultural. But that space
> must be controlled with love or it will be the control typical of
> tyranny: there will not be that much difference between Canadian
> ownership and the absentee landlord draining of the land we
> already live under.   (p. 244)

Atwood speaks out against exploitation and destruction of the
forests, urging the need to pay attention to ecological principles in a
way that the highly developed American technological society was
not doing, in order to preserve the environment for future generations. That same anxiety is expressed with increasing urgency in *The
Handmaid's Tale* (1985) and again in the stories and fables of
Wilderness Tips (1991) and *Good Bones* (1992).

Surfacing begins and ends with the forest, for just as wilderness is
significant in Atwood's version of literary history, so is it in the story
of one woman's quest to find an appropriate language in which to
write about her changing perceptions of her own identity as
Canadian and female. This novel can be approached from many
different directions, and it has already received a great deal of critical attention.[7] All I can hope to do here is to indicate some of the
main lines of inquiry as I focus my discussion on the topics of wilderness, language and narrative form. One of the first Canadian reviews
signalled the emblematic status of the novel when it described
Surfacing as 'a Canadian fable in which the current obsessions of
Canadians become symbols in a drama of personal survival: nationalism, feminism, death, culture, art, nature, pollution'.[8] This catalogue

also illustrates the parallels between *Surfacing* and *Survival*, and though it is not thematics which I wish to highlight here, it is worth noting how the novel actually offers one revisionary reading of a 'Canadian signature' as recommended in *Survival*. Explorers' journeys are refigured in contemporary Canada as individual quests for spiritual survival; victims (either Canadian or female) are urged to take responsibility for their situation and to cease to see themselves as victims; perceptions of wilderness are reshaped so that Canada no longer figures as 'exile' but is transformed into 'home ground'. The novel begins like a detective story, where the unnamed narrator goes back to the place of her childhood in the Quebec bush to search for her lost father who, as we later learn, has already drowned in the lake while looking for Indian rock paintings. Gradually she discovers that what she is really searching for is her own past. She is looking for those lost bits of herself buried in her repressed memories, and it is only in the wilderness that she finds a way to heal the split within her own psyche, thereby restoring her emotional and spiritual health. The story traces the multilayered process of rehabilitation by which a dislocated and damaged woman manages to come to terms with her past, while recognising that the past cannot ever be retrieved though it may be partially reconstructed through memory and fantasy. By the end, the narrator's perceptions of her relation to the world have changed so that she is ready to leave the wilderness to return to society. Now the only map she possesses is the network of trails on her own hand, her 'lifeline' as she calls it. This very human-centred position is one that Atwood characteristically adopts ('This above all, to refuse to be a victim') where reverence for life, a commitment to love and trust and to moral responsibility are asserted as primary values. Such a diagrammatic account of the novel leaves out many things – not only the crucial lie at its centre which is revealed in Chapter 17 when the narrator dives down into the lake, but also the visionary episodes which chart the stages of her rehabilitation in the wilderness. These will be discussed, but what I have tried to emphasise here are the ways in which this text works simultaneously on two levels. There is the outer world of landscape and society and there is the inner world of the narrator's own mind, where borders blur between realism and fantasy as the language shifts between realistic description and metaphors of psychological space.

Of course the site of this border-blur is in wilderness territory, for wilderness is not only 'geography and geology' but is also discursively located within the text as the site of dynamic transformations. It also functions as metaphor for the lost place of origin with its traces of

Amerindian prehistory in the submerged rock paintings and its forgotten Indian sacred sites. It is this spiritualised sense of place which is a significant component in *Surfacing*, for as Atwood tried to explain in an early interview:

> The only sort of good, authentic kind of a thing to have is something that comes out of the place where you are, or shall we put it another way and say the reality of your life ... Christianity in this country is imported religion. The assumption of the book, if there is one, is that there are gods that do exist here, but nobody knows about them ... The authentic religion that was here has been destroyed; you have to discover it in some other way. How that fits in with the book I don't know, but I'm sure it has something to do with it.[9]

Atwood is here sketching the metaphysical and historical dimensions of her cultural nationalism. Yet her novel begins from 'the place where you are', and one of the great strengths of *Surfacing* is its sense of specific location. The area where the novel is set has been identified as that forested part of the Canadian Shield north-west of North Bay near Lake Kipawa,[10] and the opening paragraph presents a realistic description of a journey by car into the wilderness:

> I can't believe I'm on this road again, twisting along past the lake where the white birches are dying, the disease is spreading up from the south, and I notice they now have sea planes for hire. (p. 7)

The wilderness of the early 1970s is evidently no longer the wilderness of Canadian pastoral myth. Instead, it is a territory already suffering the effects of civilisation where the trees are dying of acid rain blowing up from the United States and the area is invaded by tourist roads bringing week-end fishermen and hunters. This is cottage country on the border between two provinces, two cultures and two languages, and the district already has a history of European colonisation which goes back at least as far as the narrator's childhood memories of a paper mill and a dam. The marks of a socialised nature are already there in the small hybridised community and its exploitation of natural resources. Yet, though damaged, the forest landscape is still capable of regenerating itself and of offering its traditional protective cover: 'The peninsula is where I left it, pushing out from the island shore with the house not even showing through the trees' (p. 32).

Coming home is to enter not only another place but another time, as the narrator tracks back into an almost forgotten past which stretches beyond personal memory to the local history of the district and even further back into prehistory:

> In the cool green among the trees, new trees and stumps, the stumps with charcoal crusts on them, scabby and crippled, survivors of an old disaster. Sight flowing ahead of me over the ground, eyes filtering the shapes, the names of things fading but their forms and uses remaining, the animals learned what to eat without nouns ... Beneath it the invisible part, threadlike underground network.   (pp. 149–50)

The living forest still bears traces of the past in the present, functioning like a text in another language, signs of which are changing natural forms, for the forest is the place of dynamic transformations within a delicately balanced ecological system:

> Out of the leaf nests the flowers rise, pure white, flesh of gnats and midges, petals now, metamorphosis ... energy of decay turning to growth, green fire. I remember the heron; by now it will be insects, frogs, other herons. My body also changes, the creature in me, plant-animal, sends out filaments in me.   (pp. 167–8)

The imagery encodes not only analogy but also harmony between human and non-human at the basic level of life processes where the female biological cycle has its parallels in the life cycle of the forest. Susanna Moodie left the wilderness knowing there was something she had not learned, but the narrator of *Surfacing*, while ignorant of native traditions, reinvents 'new meanings' alone on her island, immersing herself in 'the other language' of the wilderness and the 'multilingual water' of the lake.

Indeed, *Surfacing* might be read not only as psychological and spiritual quest but also as the record of a gendered quest for a new language which is more responsive to an organic conceptualisation of reality. Some of the most interesting questions the novel raises are arguably linguistic ones and Atwood gives a hint of what these might be in an interview in 1986:

> How do we know 'reality'? How do you encounter the piece of granite? How do you know it directly? Is there such a thing as knowing it directly without language?   (*Conversations*, p. 209)

Returning to *Surfacing* with these questions in mind, it is evident that initially the narrator has a deep distrust of words, seeing them as instruments of deception and domination rather than of communication. As a woman she feels 'trapped in a language that wasn't mine' (p.106), placed in the position of victim in male power games of love and war; as an anglophone in Quebec she has to confront problems of translation 'when people could say words that would go into my ears meaning nothing' (p. 11); as a Canadian she feels compromised by American cultural influences:

> If you look like them and talk like them and think like them then you are them, I was saying, you speak their language, a language is everything you do. (p. 129)

So her quest for self-rehabilitation is also a quest to find her own 'dialect' amidst all the languages available to her: 'It was there in me, the evidence, only needing to be deciphered' (p. 76).

Her quest proceeds through a series of clearly marked stages to which the narrative structure draws our attention, for the whole of section 2 is enclosed in a curious way by the image of the narrator's clenched fist:

> From where I am now, it seems as if I've always known, everything, time is compressed like the fist I close on my knee in the darkening bedroom. I hold inside it the clues and solutions and the power for what I must do now. (p. 76)

That fist only uncloses after the series of discoveries at the centre of the novel: first the discovery of her father's drawings of the Indian rock paintings, then her dive into the lake, and finally the public announcement that her father's drowned body has been found. Only at this point does the narrative return to the present tense, and we realise that the whole of the second section (which we may also notice for the first time has been told in the past tense) has been a reconstruction from memory and that the narrator has not moved from her marginalised position in the bedroom of her father's cabin while the others are playing cards in the sitting room:

> I unclose my fist, releasing, it becomes a hand again, palm a network of trails, lifeline, past present and future, the break in it closing together as I purse my fingers. (p. 159)

Her most crucial discovery occurs when she dives down into the lake, looking for the Indian rock paintings recorded in her father's drawings. She does not find them; instead, she sees a strange blurred image which may or may not be her father's drowned body, but for her that image figures something which has not so far been revealed in the story. It is the assiduously repressed memory of her aborted child. This is the revelation of the lie at the centre of the novel, for there had never been a marriage or a child but only an affair and an abortion: 'I couldn't accept it, that mutilation, ruin I'd made, I needed a different version' (p. 143). There is a long, detailed description of how the narrator dives deep into the lake with the pale green water darkening around her; yet only with that revelation does the reader realise that the physical description has been shadowed by another dimension. Looking beyond the printed text and back to the manuscript, we find the clue to that other dimension in a scribbled marginal note: the scribbled word is 'anaesthetic'.[11] Within the novel the hint is displaced, for this text enacts the treasure hunt which the narrator is playing with her dead father and all the clues are there for the reader to decipher:

> They slipped the needle into the vein and I was falling down, it was like diving, sinking from one layer of darkness to a deeper, deepest; when I rose up through the anaesthetic, pale green and then daylight, I could remember nothing.   (p. 111)

Diving into the lake works both as realistic description and as metaphor for descent into the territory of the subconscious:

> It was there but it wasn't a painting, it wasn't on the rock. It was below me, drifting towards me from the furthest level where there was no life, a dark oval trailing limbs. It was blurred but it had eyes, they were open, it was something I knew about, a dead thing, it was dead.   (p. 142)

As that blurred image surfaces into the narrator's consciousness it signals the beginning of her recovery process ('Feeling was beginning to seep back into me. I tingled like a foot that's been asleep', p. 146). No other passage in Atwood has been so extensively interpreted and reinterpreted, so I shall merely add the comment that the redemption of her personal past is presented as sacralised response to the wilderness itself:

> These gods, here on the shore or in the water, unacknowledged or
> forgotten, were the only ones who had given me anything I
> needed; and freely.   (p. 145)

Later, when she is left alone on the island, the narrator, whom from
now on I shall call the 'surfacer'[12] has a series of wilderness encounters which have been likened to shamanistic initiation rituals.[13]
Certainly she undergoes a visionary education where psycho-spiritual
experience and sensory perceptions are presented as parallel modes
of heightened awareness which lead to re-vision and insight. Atwood
has commented in an interview on the relation her female characters have to landscape, contrasting it with some of her early poems
about male explorers:

> The only way the [male] speaker could actually get into the land-
> scape was by dying. In *Surfacing* it's a visionary experience in which
> language is transformed. There was some Indian influence on
> *Surfacing* at that point.   (*Conversations*, p. 114)

As the surfacer begins her invented 'initiation rites' she crosses
another border, this time into the territory of hallucination and
visionary experience. Suffering from exposure and near-starvation
and having eaten nothing but some wrinkled yellow mushrooms, she
has a series of visions. Significantly her first vision is that of the lost
Amerindian world of primeval forest which looms up with the clarity
of hallucination:

> The forest leaps upward, enormous, the way it was before they cut
> it, columns of sunlight frozen; the boulders float, melt, everything
> is made of water, even the rocks. In one of the languages there are
> no nouns, only verbs held for a longer moment.
>   The animals have no need for speech, why talk when you are a
>   word
>   I lean against a tree, I am a tree leaning ...
>   I am not an animal or a tree, I am the thing in which the trees
>   and animals move and grow, I am a place.   (p. 181)

In this mythic world of dynamic process, reality consists of an unin-
terrupted flow of energy in perpetual metamorphosis. The surfacer
briefly experiences that process as her body boundaries dissolve and
she has a vision of becoming vitally connected to the earth as a component of the wilderness landscape. However, to become part of that

wilderness world would mean the loss of her individual identity as a human being, and she instinctively draws away from that merging, which is the way of mysticism or madness. Irremediably human, she has to 'break surface', to 'stand' separate again, marking her difference from trees and earth. This need for separation is confirmed in the surfacer's encounter with her father's ghost as wilderness monster, standing like a terrible warning against the abolition of borders: 'He wants the forest to flow back into the places his mind cleared' (p. 186). Immediately after this vision comes the crucial moment of recovery, where at the sight of a fish jumping on the lake the surfacer undergoes a series of radical shifts in perception till her vision settles back into a frame of normalcy:

From the lake a fish jumps
An idea of a fish jumps
A fish jumps, carved wooden fish with dots painted on the sides, no, antlered fish thing drawn in red on cliffstone, protecting spirit. It hangs in the air suspended, flesh turned to icon, he has changed again, returned to the water. How many shapes can he take.
I watch it for an hour or so; then it drops and softens, the circles widen, it becomes an ordinary fish again. (p. 187)

This is an exceptionally detailed record of how subjective perceptions of an object alter it, so that a real fish becomes first a visual image, then a word and an idea in the mind of the perceiver, changing into the wooden trophy seen earlier in the village bar, then into the antlered fish in the copy of the Indian rock paintings, then into the shadow of the dead father's body, till it finally becomes a fish again, dropping into the water. These multiple transformations are effected through subjective vision and registered in language which is closer to poetry than to prose.

The surfacer is at last able to tell her life story and to offer another model for remembering when she realises that her story, like the image of the fish, is always multiple and subject to changing perceptions. Having heard the other language of the wilderness, she has also realised that words are a human necessity, for to be alienated from words is to be alienated from one's fellow human beings. The final chapter is a curious blend of definition and indeterminacy. It begins with assertion; 'This above all, to refuse to be a victim ... The word games, the winning and losing games are finished' (p. 191). However, a new language still has to be invented, and the surfacer is caught between new and old. As she contemplates the possibility of returning to her lover Joe, she faces the double possibility of love and trust but also of compromise and failure 'through the intercession of words' (p. 192). Her story ends tentatively as she stands hidden among the trees watching Joe who is calling her name, poised to step forward but not yet moving. However, the ending is optimistic, for as the surfacer realises, 'withdrawing is no longer possible and the alternative is death' (p. 191). She no longer hears the voice of the wilderness but only Joe's voice as he comes like a mediator offering her 'something', whereas the wilderness has become silent again. The novel ends, 'The lake is quiet, the trees surround me, asking and giving nothing' (p. 192).

The narrator has surfaced through patriarchal language with its definitions of 'woman' and 'victim' and she has found an appropriate form for her own story of survival within a quest narrative that mixes realism and fantasy. Yet this is a quest which is markedly incomplete and it is worth turning back now to examine the significance of the novel's title. '*Surfacing*' is a gerund (a noun made out of a verb), indicating process and activity rather than a completed action. *Surfacing* charts a change in the narrator's subjective perceptions of reality, as she shifts from a position of alienation and victimhood to a new sense of the vital relationship between herself as human and the land which she inhabits, though it also signals a further stage which she has to face in coming to terms with human beings in the modern world. That is literally her next step forward. Atwood commented on the changes registered in the novel in an interview shortly after it was published:

> You can define yourself as innocent and get killed, or you can define yourself as a killer and kill others. I think there has to be a third thing again: the ideal would be somebody who would neither be a killer or a victim, who could achieve some kind of harmony with the world ... Now in neither book [*Surfacing* or *Survival*] is that actualized, but in both it's seen as a possibility finally, whereas initially it is not.[14]

Surfacing ends with an emphasis on survival and the regenerative powers of the wilderness while *Survival* ends with two questions:

> Have we survived?
> If so, what happens *after* Survival?   (p. 246)

Twenty years later Atwood provides a sequel in *Wilderness Tips*, addressed not only to Canadians but to her international readership as well. The word 'wilderness' is there again, acknowledging the Canadian tradition out of which Atwood speaks, but now there is a marked shift away from the optimism of the 1970s towards visions of loss and disempowerment in a late modern world where the grand narratives of history and national myth are collapsing and the survival of the human race is shadowed by threats of global pollution. In this collection there are several wilderness stories, 'Death by Landscape', 'Age of Lead' and also the title story, which is the one I wish to discuss here because it gives a specifically Canadian focus to many of the anxieties about history and the future which are represented in this volume. Invoking the wilderness tradition as she had done in *Surfacing* and *Survival,* Atwood in 'Wilderness Tips' again asks the question, 'What does it mean to be a Canadian?' Twenty years on the answer is less clear, and through the multiple answers to that question wilderness is exposed as a national myth which stands in need of revision in contemporary urban multicultural Canada. This is an anxiously ambivalent story whose very title signals a shift in attitude to the wilderness myth with that slippery word 'tips': 'He [George] was not immediately sure whether this word was a verb or a noun'.[15] The story ends with a woman's vision of a drowning landscape as the forest slips slowly down into a lake.

'Wilderness Tips' is set at a lakeside cottage (probably in Ontario) in the summer of 1990, where a group of middle-aged Canadians – three sisters, one brother and the immigrant husband of one of the sisters – are spending the week-end, having driven up from the city (probably Toronto) to their pastoral retreat which the family have inherited from their great-grandfather. To all appearances, the popular myth of wilderness is in place. However, even on the first page what looks like a shared frame of reference shows its cracks in a conversation between Prue and her sister's husband George, a Hungarian immigrant who came to Canada in the late 1950s:

> 'It's the forties look,' she says to George, hand on her hip, doing a pirouette. 'Rosie the Riveter. From the war. Remember her?'
>   George, whose name is not really George, does not remember. He spent the forties rooting through garbage heaps and begging, and doing other things unsuitable for a child.   (p. 197)

George is the outsider who has learned to be a Canadian only in adult life, having first been Prue's lover and then later the husband of her younger sister Portia. It is mainly through his ambiguous vision that the tradition of wilderness is interrogated. There are a

number of complementary preoccupations here to do with cultural
and literary traditions, with problems of origin, and with questions of
inheritance and survival. As the multivoiced narrative speculates on
these matters, the question of inheritance becomes a questioning of
inheritance, played out in this most traditional of scenarios where
familiar domestic rhythms barely contain the transgressive emotional
forces which threaten its fragile order.

It is, however, the construction of the wilderness myth through literary tradition which is foregrounded here – in the name of the
cottage 'Wacousta Lodge', in the books in the great-grandfather's
library at the cottage, and in the responses of those inheritors of the
tradition living in the present. Atwood names her literary inheritance when it is explained to George on his first visit that *Wacousta* is
the title of a nineteenth-century Canadian historical romance by
Major John Richardson and that it is 'about war'. It is also about
duplicity, revenge and betrayal, for Wacousta the protagonist is a
double figure, being an English aristocrat who has come to Canada
and then gone Indian. The reference to this novel, described by a
recent critic as problematising 'the whole notion of a stable, coherent national or personal identity' for Canadians provides an important clue to the thematic patternings and shifting perspectives in
Atwood's story.[16] I would go further to suggest that not only is
Atwood aligning herself with the Ontario Gothic tradition charted by
Richardson in 1832 but that she is offering here a contemporary
revised version of *Wacousta*, voicing similar anxieties over the construction of a viable national identity more than a hundred years
later. Wacousta stalks like a totemic ancestor behind the two male
protagonists, Roland the Canadian-born traditionalist and George
the immigrant opportunist who has married Roland's favourite sister
Portia and reinvented himself as a prosperous English-speaking
Canadian. If George is the trickster figure modelled on Wacousta,
then it is Roland who has inherited Wacousta's fantasy of becoming
Indian, and borders blur when we discover that for both of them
Wacousta Lodge is 'sacred ground'. By the end of the story they are
both losers – as was Wacousta – for George has broken his private
taboo and spoiled his image of the unpolluted wilderness by seduc-
ing the third sister in the boathouse, and Roland is powerless to
prevent George's betrayal. Reduced to silence, this Canadian
brother remains fixated in his wilderness fantasies.

However, it is not only through *Wacousta* that the wilderness
tradition is examined, for there are other books on the great-
grandfather's shelves – books that only George has read. Their

titles trace the genealogy of this indigenous Canadian tradition: '*From Sea to Sea. Wild Animals I Have Known. The Collected Poems of Robert Service. Our Empire Story. Wilderness Tips*' (p. 207). When looked into, this tradition is revealed to be the invention of white male English-speaking colonialists who were fascinated by the wilderness with its alien forests and animals and its Indian lore. However, it is the last book on the shelf which highlights the ambiguities of this tradition, for *Wilderness Tips*, that most authentic-looking text which is described in detail with its date (1905), author's photograph (white male, paddling a canoe) and summary of contents, is actually a forgery. The book is Atwood's own invention and her most daring challenge as a woman writer to the male tradition of wilderness writing. This forged 'Canadian signature' raises the question of what authenticity might mean when the tradition finds its most complete representation in a pastiche text which is indistinguishable from an original. Furthermore, this imitation is embedded in a story of the same name which is itself a critique of the wilderness myth. While Atwood acknowledges the romantic appeal of wilderness as a cherished white myth of origins, she also casts doubt on the viability of this tradition in contemporary Canada. Roland, the boy who grew up reading *Wilderness Tips* and who fantasised about being an Indian, is an anachronism, a true believer in a vanished past which probably never existed outside the colonial imagination:

> All that was gone, lost, ruined, years and years before he was born. He knows this is nonsense ... How can you lose something that was never yours in the first place? (But you can, because *Wilderness Tips* was his once, and he's lost it.)   (p. 214)

Left with nothing but the pain of nostalgia, Roland is truly dispossessed – not by George whom he fears as a usurping immigrant but by the modern world of which George is one representative with its powerboats, transistor radios, its creeping urbanisation and its resultant 'acres of treelessness, of new town houses with little pointed roofs – like tents, like an invasion. The tents of the Goths and the Vandals. The tents of the Huns and the Magyars. The tents of George' (p. 211). It is through Roland's anxieties that the story articulates its anxious concerns about the survival of the wilderness tradition, which is shown to be a cherished white anglophone cultural myth in need of revision in a postmodern multicultural Canada.

In this delicately articulated story with its correspondences and border-blur, Roland's disillusion is paralleled by his sister's, for

Portia also has a wilderness vision at her moment of crisis when she
is forced to recognise the failure of her cherished fantasy of romantic love and marriage. Like her brother she takes refuge in the memories of childhood and runs down to the lake, but as she looks back
to the shore from where she lies floating in the water, suddenly
wilderness 'tips':

> It's no longer horizontal: it seems to be on a slant, as if there'd
> been a slippage in the bedrock; as if the trees, the granite out-
> crops, Wacousta Lodge, the peninsula, the whole mainland were
> sliding gradually down, submerging.   (p. 221)

Though Portia's vision shifts from one of quiet collapse into one of
cataclysmic disaster figured in the sinking of the Titanic, it is the
concept of wilderness destabilised, both as cultural myth and in its
visual figuration, which is most significant for my reading. The last
words of the story deny apocalypse by situating Portia's traumatic
moment in a wider historical context: 'And nothing has happened,
really, that hasn't happened before.' Private feelings, public crises,
literary tradition and wilderness myth all blur together here.

Though the action of the story does not move beyond visions of
collapse and disaster, Atwood does provide an ending which is
rather like the endings of *Surfacing* and *Survival*, poised on the point
of moving forward. Portia's own perceptions have changed and for
the first time she envisages how she could have lived her life differently, less bound to family expectations and traditions and making
her own choices instead. The ending functions in a shadowy way as a
springboard for revised narratives of the future beyond present
threats of collapse. As her unfaithful husband reflected earlier:
'George is not worried: he's been in countries that were falling apart
before. There can be opportunities' (p. 199).

Paradoxically through her reference to history Atwood is opening
up a space beyond calamity, suggesting that new ways might be
found to refigure the narrative of Canadian identity. It will not mean
a return to the old wilderness tradition for there has been a 'slippage in the bedrock' of English-Canadian beliefs, and traditional
assumptions no longer go unquestioned. With its reference to
Wacousta the story suggests that there never was a homogeneous
Canadian national narrative; it was always as much of a fiction as
Portia's domestic fantasies, and now its inauthenticities are being
exposed under pressure of immigrant and Native voices claiming
their right to participate in the new definitions of what being a

'Canadian' means. Canadians need to construct a new discourse of nationhood which represents cultural difference and interaction. 'Survival' is the keystone, or maybe 'Surfacing', but not 'wilderness' as any essentialist definition of Canadianness. Atwood's story suggests however that the wilderness myth for all its anachronism remains the sign of values worth preserving in some form, with its nostalgia for an unpolluted environment and the moral concepts of nobility and honour personified by the Indians in the old wilderness code. These values, she warns, are frequently lacking in contemporary life: 'When was the last time Roland heard anyone praised for being *honourable*?' (p. 213).

As in *Surfacing* and *Survival*, so in *Wilderness Tips* Atwood chronicles Canadian anxieties about identity, shifting from her early nationalist writings to her 1990s fictions which describe a postcolonial crisis where formerly dominant traditions have been permanently disrupted and where new narratives of cultural difference need to be formulated. Taking wilderness as her key motif, she addresses not only her Canadian but also her international readership, diagnosing the symptoms of a general postmodern malaise as they appear in the specifically Canadian context out of which she writes. Atwood's conception of futures being already foreshadowed by the past even as they are being shaped in the present makes for dire warnings in a world on the edge of breakdown, but she continues to write in the hope of opening up new possibilities for revisionary narratives which may avert irremediable loss and collapse, for 'nothing has happened, really, that hasn't happened before'. The final paradox may be that though Canadian wilderness may be in danger of disappearing from the earth and receding into myth, yet it is through the very power of myth to transform perceptions that hopes for regeneration and survival may lie.

3

'Feminine, Female, Feminist': From *The Edible Woman* to 'The Female Body'

Can't you see those tits aren't real? She had them done, I know for a fact; she used to be a 34A. You're in love with two sacks of silicone gel.

The Robber Bride, p. 80

These words, thought but not spoken by a rejected wife in a spirit of pained incredulity and warning ('There were some things she has the sense not to say, however') highlight the dimensions of artifice and fantasy involved in representations of the female body, while they also suggest the erotic appeal projected through an illusion of glamour. The same speaker also ponders the question: 'Male fantasies, male fantasies, is everything run by male fantasies?' (p. 392) and although in *The Robber Bride* the tables are turned through a combination of feminine witchcraft and female solidarity, the answer to that question remains ambiguous. In this chapter I shall trace Atwood's exploration of sexual power politics through social myths of femininity and representations of the female body in two texts which mark very different stages in her writing career and in the history of feminism. *The Edible Woman,* her first novel, appeared in 1969 at the beginning of 'second wave' feminism, whereas the savage little fable 'The Female Body' written 20 years later (after *Bodily Harm, The Handmaid's Tale* and a woman artist's paintings of the female body in *Cat's Eye*) belongs to the explicitly political context of feminism in the early 1990s, laying out the implications of patriarchal myths and fantasies about women with diagrammatic simplicity.[1] The differences between these texts also explain why my chapter title reverses the terms of Toril Moi's influential essay of the mid-1980s, 'Feminist, Female, Feminine', in order to indicate the direction in which Atwood's work has shifted.[2]

The Edible Woman belongs to a specific moment in the history of North American postwar feminism, which registered the first signs of the contemporary women's movement in its resistance to social myths of femininity. This is the territory charted by Betty Friedan in *The Feminine Mystique* (1963),[3] a study that Atwood herself read 'behind closed doors' like many other young women at the time, and I propose to read *The Edible Woman* in that context. Atwood and Friedan highlight the same new area of gendered social concern, and the thematic issues in *The Edible Woman* could even be classified under the chapter headings in Friedan's book. However, the very title of Atwood's novel signals significant differences with its dimensions of fantasy and metaphorical thinking which are absent from Friedan's sociological treatise, for *The Edible Woman* is an imaginative transformation of a social problem into comic satire as one young woman rebels against her feminine destiny. Whereas *The Feminine Mystique* documents the anxieties and frustrations felt by a whole generation of young women in America in the 1950s and early 1960s, *The Edible Woman* goes beyond women's anger and bewilderment in its exploitation of the power of laughter to reveal the absurdities within social conventions. This is a subversive rather than a confrontational novel which engages obliquely with social problems, adopting the form of a parodic revision of a traditional comedy of manners with its fixation on the marriage theme. Here Atwood mixes those earlier conventions with the language of 1960s advertising and cookery books, adding a dash of popular Freudianism and a few of the Jungian archetypes so fashionable in literary criticism of the 1950s and 1960s, to produce a satirical exposure of women's continuing conditions of entrapment within their own bodies and within social myths. The novel mounts its attack on social and gender ideology very wittily, though it bears the mark of its historical period with its deprecatingly feminine glance back over the shoulder when one of the characters comments, 'I don't want you to think that all this means anything' (p. 145). It is part of Atwood's playful ambiguity that the speaker here is male. That same speaker, a young graduate student in English literature, happens to be the novel's most vigorous critic of gender stereotypes, of advertising and of the consumerist ethic. Under a series of comic masks Atwood's novel

explores the relation between consumerism and the feminine mystique, where one young woman's resistance to consuming and to
being consumed hints at a wider condition of social malaise which
the new feminist movement was just beginning to address.

It would be fair to say that when *The Feminine Mystique* burst upon
the popular market in 1963 it signalled the beginning of feminism as
a political force in postwar North America. It had such a revolutionary impact for two reasons: first, because it was a 'scientific' response
to a widely recognised phenomenon ('By 1962 the plight of the
trapped American housewife had become a national parlor game.
Whole issues of magazines, newspaper columns, books learned and
frivolous, educational conferences and television panels were
devoted to the problem'; *The Feminine Mystique*, p. 25), and secondly,
because it gave a name to that widespread malaise. Suddenly, 'The
Problem That Has No Name' was named and became a public issue
rather than something confined to the area of women's private
discontents:

> There was a strange discrepancy between the reality of our lives as
> women and the image to which we were trying to conform, the
> image which I came to call the feminine mystique. I wondered if
> other women faced this schizophrenic split, and what it meant.
> (p. 9)

The Feminine Mystique, whose brilliant title derives I suspect from
Simone de Beauvoir's phrase the 'Myth of Femininity', exposes the
dimensions of mystification and inauthenticity within current
concepts of femininity which gave dissenting women a platform
for social protest as a new interest group. Friedan described the
mystique of feminine fulfilment as 'the cherished and self-
perpetuating core of contemporary American culture' (p. 18),
then subjected it to a devastating socio-economic analysis prying
behind that 'pretty picture of the American suburban housewife-
mother' to reveal the dimensions of women's loss of independence
after the Second World War which were concealed by an image of
happy domesticity:

> The end of the road ... is the disappearance of the heroine alto-
> gether, as a separate self and the subject of her own story. The
> end of the road is togetherness, where the woman has no inde-
> pendent self to hide even in guilt; she exists only for and through
> her husband and children.   (p. 47)

Friedan signals the personal dimensions of a social problem in chapter titles such as 'The Crisis in Woman's Identity' and 'The Forfeited Self', while as a sociologist she explores the link between myths of femininity, advertising and the mass market economy. In a chapter called 'The Sexual Sell' she asks in whose interest it is to keep women imprisoned in the feminine mystique, and her answer is: American business interests and the ethic of consumerism. Women are the prize victims of a conspiracy manipulated by those hidden persuaders the advertisers: 'I suddenly realised the significance of the boast that women wield seventy-five per cent of the purchasing power in America' (p. 208).[4] As Friedan presents the situation, American sociologists and educationists in the 1960s were in collusion against the development of women's powers as rational beings. In a chapter called 'The Functional Freeze, the Feminine Protest, and Margaret Mead' she condemns the pieties of social science, Freudian psychology and anthropology, all of which championed the value of women's 'adjustment' to cultural definitions of femininity:

> At a time of great change for women, at a time when education, science, and social science should have helped women bridge the change, functionalism transformed 'what is' for women, or 'what was,' to 'what should be' ... [and] so closed the door of the future on women.   (p. 135)

Some of her most vigorous condemnation is directed toward the anthropologist Margaret Mead, whose work on gender differences in primitive societies was popularly interpreted as a glorification of the female role, defined according to the biological function of childbearing. Friedan points the finger of criticism directly at Mead's study of men and women in primitive societies, *Male and Female* (1955), as the 'book which became the cornerstone of the feminine mystique'. What she criticises most is the inauthenticity of the return to 'primitive earth-mother maternity' in modern Western society, where that image of the 'natural' could only be maintained by an educated woman's negation of many of her own acknowledged capacities. As Friedan comments rather tartly:

> The role of Margaret Mead as the professional *spokesman* [my Italics] for femininity would have been less important if American women had taken the example of her own life, instead of listening to what she said in her books. Margaret Mead has lived a life of open challenge.   (p. 145)

Atwood's dramatisation of the contradictions within the concept of femininity according to the 'functional freeze' doctrine provides some of the best comedy in *The Edible Woman* in her two parodic versions of earth-mothers, one a passive victim of the feminine mystique and one (a former psychology student and evidently a devotee of Margaret Mead) whose relentless pursuit of a father for her child 'bore a chilling resemblance to a general plotting a major campaign' (*The Edible Woman*, p. 85).

In North American society of the late 1950s and 1960s where 'adjustment' for a woman meant accepting a dependent 'feminine' role, it was as Friedan says, 'very hard for a human being to sustain such an inner split – conforming outwardly to one reality, while trying to maintain inwardly the values it denies' (p. 308). In a chapter whose full title is 'Progressive Dehumanization: the Comfortable Concentration Camp', Friedan glances at the territory of female neurosis which Atwood's novel explores with such imaginative insight:

> If the human organism has an innate urge to grow, to expand and become all it can be, it is not surprising that the bodies and the minds of healthy women begin to rebel as they try to adjust to a role that does not permit this growth.   (p. 292)

Friedan cites case histories of women suffering from fatigue, heart attacks and psychotic breakdowns, a catalogue of female hysterical illness induced by women's attempts to conform to the (impossible and undesirable) codes of the feminine mystique. It is precisely in that speculative area of pathology so 'puzzling to doctors and analysts' that the nervous eating disorder of Atwood's heroine is located, where the female body becomes the site of victimisation, internal conflict and rebellion.

I think I have said sufficient to establish that *The Feminine Mystique* may be an appropriate lens through which to read *The Edible Woman* as social critique, for it is a 1960s story of a woman's identity crisis provoked by pressures against which she finds herself seriously at odds. Marian MacAlpin is a young graduate in her twenties with an independent income, living in Toronto and sharing an apartment with another young woman, Ainsley Tewce. She also has a boyfriend to whom she becomes engaged, Peter Wollander, an ambitious young lawyer with a passionate interest in guns and cameras. The narrative traces the stages of Marian's rebellion against social conformity as she becomes increasingly disillusioned with her job and her fiancé to the point where her inner conflict finds its outward expression in an eating disorder whose symptoms resemble anorexia nervosa. While the novel hints at the connection between social institutions and personal relations which would become the central theme in Atwood's collection of poems *Power Politics* (1971), it cannot easily be classified as a realist text for it insistently challenges the conventions of realism by its excursions into fantasy and its flights of metaphorical inventiveness. *The Edible Woman* is a comedy of resistance and survival which subverts social definitions from within, shown by the way Marian finally wins her independence from the feminine mystique through her traditionally feminine gesture of making a cake, which she offers to the two men in her life. Her fiancé refuses it; her strange changeling mentor and guide, Duncan the graduate student in English, helps her to eat it all up. Clearly, an iced cake in the shape of a woman is the central metaphor for Marian's perception of woman's condition and fate as decreed by the feminine mystique so that her cake-baking is both a gesture of complicity in the domestic myth and also a critique of it. Atwood described the tea ritual as 'symbolic cannibalism', with the cake as simulacrum of the socialised feminine image which Marian rejects; but it is also of course a party game with Duncan as the 'child' and Marian as the 'mother' once again in control. Eating the cake is an act of celebration which marks the decisive moment of Marian's recovery from an hysterical illness and her return to the social order. Once again she becomes a 'consumer', for it is difficult if not impossible to reconstruct one's identity outside the symbolic and social order, and individual survival is likely to mean compromises with society. This is a conclusion similar to the one in *Surfacing* (1972), and Atwood's comment on the similarities between the two books draws attention to what her female protagonists have accomplished in finding new subject positions for themselves more in harmony with the world they live in.[5]

As a woman writer Atwood has always been intensely aware of the significance of representations of the female body, both in terms of a woman's self-definition and as a fantasy object:

The body as a concept has always been a concern of mine. It's there in *Surfacing* as well. I think that people very much experience themselves through their bodies and through concepts of the body which get applied to their own bodies. Which they pick up from their culture and apply to their own. It's also my concern in *Lady Oracle* and it's even there in *The Edible Woman*. (*Conversations*, p. 187)

The originality of *The Edible Woman* lies in its exposure of the 'sexual sell' promoted by the feminine mystique, for the narrative reveals how social paradigms of femininity may distort women's perceptions of their sexuality in the interests of creating childlike or doll-like fantasy figures. A young woman like Marian, sensitised as she is to the social script of gender relations and feminine expectations, seems to have little consciousness of her own body either in terms of its maternal urges or its erotic pleasures. Female bodies and biological processes like pregnancy, childbirth and menstruation figure in the novel, but they are treated with a measure of comic detachment. When viewed through Marian's eyes, sexually mature female bodies become grotesque and rather disgusting, whether it is her friend Clara's pregnant body or the fat ageing bodies of her fellow office workers at the Christmas party or the fiasco of the coast-to-coast market research survey on sanitary napkins, where some of the questionnaires 'obviously went out to men' ('Here's one with "Tee Hee" written on it, from a Mr Leslie Andrewes', p. 110).

In contrast to Marian, her friends Clara and Ainsley celebrate women's biological destiny, though their different approaches to motherhood turn them into parodic images of the maternal principle. Clara, who enters the narrative heavily pregnant with her third child, looks to Marian 'like a boa-constrictor that has swallowed a water melon' (p. 31). Marian sees her as one of the casualties of the female life, a representation of the duplicities of the feminine mystique which could transform a girl who was 'everyone's idea of translucent perfume-advertisement femininity' into a kind of female monster, the helpless victim of her own biology:

> She simply stood helpless while the tide of dirt rose round her, unable to stop it or evade it. The babies were like that too; her own body seemed somehow beyond her, going its own way without reference to any directions of hers. (p. 37)

There are several ironies here, not least a foreshadowing of Marian's own bodily insurrection, but the most obvious is that Clara's own attitude to motherhood is quite savagely unmaternal: 'Her metaphors for her children included barnacles encrusting a ship and limpets clinging to a rock' (p. 36). Yet when Clara's baby is born, she describes the process to Marian with a kind of rapture: 'Oh marvellous; really marvellous. I watched the whole thing, it's messy, all that blood and junk, but I've got to admit it's sort of fascinating' (pp. 128–9). Marian's response is not one of sympathy but of alarm at possibly being implicated by her age and her gender, and she escapes from the maternity hospital 'as if from a culvert or cave. She was glad she wasn't Clara' (p. 132).

If Clara represents woman's passive fulfilment of her biological destiny, then Ainsley represents a more intellectualised approach to maternity as she embarks on it as a social project with the aim of becoming a single parent. (Ainsley's derogatory remarks about men and fatherhood are amusingly similar to those of Offred's mother in *The Handmaid's Tale* written 20 years later). Her programme is entirely ideological and in a curious way academic and theoretical:

> 'Every woman should have at least one baby.' She sounded like a voice on the radio saying that every woman should have at least one electric hair-dryer. 'It's even more important than sex. It fulfils your deepest femininity.'   (p. 41)

As an undergraduate Ainsley must have read Margaret Mead. Marian mentions her fondness for paperbacks by anthropologists about primitive cultures, and Ainsley herself expounds on breast-feeding habits in South America. In her quest to fulfil an anthropological concept of female 'wholeness' Ainsley displays all the contradictions between 'nature' and 'culture' identified by Friedan in her critique of Mead's theories when they are put into practice by university-educated North American women. Ainsley's pursuit of Marian's friend Leonard Slank, a notorious womaniser with a penchant for inexperienced young girls, works as a comic reversal of the traditional seduction plot exposing the dynamics of the sexual game in all its duplicity. Ainsley's artful imitation of youthful innocence ('It was necessary for her mind to appear as vacant as her face'; p. 119), and Leonard's pose of world-weary drunken lecher are equally false, as is revealed when she triumphantly announces to him that she is pregnant. He collapses in a crisis of Freudian horror:

> Now I'm going to be all mentally tangled up in Birth. Fecundity. Gestation. Don't you realize what that will do to me? It's obscene, that horrible oozy ...
>   'Don't be idiotic,' Ainsley said '... You're displaying the classic symptoms of uterus envy.'   (p. 159)

It is Leonard who is the casualty in this battle between the sexes. However, as part of the comic deconstruction of stereotypes here, the most passionate advocate for the maternal principle is a male

Jungian literary critic, the graduate student Fischer Smythe, who is obsessed with archetypal womb symbols and who in turn becomes fascinated with the pregnant Ainsley as an Earth Mother figure just as Leonard Slank recoils from her 'goddam fertility-worship' (p. 214). Indeed, it is the male characters who display far more interest in female biology than the women and whose language rises to heights of eloquence or abuse in their fantasy representations of the female body. By contrast, Marian refuses to get involved either with Ainsley's 'fraud' or Clara's domestic chaos.

Not only does Marian feel threatened by childbearing but she also feels alienated from her body in other ways as well. At the office Christmas party, surrounded by the fat and ageing bodies of her colleagues, Marian's perspective shifts from a kind of anthropological detachment to a sudden shocked recognition that she too shares this mysterious female condition:

> What peculiar creatures they were; and the continual flux between the outside and the inside, taking things in, giving them out, chewing, words, potato-chips, burps, grease, hair, babies, milk, excrement, cookies, vomit, coffee, tomato-juice, blood, tea, sweat, liquor, tears, and garbage ... At some time she would be – or no, already she was like that too; she was one of them, her body the same, identical, merged with that other flesh that choked the air in the flowered room with its sweet organic scent; she felt suffocated by this thick sargasso-sea of femininity.   (p. 167)

We begin to understand that Marian does not wish to turn into any of the models of adult women offered by society, and that behind her conventional femininity lies a horror of the body which relates to her fear of growing up signalled either by marriage, maternity or the office pension plan. She wants none of these futures, and it is in this context of challenge to the discourses of both femininity and adulthood that her hysterical eating disorder needs to be interpreted.

Marian's inability to eat may look like anorexia nervosa, but the etiology of her disease actually differs quite markedly from the clinical diagnoses as summarised by Noelle Caskey in her historical account 'Interpreting Anorexia Nervosa'.[6] Though Marian suffers from the visual and cognitive distortions which characterise semi-starvation, most of the usual symptoms of anorexia are absent. She has no phobic fear of fat and she suffers no weight loss; she does not feel any of that enhanced sense of autonomy which Sheila MacLeod describes in *The Art of Starvation* (1982). Marian suffers from a condition of self-division which Dennis Cooley has identified in *Power Politics*:

> We find in *Power Politics* what we find in so many Atwood books of the 1970s especially (I include the novels): namely, a division of head and body at the neck. The neck figures as pinched conduit between faculties (mind/body) whose schism is disastrous.[7]

With Marian this division signals two powers of agency within herself, will and instinct acting in opposition to each other in a pattern which becomes the main line of narrative action:

> Whatever it was that had been making these decisions, not her mind certainly, rejected anything that had an indication of bone or tendon or fibre. (p. 152)

Though she sees this as a malignant, possibly life-threatening condition, she is powerless to control it. At the peak of her disease she reaches the point where she cannot eat or drink anything at all:

> It had finally happened at last then. Her body had cut itself off. The food circle had dwindled to a point, a black dot, closing everything outside. (p. 257)

Of all the diagnoses of anorexia, the one closest to Marian's case would appear to be what Caskey calls 'a thought disorder',[8] where the body's refusal to eat forms part of a discourse of hysterical protest. It is an example of that disturbed female vision which signals the collapse of boundaries between personal trauma and social crisis that Atwood will use much later in *Wilderness Tips*. In this early feminist text the personal is fused with the political as Marian's body speaks its language of rebellion against the socialised feminine identity that she appears to have already accepted. Marian can quote the received 1960s wisdom about the influence of the subconscious on behaviour, 'It was my subconscious getting ahead of my conscious self, and the subconscious has its own logic' (p. 101), though it is typical of her lack of self-knowledge that she should so disastrously misinterpret its messages in her own case. Marian's hysteria is a mode of metaphorical discourse popularised first by Freudian psychoanalysis as the language of the subconscious and of dreams, and then appropriated by feminist writers and critics as a distinguishing mark of female subjectivity, where the feminine 'imaginary' disrupts the logic of a masculine 'symbolic' order.[9] Marian's rebellion occurs at a level below consciousness and then manifests itself in hallucinations and body language. As Freud has shown, the body evades the repression of conscious will by speaking out in the language of metaphor, so that Marian's anxiety at the prospect of her 'erasure' as an independent social being within the patriarchal system through marriage to Peter is externalised first in images of metamorphosis where she becomes identified with animal victims, and then even more overtly by her body's panic protest in its refusal to ingest food or drink. The social system 'makes her sick'. It is not insignificant that Peter represents the law-giver and the hunter in Marian's scenarios of violence, whereas she is the escape artist identified with the spaces of the wilderness. The pattern is signalled in her first attempt at flight, when she runs away from the Park Plaza Hotel and the talk of her male companions, Peter and Leonard Slank, about cameras and hunting. That attempt is fuelled by Marian's subconscious identification with the disembowelled rabbit in Peter's story and then confirmed by the description of her recapture:

> I felt myself caught, set down and shaken. It was Peter, who must have stalked me and waited there on the side-street, knowing I would come over the wall. 'What the hell got into you?' he said.   (p. 74)

Of course, she is accused by the two men of emotional instability: 'Didn't think you were the hysterical type.' Marian's own silent response offers a different interpretation of 'hysteria' with its suggestion of unconscious resistance:

> Once I was outside I felt considerably better. I had broken out; from what, or into what, I didn't know. Though I wasn't at all certain why I had been acting this way, I had at least acted. Some kind of decision had been made, something had been finished.   (p. 78)

The hunting imagery is continued in the narrative, for the trap is sprung with Peter's marriage proposal that same night. Though Marian makes every effort to adjust herself to the socially acceptable image of adoring female partner, her eating disorder is clearly a continuation of this pattern of psychic resistance, a metaphorical expression of panic at the idea of marriage. It is Marian's imagination which is the subversive force, the place where food is metamorphosed into living flesh and blood:

She looked down at her own half-eaten steak and suddenly saw it as a hunk of muscle. Blood red. Part of a real cow that once moved and ate and was killed. ... and she had been devouring it. (pp. 151–2)

The cannibalism motif which carries through to the end with the cake is a sign of hallucinatory displacement, where metaphor inscribes Marian's unconscious fears of becoming an object of consumption herself. As her marriage gets closer, so her disorder gets worse and the list of 'forbidden foods' gets longer, until the point where she can eat nothing at all.

However, this is to leap ahead, neglecting the circumstances which produced Marian's rebellion in the first place. On the surface she would seem to be content with her destiny – with her job in the marketing firm which promotes sexual stereotyping, and then her forthcoming marriage and entry into domesticity. Reading back from the crisis, however, there are early warning signs of Marian's dissent in her antipathy to the maternal projects of Clara and Ainsley and her futile escape attempts from Peter. Even the marriage proposal itself, made unexpectedly in the midst of a furious argument and with an electric storm raging, is a parodic version of the female romance plot. So is Marian's capitulation to the myth of feminine submissiveness:

'When do you want to get married?' he asked, almost gruffly.
My first impulse was to answer, with the evasive flippancy I'd always used before when he'd asked me serious questions about myself, 'What about Groundhog Day?' But instead I heard a soft flannelly voice I barely recognized, saying, 'I'd rather have you decide that. I'd rather leave the big decisions up to you.' (p. 90)

This puppet voice imitates Friedan's helplessly dependent women: 'They had no thought for the unfeminine problems of the world outside the home, they wanted the men to make the major decisions' (p. 18). By the end of the first section, Marian's submission to the feminine mystique is almost complete as she throws away her university textbooks and prepares to think about what a 'well-organised marriage' might mean.

There is only one disruptive element in her scenario of social conformity. This is represented by the oddly childlike figure of Duncan, the young man who alone had challenged the rhetoric of Marian's Moose Beer questionnaires:

'First, what about "Deep-down manly flavour?" '

He threw his head back and closed his eyes. 'Sweat,' he said, considering. 'Canvas gym shoes. Underground locker-rooms and jock-straps.'   (p. 52)

He is also the man in the laundromat who stares at the washing machines in their endlessly repetitive cycles and with whom Marian feels an inexplicable affinity:

I still can't quite fit in the man at the laundromat or account for my own behaviour. Maybe it was a kind of lapse, a blank in the ego, like amnesia ... he has nothing at all to do with Peter. (p. 103)

Duncan is the unaccommodated remainder whose role is to unsettle the whole structure of Marian's expectations by revealing its lack.

The design of the narrative with its radical shift from the first person narration in Part 1 to the third person in Part 2 underlines Marian's loss of an independent sense of self; it is also Part 2 which signals the onset and crisis of her nervous disease. As the bride to be, she has already opted out of the professional world and has nothing to do but wait passively for her wedding: 'It was all being taken care of, there was nothing for her to do. She was floating, letting the current hold her up' (p. 115). Under the spell of the feminine mystique, she is merely biding her time, yet there are signals that this is for Marian what Friedan would call 'The Mistaken Choice'. Though an apparently willing victim, Marian is troubled by her strange eating disorder and by inexplicable intimations of 'sodden formless unhappiness'. Perhaps the best gloss on her state is provided by another victim of the feminine mystique in the late 1950s, the American poet Adrienne Rich, who writes about her own condition using similar imagery of drifting and self division: 'What frightened me most was the sense of drift, of being pulled along on a current which called itself my destiny, but in which I seemed to be losing touch with whoever I had been, with the girl who had experienced her own will and energy almost ecstatically at times, walking around a city or riding a train or typing in a student room'.[10] It is the concept of freedom which Duncan represents, enhanced in his case by a Peter Pan pose of childlike irresponsibility as he refashions the world according to his own wishes and so fantasises an alternative reality. He challenges all Marian's traditional ideas of masculinity, romantic love and parent–child relations, while his 'family' of two other male graduate students, Trevor and Fish, forms a gaily subversive trio who transgress traditional gender roles, dedicated as they are to the domestic arts of washing and ironing, cooking and parenting. Caught between this playful student world and the world of social conformity, Marian loses any sense of herself as a unified subject, beginning to hallucinate her emotional conflict in images of bodily dissolution and haunted by hallucinations of fragmentation. Lying in the bath on the evening of the first party which she and Peter are giving as an engaged couple, she begins to believe that her body is 'coming apart layer by layer like a piece of cardboard in a gutter puddle' (p. 218).

That party, to which all the main characters in the novel are invited, represents the climax of Atwood's 'anti-comedy':

> I think in your standard 18th-century comedy you have a young couple who is faced with difficulty in the form of somebody who embodies the restrictive forces of society and they trick or overcome this difficulty and end up getting married. The same thing happens in *The Edible Woman* except the wrong person gets married ... The comedy solution would be a tragic solution for Marian. (*Conversations*, p. 10)

Atwood's fictional method is what is now recognised as a feminist revision of a traditional genre highlighting the artifice of literary conventions and the social myths they inscribe. There are other divergences from traditional comic patterns here as well. Not only is the artifice of femininity exposed ('You didn't tell me it was a masquerade', says Duncan, looking at Marian's lacquered hair and her slinky red dress) but the party provides the first occasion when the male protagonists speak about femininity from their own perspective, revealing a surprisingly high level of masculine anxiety about this topic. The most devastating attack on the feminine mystique comes from Clara's husband Joe, the philosophy lecturer, who earnestly challenges such mythologising, making a political statement from his personal point of view as a husband and a teacher:

> She's hollow, she doesn't know who she is any more; her core has been destroyed ... I can see it happening with my own female students. But it would be futile to warn them. (p. 236)

There is also a confrontation between the glowingly pregnant Ainsley and Leonard Slank whose masculinity is revealed to be a fragile structure. When she makes her public announcement of his paternity he collapses in a drunken heap, only to be cast aside as Ainsley finds a new father figure for her unborn child in the scholarly Fischer Smythe. That Jungian enthusiast sees her as the living embodiment of the mythic feminine and he pats her belly tenderly, 'his voice heavy with symbolic meaning' (p. 241).

Such comedy coexists with a more serious crisis of realisation for Marian, who looks into her vision of the feminine mystique only to find that she is herself absent from her fantasy of future married bliss in the suburbs:

> There was Peter, forty-five and balding but still recognizable as Peter, standing in bright sunlight beside a barbecue with a long fork ... She looked carefully for herself in the garden, but she wasn't there and the discovery chilled her.   (p. 243)

That self-obliteration prefigures Marian's disappearance from the party for it combines with the traumatic moment when Peter tries to take her photograph, and Marian suddenly sees her predicament as she slips back into her wilderness fantasy:

> She could not let him catch her this time. Once he pulled the trigger she would be stopped, fixed indissolubly in that gesture, that single stance, unable to move or change.   (p. 245)

At last Marian knows what she does not want, and so she escapes from the social script to her unscripted meeting in the laundromat with Duncan and into their brief liaison in a sleazy hotel. Though it begins as a parody of lovemaking with Duncan's complaint that there is 'altogether too much flesh around here' (an echo of Marian's own disgust with female bodies), it ends rather differently with him gently stroking her 'almost as though he was ironing her'. There is also a suggestion of their wilderness affinity as Duncan's face nudges into her flesh, 'like the muzzle of an animal, curious, and only slightly friendly' (p. 254), and it is in the wilderness of a Toronto ravine to which he guides her that Marian's undramatised clarification of mind occurs. Duncan's action in leaving her alone there is exactly what Friedan might have prescribed for bewildered dissenters from the feminine mystique, 'for that last and most important battle *can* be fought in the mind and spirit of woman herself' (*The Feminine Mystique*, p. 369).

By following her own line of metaphorical thinking, Marian discovers a way to solve what for her is an ontological problem, 'some way

she could know what was real: a test, simple and direct as litmus-paper'
(p. 267). The test is of course the cake which she bakes and then ices
in the shape of a woman, a transformation of science into domestic
ritual. Gazing at the cake lady and thinking of her destiny she says,
'You look delicious ... And that's what will happen to you; that's what
you get for being food' (p. 270). However, when offered the cake
Peter flees, either from Marian's literalised metaphor or from her
undisguised hostility, probably into the arms of Lucy, one of Marian's
office friends with 'her delicious dresses and confectionery eyes'
(p. 112). Maybe Marian was right and an 'edible woman' was what
Peter had really wanted all along. It is as if a spell has been broken:
Marian's confusion falls away, and recognising that 'the cake after all
was only a cake' (p. 272), she starts to eat it. Only Ainsley, ever alive to
symbolic implications, bothers to translate the significance of Marian's
cake eating, ironically echoing Peter's earlier accusations. 'Marian!'
she exclaimed at last, with horror. 'You're rejecting your femininity!'
This interpretation is confirmed by Marian's 'plunging her fork into
the carcase, neatly severing the body from the head' (p. 273). That
violent gesture with its parody of vampire slaying carries a further
implication that the feminine image has been draining Marian's life
blood but will have the power to do so no more.

The third section with its energetic return to a first person narrative, 'I was cleaning up the apartment' (p. 277), is devoted to tidying
up the plot in a comic *dénouement* where it is significant that the
three women protagonists survive better than the men: Peter has left
and Marian is once again independent; Leonard Slank has had a
nervous breakdown and is being cared for by Clara like another of
her numerous children, while Ainsley has fulfilled her biological
mission while managing to conform neatly to social convention by
marrying Fischer Smythe and going off to Niagara Falls for their
honeymoon. Marian's house-cleaning works as another domestic
analogy for her own rehabilitation, as her response to Duncan's
phone call suggests: 'Now that I was thinking of myself in the first
person singular again I found my own situation much more interesting than his' (p. 278). Their tea is a replay of Peter's visit, though
with the important differences that Duncan eats the cake (described
by Marian as 'the remains of the cadaver') and that they talk together in a way that she and Peter did not manage to do. It is a curious
conversation in which Duncan casually offers five possible interpretations of the preceding narrative action as if he were commenting
on a literary text in a graduate seminar. The one reading he categor-
ically rejects is Marian's assertion that Peter was trying to destroy her:

'That's just something you made up' (p. 280). Instead, he multiplies the possibilities around the question: Who has been trying to destroy whom? Duncan's ironising (like his passion for ironing things out flat) represents a deliberate distancing from Marian's personal crisis in a general comment on human behaviour. Such a device with its opening up of multiple perspectives shifts any reading of this novel beyond a single feminist focus, implying that the politics of gender is only one example of the power struggles in any relationship. It is Duncan who has the last word, transforming this into a comedy of good manners as he finishes cleaning up the cake: '"Thank you," he said, licking his lips. "It was delicious"' (p. 281). He is the good child who says thank you as Marian the mother regards him with a smile. Yet the ending is not quite the sentimental resolution it may look at first glance, for Duncan remains an enigma,[12] and on a psychological level his eating of the cake resembles nothing so much as the activity of the Sin Eater, a role assigned to the therapist in one of Atwood's later stories.[13]

The domestic scenario raises one last point which relates to the important question of female creativity. It is significant that Marian has chosen to make her protest through a traditionally feminine mode which bypasses language: 'What she needed was something that avoided words, she didn't want to get tangled up in a discussion' (p. 267). She thinks that she has accomplished her purpose, though as any reader in the 1990s would note, none of the three young women – Marian, Ainsley nor Clara – has escaped from their culturally defined gender roles; they are still producing cakes and babies. This leaves unresolved the issue of women's attempts to establish themselves as independent speaking subjects working creatively through writing or painting, a topic to which Atwood will return in *Surfacing*, *Lady Oracle* and *Cat's Eye*.

Twenty years later Atwood is still preoccupied with 'writing woman', both in the sense of woman as writer and woman as written about, though we might expect that a fable belonging to the 1990s like 'The Female Body' would show a more explicitly feminist awareness of the political and theoretical dimensions within representations of the feminine than a novel written at the end of the 1960s. In both texts the focus is on woman as spectacle or fantasy object of desire and violence, and representations of the female bodies in the later text double back to take in the same images of fashionable femininity or women's captivity as in *The Edible Woman*. In both, women are represented as victims: a woman being eaten alive (playfully figured as a sponge cake) and woman as murder victim. ('The

Female Body' occurs in a collection entitled *Good Bones*: 'This is the cemetery. The good bones are in here, the bad bones are out there, beyond the church wall, beyond the pale, unsanctified'; p. 151). And in both these texts the female figures are created by a woman writer, which raises an obvious problem in relation to gendered representation and interpretation. It has been neatly formulated by Mary Ann Caws in relation to women art critics:

> For how could we possibly think that a seeing woman writing about women being touched with the brush, perfectly *captured* in paint, or accurately shot by a camera's eye ... would have an 'objective' point of view? ... She, we are bound to think and say, is implicated, heavily.[14]

As indeed is Atwood, who explores these questions in her feminist fable of resistance 'The Female Body'.

Taking as my starting point another essay on representation, Nancy K. Miller's exemplary essay, 'Rereading as a Woman: the Body in Practice', I shall begin by shifting attention to women writers:

> What is it possible for a woman to read [write] in these conditions of effacement and estrangement; in a universe ... where the rules of aesthetic reception and indeed of the hermeneutic act itself are mapped onto a phallomorphic regime of production?[15]

Such theoretical language would seem appropriate here in a way it would not have been for *The Edible Woman*, for Atwood directly addresses the question of the female body as text to be written and read. Her epigraph focuses the reader's attention:

> ' ... *entirely devoted to the subject of "The Female Body". Knowing how well you have written on this topic ... this capacious topic ...* '
>
> – letter from the *Michigan Quarterly Review*[16]

Atwood's reply to this letter directly addresses problems of representation faced by a woman writer where she plays with the double meaning of 'subject' – woman as writing subject and woman's exclusion from subjecthood when the female body becomes the subject of patriarchal discourse. The speaking 'I' begins by describing herself playfully and multiply, then embarks on an anatomy in seven sections of male representations of the female body, all of them reductive, exploitative or misogynist. These are discursive constructions of women as *non*-subjects – mute bodies to be gazed at, fantasised about, probed, used and abused, fabricated as commodities, exploited as saleable goods or expendable national resources – a terrifying catalogue written in language which imitates the 'objectivity' of the male gaze in a spirit of ferocious parody. The resulting fable presents an angry feminist history of sexual politics where the female is fetishised and deprived of language and choice. There is a shift in focus at the end, which reveals the blind spots in masculinist discourse when seen from a feminine perspective. However, this is no escape fantasy; rather, it is a no-exit situation for women, at least within the traditional male symbolic order.

The disarmingly conversational opening signals the writer's sense of subjective involvement with her 'topic' for the narrating 'I' starts by writing about her own body, with the caveat that there cannot be any essentialist discourse about Woman capital W: 'I agree, it's a hot topic. But only one? Look around, there's a wide range. Take my own, for instance' (p. 39)

Writing from within her own body as the focus of sensation, thought and desire, the narrator (not Atwood but the speaking 'I' of fiction) plays across the gap between language and reality, creating a self portrait which is a kaleidoscope of shifting perspectives:

> away goes my topic, my topical topic, my controversial topic, my capacious topic ... my vulgar topic, my outrageous topic ... hunting for what's out there, an avocado, an alderman, an adjective, hungry as ever.   (p. 40)

This list with its proliferating metaphors challenges the masculine order of discourse by its dazzling parody of the language of poststructuralist theory. It presents a domesticated translation of some of the key concepts formulated by the French deconstructionist Jacques Derrida in his essay 'Structure, Sign and Play' where he rejects the concept of absolute presence within language in favour of an endless play of verbal signifiers without fixed meanings.[17] At the same time and for all her jokiness, the narrator manages to establish herself as a woman writing about her relationship to the world before she embarks on the more difficult task of cataloguing the shifting representations of woman within a male-dominated economy.

Every section until the last offers a different series of images of the female body, highlighting both the contradictions within such figurings and their one common denominator: none of the female bodies here seems to be made of flesh and blood. They are all mas-

culine constructions of woman as 'other' than fully human – as
child, doll, object of male pleasure or power, but never woman with
an identity or a voice to express her own feelings and desires.
Atwood's catalogue illustrates women's 'underdeveloped condition
stemming from their submission by/to a culture which oppresses
them, uses them, cashes in on them'.[18] Her projection of the feminine here is close to the speculations on sexual power politics of
French feminist theorists such as Luce Irigaray and Hélène Cixous,
whose essays would seem to provide a kind of running commentary
on many of the positions to which women are subjected in this text.
However, we need to be wary of the distorting effects likely to be
produced by reading through any ideological lens. (We might also
bear in mind Atwood's comments on literary criticism: 'I really feel
that it ought to be graspable. It should not be full of too many of
those kinds of words which only the initiated can understand';
Conversations, p. 209). In my brief discussion of three sections of 'The
Female Body' I shall try to demonstrate the stylistic range of
Atwood's reflections on its representation.

3.   The Female Body is made of transparent plastic and lights up
when you plug it in. You press a button to illuminate the different
systems. The Circulatory System is red, for the heart and arteries,
purple for the veins; the Respiratory System is blue, the Lymphatic
System is yellow, the Digestive System is green, with liver and
kidneys in aqua. The nerves are done in orange and the brain is
pink. The skeleton, as you might expect, is white.   (p. 41)

Is this a biological model of femaleness? Not really, for the model is
synthetic, made of plastic which 'lights up' when it is plugged in.
This is female body as educational toy, a reductive version of woman
as object to be probed for scientific experiment, possibly even a
parodic version of Irigaray's image in *Speculum de l'autre femme* (1974)
where the 'speculum', as Toril Moi explains, is a 'surgical instrument
for dilating cavities of the human body for inspection, a concave
mirror which gynaecologists use to inspect the cavities of the female
body'.[19] Here the 'scandal' of female sexuality is both hinted at and
evaded by the language of advertising: 'The Reproductive System is
optional, and can be removed ... We do not wish to frighten or
offend.' The satire works in several ways here, though always denying
any connection between the female body and feminine subjecthood.
    In the following section there is a shift in focus and narrative
event, though continuities are plain in the image of a doll-woman

subjected to the law of the father within the family and propelled
toward self destruction. This is the most disturbing and violent scene
in the text, where the adolescent girl figures as broken disjointed
Barbie doll:

> 4.   She came whizzing down the stairs, thrown like a dart. She was
> stark naked. Her hair had been chopped off, her head was turned
> back to front, she was missing some toes and she'd been tattooed
> all over her body with purple ink, in a scroll-work design. She hit
> the potted azalea, trembled there for a moment like a botched
> angel, and fell.
>   He said, I guess we're safe.   (p. 42)

Again in this depiction of the female body boundaries are blurred
between human and non-human, as between volition and the robotic
movements of this 'living doll'. She is naked, mutilated, scrawled
upon, her body deprived of any meaning but that of bizarrely deco-
rated object. She cannot see, she does not speak; reduced to exotic
alien object in a domestic scenario, she hits the 'potted azalea' at the
bottom of the stairs and falls down. But before she falls, there is the
moment of shock when the referential terms of the image shift to
Christmas angel or Miltonic fallen angel (both interpretations are
possible here) giving a glimpse of grace which is immediately denied
in the 'fall'. As doll, punk and fallen angel overlap, the image is one
of irretrievable damage, illustrating the catastrophe of teenage rebel
as female victim. Yet this moralised reading is always second to the
disturbing power of the dismembered doll's body, a surreal image
like those of female bodies distorted or truncated into art objects in
the paintings of René Magritte or the photographs of Man Ray.[20] I
would also suggest that the woman writer's angle is strongly indicated
here in her savage recording of the father's voice at the end, when
safety for his daughter is out of the question.

This image of the female body as the site of victimisation and pain
lurks as subtext beneath the sections on women as objects of
exchange: 'The trade that organizes patriarchal societies takes place
exclusively among men. Women, signs, goods, currency, all pass
from one man to another'[21] Images of female bodies are fabricated
as domestic appliances like door-knockers and bottle-openers, just
as women are exploited in advertisements for 'cars, beer, shaving
lotion, cigarettes, hard liquor'. These repetitive images signal the
extent to which women's bodies have been fetishised within popular
culture, while women's role as collaborators is underlined by the

image of prostitution in the same section, where women are persuaded to sell their bodies for the good of the state: 'Listen, you want
to reduce the national debt, don't you? Aren't you patriotic?' Within
a patriarchal economy women's bodies may be counted as 'a natural
resource' (by the same logic presumably that rape becomes an
instrument of war) but they are also expendable. The connection
between woman and nature blurs among images of shoddy goods
and worn out rags, so that women's postulated relation either to
nature or to culture works to their disempowerment when 'woman is
traditionally use-value for man, exchange-value among men'.[22]

With a characteristic shift of balance which in a theoretical text
would probably be described as a deconstructive move, the final
section opens out from its satirical exposure of patriarchal attitudes
towards interrogation of those positions through language which
mixes the discourses of science, Freudian psychoanalysis and fairy
tale. The section opens with a 'scientific' discussion of the structure
of male and female brains and possible physiological grounds for
psychological theories of sexual difference. According to this model
of the different functions of the right and left brain, which Atwood
has discussed elsewhere in relation to processes of artistic creativity,
women are programmed to have a stronger sense of interrelatedness
than men because the two halves of the female brain are more
strongly connected together.[23]

By contrast, a man's mental functions are more compartmentalised:

> The male brain, now, that's a different matter. Only a thin con-
> nection. Space over here, time over there, music and arithmetic in
> their own sealed compartments. The right brain doesn't know
> what the left brain is doing ... That's the male brain for you.
> Objective. (p. 45)

Then we notice a change from such claims of objectivity and
images of male domination to representations of male subjectivity:
'This is why men are so sad, why they feel so cut off, why they think
of themselves as orphans cast adrift', all indicative of the shift
towards a feminine focus. Then a second female voice speaks, questioning masculine constructions of the universe (or of 'universals'):

> What void? she says. What are you talking about? The void of the
> Universe, he says, and she says Oh and looks out the window and
> tries to get a handle on it, but it's no use, there's too much going
> on. (p. 45)

When the female subject speaks at last, her 'womanspeak' (Irigaray's '*le parler femme*') offers a totally different perception of the world as multiple and full of meanings, the very condition of the 'feminine' which Irigaray claims both escapes and irritates patriarchal logic:

> 'She' is indefinitely other in herself. That is undoubtedly the reason she is called temperamental, incomprehensible, perturbed, capricious – not to mention her language in which 'she' goes off in all directions and in which 'he' is unable to discern the coherence of any meaning.[24]

This may look suspiciously like another essentialist definition of woman, but clearly it is useful to Atwood to mark gender difference and to justify the male stance of alienation from her, 'not just alone but Alone, lost in the dark, lost in the skull' (p. 46). We are reminded of Atwood's comment on gender difference in an interview in 1985:

> Kierkegaard would never have been a woman, you know. And I think a lot of the speculation about the void and things like this are very male. Why? Because they could afford to do that, again. I think women are much more grounded in the world because they have had to be.   (*Conversations*, p. 187)

The voice of the female speaking subject creates the space for the woman writer's crucial exposure of the blind spot within male logic, as she goes on to challenge Freudian theories of female deficiency (penis envy) in a neat feminist reversal of traditional models of dependency and lack:

> Then it comes to him: he's lost the Female Body! Look, it shines in the gloom, far ahead, a vision of wholeness, ripeness, like a giant melon, like an apple, like a metaphor for *breast* in a bad sex novel; it shines like a balloon, like a foggy noon, a watery moon, shimmering in its egg of light.   (p. 46)

This scenario from the Oedipal plot of infantile male attachment to fear of loss of the mother is figured through a range of unambiguously female imagery in a persuasive argument against the notion that woman is man's negative mirror image. Instead she becomes the object of his keenest desire, but it is an unspeakable desire which he in turn projects as unspeaking or silent woman. Atwood would argue that woman is not only silent but silenced, for this revelation of the primacy of the Mother may also be bad news for women; desire and need do not necessarily change the pattern of male domination but may result in an 'intensified misogyny'.[25]

The fable ends with a grim return to the patriarchal order as women are captured and imprisoned, reinscribed in the language of fairytales and nursery rhymes which is both infantile and sinister: 'Catch it. Put it in a pumpkin, in a high tower.' Peter Pumpkin Eater, Rapunzel, Bluebeard are all stories of women's punishment where the female body is locked up, 'so it can never get away from you again' (p. 46). As the Handmaid would say, 'I wish this story were different' (*The Handmaid's Tale*, p. 279), and possibly this old story of repression *is* different for it is being retold by a woman writer who is mocking male power fantasies by mimicking their language and exposing both their arrogance and their incomplete mastery. The discourse of domination looks less authoritative when it is mixed in with fragments of failed family romance, surrealistic images, and the language of the nursery, all of which are shown to feature in male representations of the Female Body.

Written from the perspective of a female writer who is by definition implicated in the topic of the Female Body as 'my own topic', this fable is of course not objective ('How could we possibly think that a seeing woman writing about women's [bodies] would have an "objective" point of view?'). Moreover, it exposes the non-objectivity of patriarchal constructions of the female body. 'Male fantasies, male fantasies, is everything run by male fantasies?' (*The Robber Bride*, p. 392). The answers to this question are canvassed in the novels themselves, where the stories are told from a variety of female perspectives generated by a woman writer's imagination and through which 'the stories of sexual difference would have to be figured otherwise'.[26]

On the other hand [as Atwood wryly remarks] it could be argued that men don't have any bodies at all. Look at the magazines! Magazines for women have women's bodies on the covers, magazines for men have women's bodies on the covers.[27]

4

Atwoodian Gothic: From *Lady Oracle* to *The Robber Bride*

Atwoodian Gothic is both sinister and jokey, rather like the scary game which Atwood describes in *Murder in the Dark*, a game about murderers, victims and detectives played with the lights off. The only other thing the reader needs to know is that the victim is always silent and that the murderer always lies:

> In any case, that's me in the dark. I have designs on you, I'm plotting my sinister crime, my hands are reaching for your neck or perhaps, by mistake, your thigh. You can hear my footsteps approaching, I wear boots and carry a knife, or maybe it's a pearl-handled revolver, in any case I wear boots with very soft soles, you can see the cinematic glow of my cigarette, waxing and waning in the fog of the room, the street, the room, even though I don't smoke. Just remember this, when the scream at last has ended and you've turned on the lights: by the rules of the game, I must always lie.[1]

This game is emblematic of Atwoodian Gothic; its aim is to scare, yet it is a sort of fabricated fright; there are rules and conventions and we enter into a kind of complicity because we want to be frightened. Atwood suggests, 'You can say: the murderer is the writer' and then either the book or the reader would be the victim, which makes an interesting identification between Gothic storyteller and murderer, trickster, liar. We could take that one stage further with Atwood's female Gothic storytellers, Joan Foster in *Lady Oracle*, Zenia in *The Robber Bride* and Atwood herself, identified as sybils, witches, supreme plotters all ('I have designs on you').

So, what is Gothic? At the core of the Gothic sensibility is fear – fear of ghosts, women's fear of men, fear of the dark, fear of what is hidden but might leap out unexpectedly, fear of something floating around loose which lurks behind the everyday. The emblematic fear within Gothic fantasy is that something that seemed to be dead and buried might not be dead at all. Hence the Gothic outbreaks of terror and violence as things cross forbidden barriers between dream and waking, life and death. It is easy to recognise a Gothic novel for it is characterised by a specific collection of motifs and themes, many of which come through folklore, fairytale, myth and nightmare. One of the most succinct accounts of the Gothic as a literary genre is Eve Kosofsky Sedgwick's critical study *The Coherence of Gothic Conventions*, which identifies two key terms to define the Gothic: the Unspeakable and Live Burial.[2] Arguably those terms might be seen as different images for the same thing for they both relate to what is hidden, secret, repressed, and which is threatening precisely because it is still alive and blocked off from consciousness though ready to spring out, transformed into some monstrous shape – like Freud's *unheimlich*, both familiar and alien to us.[3] It is this uncanny quality of Gothic which is embodied in its obsession with the transgression of boundaries and with transformations – 'change from one state into another, change from one thing into another'.[4] On the level of the supernatural, there is the phenomenon of ghosts transgressing boundaries between life and death, while on the psychological level there is the erosion of boundaries between the self and the monstrous Other. (What does a Gothic protagonist see or fear to see when she looks in the mirror?) In the borderline territory between conscious and unconscious, a space is opened up for doubles and split selves, which are not total opposites but dependent on each other and linked by a kind of unacknowledged complicity, like Dr Frankenstein and his monster. To return to that game in *Murder in the Dark*: Atwood reminds players that they may take turns to be murderer or victim, for one role does not preclude the other. Gothic finds a language for representing areas of the self (like fears, anxieties, forbidden desires) which are unassimilable in terms of social conventions. In relation to fiction, the major point to consider is how these transgressions are expressed through narrative, most obviously in the shifts from realism to fantasy signalled in dreams and hallucinations, when frequently the working out of dreams is crucial to the plot. There is also the difficulty any Gothic story has in getting itself told at all: Gothic plots are characterised by enigmas, multiple stories embedded in the main story, multiple narrators and shifting points of view, and mixed genres, where fairy tale may blur into history or autobiography. At all times the Gothic narrative suggests the co-existence of the everyday alongside a shadowy nightmarish world.[5]

Not surprisingly, the Gothic romance has traditionally been a favourite genre for women writers, from Ann Radcliffe's *The Mysteries of Udolpho (1794)*, Mary Shelley's *Frankenstein* (1818), the Brontës' *Wuthering Heights* and *Jane Eyre* (1840s), through to Daphne Du Maurier's *Rebecca* (1938), Jean Rhys's *Wide Sargasso Sea* (1966), and the contemporary fiction of Margaret Atwood, Angela Carter, Beryl Bainbridge, Alice Munro. It is a devious literature through which to express female desires and dreads, and in Atwood it is easy to see the traditional forms surviving, updated but still retaining their original charge of menace and mystery, while balancing women's urge toward self-discovery and self-assertiveness with self-doubts, between celebration of new social freedoms and women's sense of not being free of traditional assumptions and myths about femininity. It is to this territory of Gothic romance that Atwood returns again and again, using its images and motifs and its narratives of transgression. To glance briefly at the pervasiveness of Gothic in Atwood, one would need to start with her early watercolours from the late 1960s where sinister knights in armour with hidden faces peer at damsels dressed in red, or dark male figures hold unconscious purple female bodies in their giant arms.[6] *Surfacing* might be construed as a ghost story in the Canadian wilderness, a reading suggested by Atwood in an early interview when she explained that she was writing in the tradition of the psychological ghost story:

> You can have the Henry James kind, in which the ghost that one sees is in fact a fragment of one's own self which has split off, and that to me is the most interesting kind and that is obviously the tradition I'm working in.[7]

The motifs of haunted wilderness and the split self are still there 20 years later in the story 'Death by Landscape' in *Wilderness Tips*, just as the werewolf image which was there in *The Journals of Susanna Moodie* recurs in 'Age of Lead' in that same collection. The title story in *Bluebeard's Egg* (1983) is a modern revision of fairy tale,[8] while *Bodily Harm* (1981) and *The Handmaid's Tale* (1985) exploit traditional Gothic motifs in their representation of classic female fears of sexual violence or imprisonment. In *Cat's Eye* (1988) the protagonist is haunted by the past and by her doppelganger Cordelia ('Lie down,

you're dead!') who represents the other half of herself, her dark
mad twin. There is also a poem 'The Robber Bridegroom' in
Interlunar (1984), and it is interesting to note that 'The Robber
Bridegroom' was considered by Atwood as a possible title for *Bodily
Harm*. In this recirculation of images and themes, we note very repetitive patterns which are the identifying marks of a literary genre. The
same stories are being retold, as the reader is constantly reminded
through intertextual allusions to fairy tales and old Gothic
romances, so that versions that might look contemporary and new
circle around old enigmas. It is from this Gothic continuum that I
wish to single out *Lady Oracle* (1976) and *The Robber Bride* (1993) in
order to examine what transformations of Gothic conventions
Atwood has managed in novels that are nearly 20 years apart; to see
how her changing use of Gothic conventions reflects her responses
to shifts in cultural mythology, especially in her thinking about
women. What we find is the reworking of traditional Gothic motifs
within the frames of realistic fiction, for unlike her protagonist Joan
Foster in *Lady Oracle*, Atwood does not 'write with her eyes closed'.
On the contrary, Atwood is an attentive and often satirical critic of
contemporary Canada, exposing popular myths and social ideologies
for Atwood has designs on us. But then, of course, so did Joan
Foster, and so did Zenia, the Robber Bride.

Atwood described *Lady Oracle* as 'a realistic comic novel colliding
with Gothic conventions – I give you *Northanger Abbey*', as she
explained for a lecture in 1982.[9] It is also a fictive autobiography,
told by a woman who is a novelist and a poet, suggesting shadowy
parallels with Atwood herself in her early days of fame when she was
becoming a cultural ikon in Canada. More to the point because this
novel is not autobiography but an autobiographical fiction, there are
strong parallels with *Cat's Eye* told by that other successful woman
artist, Elaine Risley the painter. In both cases a woman struggles to
find her voice, to define her identity through telling her life story in
different versions. *Lady Oracle* and *Cat's Eye* are curiously similar autobiographical projects because the stories the protagonists tell offer
multiple versions of their lives which never quite fit together to form
the image of a unified and coherent self. Who is Joan Foster, who
writes popular Gothic romances under the pseudonym Louisa K.
Delacourt? What is the significance of Lady Oracle, Joan's other
pseudonym when she writes poetry? The one thing the reader can be

sure about with Joan is that she is a fantasist, and a trickster: 'All my life I'd been hooked on plots'.[10]

Lady Oracle is a story about storytelling, both the stories themselves and the writing process, for Joan offers us multiple narratives figuring and refiguring herself through different narrative conventions. The novel is structured through a series of interlocking frames. First, there is the story of Joan's real life in the present, set in Italy where she has escaped after her fake suicide in Toronto, Canada. Enclosed within this is her private memory narrative of a traumatic childhood filled with shame, pain and defiance centring on her relationship with her neurotic mother, of an adolescence when she escapes to London and becomes a writer of popular Gothics, her marriage to a Canadian, her celebrity as a poet, to be followed by the threat of blackmail and her second escape from Canada to Italy. Embedded within this narrative are snippets from Joan's Gothic romances ('Bodice Rippers' as she calls them), which provide more glamorous and dangerous plots than everyday life in Toronto, or even in Italy, during the late 1960s and early 1970s. Then there is a fourth narrative thread, the curiously mythic 'Lady Oracle' poems, produced as Joan believes by Automatic Writing when she looks into a dark mirror in her bedroom in Toronto. These shifting frames generate a series of comic collisions, confrontations and escape attempts, but there are no clear boundaries between them as borders blur between present and past, art and life. Joan's fantasies of escape and transformation are always duplicitous and riddled with holes, so that one story infiltrates another and fantasy is under continual barrage from the claims of real life. Joan may adopt multiple disguises in the form of fancy costumes, wigs, different names and different personas, but 'it was no good; I couldn't stop time, I could shut nothing out' (p. 277). Through this shimmer of different figures, the reader wonders if there is any chance of getting beyond the veils to the centre of the plot or to the enigma of Joan Foster herself. Do we ever get beyond the distorting funhouse mirrors? Joan is nothing if not a self-caricaturist as well as a parodist of Gothic romance conventions, as she switches between real life and fantasy roles in a continual process of double coding. All these fantasies are arguably distorted versions of herself, a process described by Paul de Man in his essay, 'Autobiography as Defacement': 'Autobiography deals with the giving and taking away of faces, with face and deface, figure, figurations and disfiguration' in images of the self endlessly displaced and doubled.[11]

It is arguable that Joan constructs the Gothic plots in her own life.

From her point of view even her life story could be seen as a tale told by a ghost, speaking from beyond her watery grave in Lake Ontario: 'I planned my death carefully; unlike my life, which meandered along from one thing to another, despite my feeble attempts to control it' (p. 7). Of course this 'death' is another of her contrived plots for Joan is not dead at all. One of the things that frightens her most in Italy is that people at home in Canada will think that she is really dead, and not even miss her. Having escaped from her husband Arthur in Toronto, Joan realises that the other side of her escape fantasy is isolation:

> The Other Side was no paradise, it was only a limbo. Now I knew why the dead came back to watch over the living: the Other Side was boring. There was no one to talk to and nothing to do. (p. 309)

Such reflection is a result of Joan's rueful recognition of the gap between real life and fantasy, for she is haunted by memories of her visit to this same Italian village the previous year with her husband and is now filled with the longing that he will come to rescue her from her own perfect plot which begins to look 'less like a Fellini movie than that Walt Disney film I saw when I was eight, about a whale who wanted to sing at the Metropolitan Opera ... but the sailors harpooned him' (p. 9). Critics have been rather fond of saying that Joan's real-life narrative and the Gothic novel she is writing in Italy start off separate and gradually become entwined till at the end of the narrative borders blur and Joan enters the Gothic maze in *Stalked by Love*.[12] That observation is true as far as it goes, but that is not far enough. Borders between realism and fantasy are blurred from the beginning as Joan continually slides from the embarrassments of the present into fantasy scenarios and back again, for she is an escape artist who is beset by one inconvenient insight, 'Why did every one of my fantasies turn into a trap?' (p. 334).

However, before going any further into Joan's Gothic plotting, it is advisable to look at the title *Lady Oracle* in order to see what it signifies about Joan as a woman writer who faces the challenging questions: How do you find a voice to speak for yourself, and what do you say when you do? The most significant thing about an Oracle is that it is a voice which comes out of a woman's body and is associated with hidden dangerous knowledge, but that it is not her own voice. The voice of the Delphic Oracle was the voice of the god Apollo, or earlier the voice of the Earth Goddess. Atwood's research notes for her novel contain a significant amount of material on oracles (from Robert Graves, *The Greek Myths*), on Pythia the priestess of Apollo at Delphi (from Lamprière's *Classical Dictionary*), and on the Sybil of Cumae (from Virgil's *Aeneid*, translated by C. Day Lewis, and from Ovid's *Metamorphoses,* Book XIV, in Loeb's Classical Library).[13] Both Pythia and the Cumaen Sybil are described as 'possessed', the Pythoness speaking 'in a convulsive state ... the oracles of the god, often with loud howlings and cries', and the Sybil whose 'fey heart swelled in ecstasy ... More than mortal her utterance.' The role of prophetess is here in danger of being reduced to the role of the hysteric, for the oracle is 'beyond herself' and not conscious of what she is saying. Joan Foster presents herself as uncomfortably close to this model – not only in the automatic writing of her Lady Oracle poems but also in her costume Gothics. They too are a form of automatic writing, for Joan is writing through Gothic romance formulas and she types with her eyes closed. The very name 'Lady Oracle' is not her own choice but is chosen for her by her male publishers: 'You write, you leave it to us to sell it' (p. 234). When she becomes a celebrity, Joan even begins to feel a certain paranoia about her persona:

> It was as if someone with my name were out there in the real world, impersonating me ... doing things for which I had to take the consequences: my dark twin ... She wanted to kill me and take my place, and by the time she did this no one would notice the difference because the media were in on the plot, they were helping her. (pp. 250–1)

In other words, Joan starts to feel like one of the victims in her Gothic romances written under her other *nom de plume* 'Louisa K. Delacourt' borrowed from the name of her deceased Aunt Lou. In her fiction, her poetry and her interviews, Joan refuses to take responsibility for what she says; though from another point of view her double identities also provide her with a kind of escape, for she cannot be defined by any statement made in her name and the name is always changing. There is Lady Oracle for whom Joan is merely the medium and Louisa K. Delacourt is the name of her dead aunt. Joan uses the names as alibis:

> The really important thing was not the books themselves, which continued to be much the same. It was the fact that I was two people at once, with two sets of identification papers, two bank

accounts, two different groups of people who believed I existed. I was Joan Foster ... But I was also Louisa K. Delacourt.

As long as I could spend a certain amount of time each week as Louisa, I was all right.   (p. 213)

Jean is a very slippery subject, parallel with Elaine Risley in *Cat's Eye* who does not take on the interpretative responsibility for arranging the paintings at her first retrospective exhibition but leaves it to the gallery directors and who says, 'I'm what's left over'.[14] In turn, Joan and Elaine are like Offred in *The Handmaid's Tale* whose voice tapes are edited years after she is dead by someone else. All these women are 'missing persons'; they have no authoritative voice over their work, and they are all escape artists. Joan gives her readers multiple versions of the truth about herself, cultivating duplicity with an energy that suggests the forces of repression behind her performances:

It was true I had two lives, but on off days I felt that neither of them was competely real ... If I brought the separate parts of my life together (like uranium, like plutonium, harmless to the naked eye, but charged with lethal energies) surely there would be an explosion.   (pp. 216–17)

Indeed, Joan never does take the consequences for the minor explosion she participates in when she and her lover the 'Royal Porcupine' (whose less picturesque real name is Chuck Brewer) stage an absurdly sixties happening in a snowy park using the sticks of dynamite which Joan is supposed to be carrying around Toronto for a crazy Canadian nationalist plot to blow up the Peace Bridge at Niagara Falls. She even uses those explosives as the basis for another of her fantastical plots, her fake suicide which is transformed in her absence into a real life murder mystery.

Joan assumes no responsibility for what she writes and yet through this pose she tells us a great deal about herself – her fears and ambitions and her forbidden feelings. It is through her memory narrative of a middle class Toronto childhood, that 'can of worms' as she calls it, that Joan reveals the sequence of humiliations and betrayals against which she has constructed her multiple self-defences. Joan's life story is a tale of grotesques and monsters for Joan is an only child, the unwanted product of an unhappy wartime marriage, who cannot please her neurotic mother and who in a rage of adolescent defiance overeats till she looks like 'a beluga whale':

I ate to defy her, but I also ate from panic. Sometimes I was afraid I wasn't really there, I was an accident; I'd heard her call me an accident. Did I want to become solid, solid as a stone so she wouldn't be able to get rid of me? What had I done? Had I trapped my father ... had I ruined my mother's life? I didn't dare to ask.   (p. 78)

For Joan, everyone is shadowed by their opposites. The most import-ant and duplicitous figure is her mother, who 'puts on her face' with its larger-than-life lipsticked mouth, 'the real one showing through the false one like a shadow' (p. 68). Her small daughter really believes her to be a 'triple headed monster', and that mother returns to haunt her throughout her adult life. Joan's father, the benevolent anaesthetist also had a double career as a French-speak-ing Canadian who had been an assassin for the Resistance during the war, a fact which causes his daughter as much bewilderment as the flasher in the ravines who might also have been the Daffodil Man who rescued Joan when she was tied up and left behind by her girl friends after Brownies. There is also her fat fairy godmother Aunt Lou, who leaves Joan enough money in her will to escape from home but only on condition that she loses weight. It is no wonder that Joan suspects everybody of having a secret life and that she sees herself too as a 'duplicitous monster' whose only means of expres-sion is through disguise. Joan knows the value of this double coding when she becomes a self parodist at the age of seven in a dance recital, where instead of being the fairy, the fat little girl is tricked into being a mothball in a furry suit. Her 'dance of rage and destruc-tion' is interpreted by the watching parents as a comic entertain-ment to be applauded ('Bravo Mothball!', p. 50). Behind the performance Joan's anguished childhood self remains hidden. It is no wonder that as an adult Joan cannot bring herself to tell her raw-boned idealist husband that she writes costume Gothics for 'He wouldn't have understood' and she is afraid of losing his affection and respect. Indeed, Joan's primary motivating force is fear – fear of the past, fear of blackmail, fear of the loss of Arthur's love, and above all, fear of being found out. After all, 'when it came to fantasy lives I was a professional' (p. 216).

In such a context Joan's insistence on the 'automatic writing' of the *Lady Oracle* poems begins to look like a psychological necessity, though Atwood's own comments on such a method of production are sceptical:

In my experience, writing is not like having dreams ... It's much more deliberate ... You can shape your material into a coherent pattern. (*Conversations*, p. 48)

An examination of the *Lady Oracle* manuscript materials bears out this conscious construction, for in the Atwood Papers there is a letter to her research assistant in which Atwood asks for a map of Italy, an English–Italian dictionary, details of the water fountains in the Villa D'Este at Tivoli, 'especially; the sphinxes with water squirting out their tits and the statue of Diana of Ephesus which is covered with breasts', an Italian *photoromanze*, and a copy of *Jane Eyre*. 'Later, I'll tell you what all this is for'.[15]

The connections between *Jane Eyre* and Joan's popular Gothic romances are plain, though we may question why anyone would write them and why so many women read them. Joan's short answer would be, 'The pure quintessential need of my readers for escape, a thing I myself understood only too well' (p. 34). Joan explains and justifies her project to herself: 'The truth was that I dealt in hope, I offered a vision of a better world, however preposterous. Was that so terrible?' (p. 35). However, the fact remains that there is more anguish and violence than pleasure in these Gothic scenarios of *Escape from Love*, *Love My Ransom*, and *Stalked by Love*. As Atwood remarked when discussing *Lady Oracle* in an interview with Joyce Carol Oates in 1978:

I've always wondered what it was about these books that appealed – do so many women think of themselves as menaced on all sides, and of their husbands as potential murderers? And what about that 'Mad Wife' left over from *Jane Eyre*? Are these our secret plots? (*Conversations*, p. 75).[16]

Janice Radway in *Reading the Romance* would seem to agree with Atwood when she argues that the appeal of popular romance fiction relates less to escapism than to women's fears about the loss of independence, male indifference and male violence. These issues are recuperated under the happy endings of romance, though women know such endings to be illusory.[17] Possibly women read these novels out of lack and dissatisfaction, which is why they need to keep on reading them – or, in Joan's case, to keep on writing them.

How does Joan figure out her life (while stepping aside from her real life) through her Gothic plots, which are as grotesquely distorted as the fantasy of the discarded sodden clothes which come back to haunt her dreams in Italy, or the Fat Pink Lady fantasy of her childhood? This last is an extraordinarily interesting fantasy which is both reflection and sublimation for Joan, a grotesque fairytale image of 'The Biggest Modern Woman in the World' who walks across Canada on a tightrope, much to everyone's amazement, but who in real life is nothing but a circus freak. As Joan insists, it's all a trick, but like her other more sinister Gothic narrative tricks, 'it's still not so simple' (p. 203). The Charlottes, Felicias, and Penelopes are all partial figurings of her fantasies of desirable femininity, while their persecutions are displacements of her own sense of inadequacy and dread. These Costume Gothics also allow Joan to indulge her New World fascination with Europe – its history, its decaying aristocracy, and its words for outmoded female fashions like 'fichu', 'paletot' and 'pelisse'. It is no accident that her first lover was a Polish count who rescued Joan when she fell off a bus in London. It was Paul who encouraged her to write costume Gothics while he indulged his own fantasies by writing nurse novels under the pseudonym 'Mavis Quilp' a name he had found in Dickens. The titles of Paul's Nurse novels are as formulaic of that genre as Joan's Gothics: *Janet Holmes, Student Nurse, Helen Curtis, Senior Nurse, Anne Armstrong, Junior Nurse,* and finally – after he comes to Canada, *Nurse of the High Arctic.* It is also symptomatic of Joan's imaginative transformations of real life that she would fall in love with Arthur Foster, a graduate student from the Maritimes, not in their native Canada but in Hyde Park, London, when she happened to bump into him while he was distributing leaflets for Ban the Bomb and she was walking the course for one of her costume Gothics. This chance encounter gives Arthur a Byronic tinge which is entirely imaginary:

> I looked at him more closely. He was wearing a black crew-neck sweater, which I found quite dashing. A melancholy fighter for almost-lost causes, idealistic and doomed, sort of like Lord Byron, whose biography I had just been skimming. We finished collecting the pamphlets, I fell in love.   (p. 165)

Joan spells out her Gothic formula when she is looking over the proofs for her *Lady Oracle* poems:

> On re-reading, the book seemed quite peculiar. In fact, except for the diction, it seemed a lot like one of my standard Costume Gothics, but a Gothic gone wrong. It was upside-down somehow.

There were the sufferings, the hero in the mask of a villain, the villain in the mask of a hero, the flights, the looming death, the sense of being imprisoned, but there was no happy ending, no true love. The recognition of this half-likeness made me uncomfortable. Perhaps I should have taken it to a psychiatrist instead of a publisher ... and no one would understand about the Automatic Writing. (p. 232)

Joan does not understand it herself but Atwood does. There is a passage in an essay Atwood wrote in 1965 on Rider Haggard's novel *She*, which casts light on her attitude to Joan's psychological riddle. Haggard claimed that he had written his novel in a trance, and Atwood quotes one of his biographers as saying, 'Haggard was writing deep, as though hypnotized'; that biographer proceeded to connect *She* with Haggard's childhood traumas and his interest in myth – all of which sounds uncomfortably close to the psychological and mythic interpretations of *Lady Oracle*.[18] However, Atwood's wry comment is worth noting: 'Haggard may have been writing "deep, as though hypnotized"; but if so the unconscious experience he was drawing upon was the creation of his [five] previous books.'[19]

While this does not rule out psychological and mythic interpretations of the narrator's experience in *Lady Oracle*, it does point to the location of Joan's sources of reference within her own real-life experience which is already written into this novel. Of special significance are her experiences with Aunt Lou and the spiritualists and her guilts about her mother – one of those terrible War Bride mothers, monsters with triple heads – who turns up again tripled, as three mothers in *The Robber Bride* and who are responsible for generating their daughter's insecurities and escape fantasies. The Gothic images of the 'Lady Oracle' title poem deriving from *She*, Tennyson's 'The Lady of Shallott', Khalil Gibran and Rod McKuen, display an excess of signification which hints at complex energies incompletely understood by the subject herself for most of the novel. Joan's tormented relationship with her mother forms the 'unspeakable' subtext throughout her real life narrative, for even after she leaves home (where her mother in a fit of rage and frustration plunges a kitchen knife into Joan's arm) she is haunted by her mother's 'astral body' and her mother's face remembered from childhood 'crying soundlessly, horribly; mascara was running from her eyes in black tears' (p. 173). More disturbingly this visionary visit to London signals her mother's death, which was apparently accidental but which Joan in her Gothic imaginings speculates might have been suicide or even

murder by her father. The unacknowledged symbiotic relation
between mother and daughter is signalled by a narrative switch from
this memory of her mother's death to Joan's present forlorn condition in Italy suffering from her own fake suicide: 'I'm not really
dead', Joan writes to Arthur on a postcard.

The 'Lady Oracle' title poem adopts traditional symbolism which
both veils and reveals Joan's repressed memories of her mother,
whose ghost she had failed to recognise as the figure standing
behind her when she looked into the dark mirror during her occult
experiments:

> She is one and three
> The dark lady   the redgold lady
> the blank lady   oracle
> of blood, she who must be
> obeyed   forever   (p. 226)

Though the words which come to Joan in her automatic writing
experiment cry out for interpretation with 'iron', 'throat', 'knife'
and 'heart', they are sufficiently indeterminate for her to be able to
repress any recognition of the dark figure who 'certainly had
nothing to do with me' (p. 222). Only near the end of the novel
when she is at her wit's end and cannot think of any way out of her
Italian escape fantasy does Joan realise that she too is capable of
hurting people and so learns to recognise some similarities between
them. She is able finally to forgive her mother's ghost and so to free
herself from guilt:

> It had been she standing behind me in the mirror ... My mother
> was a vortex, a dark vacuum, I would never be able to make her
> happy. Or anyone else. Maybe it was time for me to stop trying.
> (p. 329)

This revelation occurs at the same time as Joan's growing unease
with her Gothic plots, in real life and in fiction. Whereas up to this
time her novel *Stalked by Love* had been progressing according to its
set formula while her real life narrative spiralled and twisted, now
Joan's novel also swings out of control when she finds that she is
identifying with the villainess rather than with the heroine. Her fake
suicide begins to have real life consequences when reports reach her
that the two friends who had helped her have been arrested on a
murder charge in Toronto:

POETESS FEARED SLAIN IN TERRORIST PURGE!   (p. 337)

Joan finds herself trapped in a bizarre plot not of her own making: 'I'd have to go back and rescue them. I couldn't go back' (p. 338). As borders blur, the only thing Joan knows for certain is that she is going to have to let her heroine Charlotte go into the maze in *Stalked by Love*: 'She'd wanted to go in ever since reaching Redmond Grange' (p. 331). This is a classic piece of Gothic plotting, but again 'it's not so simple' as Atwood reminded an interviewer when discussing *Lady Oracle*:

> In Gothic tales the maze is just a scare device. You have an old mansion with winding passages and a monster at the center. But the maze I use is a descent into the underworld.   (*Conversations*, p. 47)

We are reminded of the winding passages which Joan encountered in her walk into the dark mirror of her unconscious. Is this the maze into which Joan must go to answer the sphinx's riddle in order to live? And who is Joan's double – the Gothic heroine or the villainess? Is Joan an innocent victim or is she a witch (as the Italian villagers believe her to be)? Faithful to habit, Joan closes her eyes and follows Charlotte into the conventional Gothic plot design, but much to her surprise, this time the plot does not conform to stereotype: 'I'd taken a wrong turn somewhere' (p. 333). When Joan resumes her storytelling after some accidental disruption, there is a crucial shift which infringes the Gothic formula, for this time it is not the heroine who enters the maze but the villainess Felicia; now it is she who is determined 'to penetrate the secret at last' (p. 341). There is a further slippage of conventions in the scenario of the plot so that Joan's book begins to look less like a Gothic romance than like a Fellini film, for Felicia finds herself confronting four women all of whom claim to be what she is herself, 'Lady Redmond'. There is no way out for Felicia – or for Joan – except through a door which looks the same from both sides. When this opens to reveal Redmond (husband or killer?) standing on the threshold, Felicia addresses him as 'Arthur', which is the name of Joan's husband. The final Gothic image is of Redmond–Arthur, the demon lover, reaching for Felicia's throat. He undergoes a dazzling series of transformations which shadow all the men with whom Joan has ever been involved: her father, her lovers, her husband and the villain of the Lady Oracle poems, till finally they collapse into the figure of death:

> *The flesh fell away from his face, revealing the skull behind it; he stepped*
> *towards her, reaching for her throat ...*   (p. 343)

Romance fantasy, violence and death are telescoped in the final
scenario but nothing is resolved, for Joan is interrupted by the sound
of footsteps coming down the path. Does she think it is Arthur or
does she think it is the figure of death? And are they the same? (Why
do women see their husbands as 'potential murderers'?) In this crisis
Joan acts with the energy of one of her Gothic protagonists, bashing
the male stranger on the head with an empty Cinzano bottle when
he appears at her door and knocking him out. This is the explosion
which she had feared as real life and the shadows of fiction come
into collision.

The ending is deliberately bathetic, for the man who Joan fears
has come for her life has in fact come for her life story. He is a
reporter and Joan tells him her story, which we realise is the novel
we have just been reading. Joan decides to give up costume Gothics
and to write science fiction instead, as 'the future is better for you',
facing up to responsibility for her own life and returning to Toronto.
Like *Northanger Abbey* this novel is about the perils of Gothic thinking, just as it is also about the heroine's moral education: 'Joan's
gotten as far as saying, I am who I am – take it or leave it'
(*Conversations*, p. 66). Through telling her stories and coming to
recognise their distortions and limits, Joan seems to be on the point
of finding her way back into real life with all its messiness; 'I don't
think I'll ever be a very tidy person' (p. 345). However, again like
Jane Austen, Atwood gives her plot a mischievous twist at the end:
Joan reveals that she has not yet returned to Toronto but that she is
still in Rome looking after the man whom she knocked on the head,
'I've begun to feel that he's the only person who knows anything
about me.' Like the surfacer on the edge of the wilderness about to
step forward, this is a suspension bridge ending.

The Robber Bride could be classified as a mutant form of female
Gothic romance with the return of a 'demonic woman' from the
dead in a story about transgressions, magic mirrors, shape changers
and dark doubles, betrayals and omens of disaster, until the final
defeat of the demon by three women friends when her body is
burned up and its ashes scattered over the deepest part of Lake
Ontario. There is also a multiple homecoming and the restoration of

social and family order at the end. Here we find the key Gothic elements of the unspeakable and the buried life, together with a whole range of traditional motifs like vampires, spells, soul stealing and body snatching. It could also be argued here that the traditional Gothic plot is 'upside-down somehow', for though there are female victims there are no rescuing heroes, just as there are no tombs, mazes or haunted houses; in this story the blood belongs to history and to metaphor. All of which highlights the fact that *The Robber Bride* is a postmodernist fiction which exploits the shock effects that occur when Gothic fairy tale migrates into totally different genres like the failed family romance, the detective thriller, and documentary history. Tony, the professional historian among the three friends, knows this technique and how it might be used to engage the interest of listeners and readers:

> She likes the faint shock on the faces of her listeners. It's the mix of domestic image and mass bloodshed that does it to them.[20]

The novel is both like a fairy tale as its title indicates and like history, which – as Tony explains – is always 'a construct' (p. 6), being the combination of different kinds of textual evidence: social documentary, private memory narrative and imaginative reconstruction. History is a discontinuous text with crucial gaps, so that different interpretations of the facts are always possible. Tony's words recall those of the American historiographer Hayden White, who suggests that the narratives of history always reconstruct the available facts of the past for readers in the present according to congenial ideological perspectives and identifiable literary patterns like the quest of the hero or fables of decline and fall.[21]

The Robber Bride is the story of Zenia, another of Atwood's missing persons like Offred in *The Handmaid's Tale* or Cordelia in *Cat's Eye*, told through the multiple narratives of her three friends, Antonia Fremont (Tony), Roz Andrews, and Charis. As each of the three tells her own life story, different overlapping frames of reference are set up through which Zenia's character and significance are given meaning, though Zenia never exists independently of the stories of others. It is through her relationships that Zenia's identity is constructed, but it is also transformed as it is refigured through the perspectives of a military historian (Tony), a successful businesswoman (Roz) and a New Age mystic (Charis). These women are all living in Toronto on 23 October 1990, a crucial date for the narrative as on that day they are having lunch together at a fashionable Toronto restaurant called the Toxique and 'Zenia returns from the dead' (p. 4). Through the swirl of contemporary history which Atwood sketches as a globalised scene of disasters the novel focuses on this one particular event, the kind of 'definitive moment' so useful to historians – and to novelists – after which 'things were never the same again. They provide beginnings for us, and endings too' (p. 4). The postmodern self-reflexivity of the narrative is signalled in the first and last sections, entitled 'Onset' and 'Outcome', told by Tony who has a 'historian's belief in the salutary power of explanations' while realising the 'impossibility of accurate reconstruction.' Yet for all its enigmas and secrets and dark doubles – traditional Gothic elements which we are reminded are also the features of historical and psychological narratives – the novel is structured quite schematically, moving out from the crisis of Zenia's Gothic reappearance in the restaurant five years after her memorial service, then scrolling back through the life stories of all three in an attempt to track Zenia down, only to return to the Toxique again about a week later where the final crisis occurs. Though the three friends have met to exchange stories of their confrontation with Zenia, whom they have all tracked down on the same day and to celebrate their resistance and her defeat, they discover something even more startling has happened: Zenia is dead, really dead this time. As Tony's husband West says, 'Again? I'm really sorry' (p. 449), and there is a second memorial service for Zenia a year later which is a replay of the earlier one, when the friends scatter her ashes and return to Charis's house to tell stories about Zenia all over again.

Within that contemporary frame the memory narratives of Tony, Charis and Roz all occur in chronological sequence charting the history of changing cultural fashions in Toronto over the past 30 years. Tony's section ('Black Enamel') recounts her memories of meeting Zenia as a student in the 1960s as it tracks back through Tony's unhappy childhood, and recounts Zenia's many attempts to rob Tony of her money, her professional reputation, and her beloved West. Charis's section ('Weasel Nights') focuses on her memories of Zenia in the 1970s, the era of hippies and draft dodgers, her American lover Billy and their daughter August, with flashbacks to her childhood as a victim of sexual abuse; it ends with Zenia's seduction of Billy and his disappearance. Roz's section ('The Robber Bride') recounts her meetings with Zenia in the 1980s and follows a similar pattern of recall: childhood memories, marriage, motherhood and a successful business career, up to Zenia's seduction of Roz's husband Mitch and his eventual suicide. Only Tony survives with her man, and it is left to her to give a narrative shape to the fragments of Zenia which exist in the multiple anecdotes of these women: 'She will only be history if Tony chooses to shape her into history' (p. 461).

For all three Zenia is the 'Other Woman', and her existence challenges the optimistic assertion of the early 1970s feminists which Roz recalls with some scepticism in 1990:

> 'The Other Woman will soon be with *us*', the feminists used to say. But how long will it take, thinks Roz, and why hasn't it happened yet?' (p. 392).[22]

Zenia represents a powerfully transgressive element which continues to threaten feminist attempts to transform gender relations and concepts of sexual power poliics. It is the otherness of Zenia which is figured in her three avatars in this novel, identified in the different life stories told by the three friends. One avatar is from fairy tale: *The Robber Bridegroom* by the Brothers Grimm, which is here feminised by Roz's twin daughters and savagely glossed by her through the parodic mode of double-coding:

> *The Robber Bride*, thinks Roz. Well, why not? Let the grooms take it in the neck for once. The Robber Bride, lurking in her mansion in the dark forest ... The Rubber Broad is more like it – her and those pneumatic tits. (p. 295)

A second avatar is from the Bible, the figure of Jezebel in the Old Testament (1 Judges: 21). This is prefigured in Charis's childhood when with her grandmother she used to choose revelatory passages from the Bible at random and once lit on the death of Jezebel; that 'message' is confirmed on the very day of her last confrontation with Zenia by her morning Bible reading:

> She realized it as soon as she got up, as soon as she stuck her daily pin into the Bible. It picked out Revelations Seventeen, the chapter about the Great Whore. (p. 420)

There is a third avatar advanced by Tony near the end, that of the medieval French Cathar woman warrior, Dame Giraude, who in the thirteenth century defended her castle against the Catholic forces of Simon de Montfort. She was finally defeated and thrown down a well. This is the most unsettling of Zenia's avatars because it introduces a new perspective on her otherness which extends beyond the demonic. Just as Tony very much admires the reckless courage of Dame Giraude fighting for a lost cause so too she has a sneaking admiration for Zenia as a guerrilla fighter, despite her own humiliations at her hands:

> Zenia is dead, and although she was many other things, she was also courageous. What side she was on doesn't matter; not to Tony, not any more. There may not even have been a side. She may have been alone.   (pp. 469–70)

This is a recognition of the 'otherness' of Zenia, which cannot be accommodated within the parameters of the friends' stories. Tony has always associated Zenia with war – or 'Raw' in terms of her own subjective life. As a result of having known Zenia, Tony contemplates writing a book about female military commanders: '*Iron Hands, Velvet Gloves*, she could call it. But there isn't much material' (p. 464). It is also Tony who wishes to give Zenia's ashes a sort of military burial on Armistice Day: 'An ending, then. November 11, 1991, at eleven o'clock in the morning, the eleventh hour of the eleventh day of the eleventh month' (p. 465).

Whichever way we look at it, the most interesting figure in the novel is Zenia, the 'demonic woman'; she is there in the title and it is her story which defines and focuses the narrative. How is it that this traditionally Gothic figure survives as such a powerful force in Atwood's novel about contemporary social reality in 1990s Toronto? I wish to suggest that Atwood herself has done a Dr Frankenstein performance here, reassembling parts of old legends and fairy tales in order to create her female monster who strides through three Canadian women's stories from the 1960s to the 1990s haunting their lives and wreaking havoc. However, Atwood revises the *Frankenstein* ending for it is the monster who destroys herself and it is the three friends who survive, though their memories of Zenia will live on. This is perhaps putting it rather melodramatically, but what Zenia represents will always exceed the bounds of decorum. Her power is the power of female sexuality, and the figure of Zenia relates directly to contemporary social myths about femininity; it also relates to male (and female) fantasies about the feminine; and in addition it challenges feminist thinking about gender relations. In her reading from *The Robber Bride* at the National Theatre in London in 1993 Atwood offered an important clue to an interpretation of her new novel when she said, 'It's a book about illusion: now you see it, now you don't.' Through Zenia's story Atwood confronts the ideology of traditional female romance where 'getting the power means getting the man, for the man *is* the power' (a statement made by Atwood in Wales in 1982). In this novel Atwood is investigating the extent to which that old proposition about power still holds true in the feminist – or post-feminist – 1990s. In answer to a question asked at the National Theatre, 'Why should women now mind much about having men taken away from them by other women?', Atwood replied, 'This is not ideology; it's real life.' I would add that *The Robber Bride* is also fantasy, for this is a fantastic tale which examines once again the fantasies that underpin real life as well as fiction. Female sexuality has always been a problem for real women and real men, just as it is a problem for feminism: 'Male fantasies, male fantasies, is everything run by male fantasies?' (p. 392). Have women internalised these fantasies to such an extent that as Roz fears, 'You are a woman with a man inside watching a woman'? Atwood answers Roz's rhetorical questions by investigating the effects of fantasies of desirable femininity on women themselves. Zenia inhabits that fantasy territory:

> The Zenias of this world ... have slipped sideways into dreams; the dreams of women too, because women are fantasies for other women, just as they are for men. But fantasies of a different kind. (p. 392)

Who is Zenia? And what kind of fantasy is she for her three contemporaries? Zenia seems to be real but she has a double existence for she belongs to two different fictional discourses, that of realism and of fantasy. She is a very transgressive figure who exists both as a character in the realistic fiction and also as the projection of three women's imaginations. As the Other Woman, her identity is fabricated through their stories about her, which are all stories of seduction, betrayal and humiliation. She herself is an enigma. Indeed she derives meaning only within the signifying structures of other people's stories and then always retrospectively. Zenia is a liar, a floating signifier, possibly a void and certainly a fraud. There is no indication that she has any independent subjective life, unless it is her 'aura' which is savagely at variance with her glamorous appearance; it is according to Charis, 'a turbulent muddy green ... a deadly aureole, a visible infection' (p. 66). At least this is how Zenia appears to one of her victims, always on the loose and ready to rob them of whatever is most precious to them. Zenia is everything they want

most and everything they fear, for she represents their unfulfilled
desires just as she represents their repressed pain-filled childhood
selves. She is the dark double of them all, having multiple identities
but no fixed identity. As Tony discovers after systematic research:

> Even the name Zenia may not exist ... As for the truth about her,
> it lies out of reach, because – according to the records, at any rate
> – she was never even born.   (p. 461)

Indeed, there are three different versions of Zenia's life story which
have been tailored to fit the lives of Tony, Charis, Roz. She is what
they most desire and dread to be. They all think occasionally that
they would like to be someone other than the persons they are; most
of the time they would like to be Zenia. It is no wonder that Tony
reaches this conclusion:

> As with any magician, you saw what she wanted you to see; or else
> you saw what you yourself wanted to see. She did it with mirrors.
> The mirror was whoever was watching, but there was nothing
> behind the two-dimensional image but a thin layer of mercury.
> (p. 461)

Why cannot the three women let Zenia go, when they believe she
is dead and when they have been to her memorial service five years
earlier? Having been tricked and robbed by Zenia of men, money
and self confidence, they keep on meeting once a month for lunch
because of her. The positive outcome is that they become fast
friends, and it is worth noting that this is the first time such a group
of loyal female friends has appeared in Atwood's fiction. However,
the fact remains that they meet to tell stories about Zenia, and actually it is their collective need of her which brings her back from the
dead – or would do so, if she were really dead. When she commits
suicide the three friends stand looking at her, still needing to believe
that she is looking at them:

> Zenia revolves slowly, and looks straight at them with her white
> mermaid eyes.
>   She isn't really looking at them though, because she can't. Her
> eyes are rolled back into her head.   (pp. 446–7)

The switch in narrative perspective reminds readers of whose is the
active needy gaze and it is not Zenia's. Even when they have scat-

tered her ashes in Lake Ontario at the end, their stories will still be about Zenia. They need her, or their stories about her, in order to define themselves, for the 'good' women are shown to be as dependent on the 'Other Woman' as she is on them. Zenia is inside each one, for she represents their unfulfilled shadow selves: 'Was she in any way like us? thinks Tony. Or, to put it the other way around: Are we in any way like her?' (p. 470). The dark reflection in the magic mirror is still there, in that 'infinitely receding headspace where Zenia continues to exist' (p. 464).

As Alison Light wrote of Daphne du Maurier's *Rebecca*, that story of another 'demonic' woman:

> It demarcates a feminine subjectivity which is hopelessly split within bourgeois gendered relations ... [it] makes visible the tensions within the social construction of femininity whose definitions are never sufficient and are always reminders of what is missing, what could be.[23]

Light's remark about a woman's novel of the late 1930s needs very little updating in relation to *The Robber Bride* written nearly 60 years later where the concept of split feminine subjectivity is shared by all three of Atwood's protagonists. Signalled in their doubled or tripled names (Tony/Antonia Fremont/Tnomerf Ynot; Roz Andrews/Rosalind Greenwood/Roz Grunwald; and Charis, formerly known as Karen), it is commented on explicitly in all three. Since childhood Tony has always been able to write and spell backwards: 'It's her seam, it's where she's sewn together; it's where she could split apart' (p. 19). Similar comments are offered about Charis, who was 'split in two' as a sexually abused child (p. 263) and about Roz, whose life was 'cut in two' when her Jewish father returned to Toronto after the Second World War (p. 332). All three have a seam, a split, which is the space of repression occupied by their 'dark twins' and Zenia operates on this edge of desire and lack which is the borderline territory of the marauding Gothic Other.

Zenia is a threat because of her flaunting sexuality, her deceptions and betrayals, her ruthless contempt for others and her random destructiveness. With her siren song she seduces men and pulls them inside out and then abandons them, though as Tony realises there is nothing gender-specific about this with Zenia:

> How well she did it, thinks Tony. How completely she took us in. In the war of the sexes, which is nothing like a real war but is

instead a kind of confused scrimmage in which people change allegiances at a moment's notice, Zenia was a double agent. (p. 185)

The otherness which Zenia represents has to be construed as deviant, dangerous and threatening, and it has to be annihilated again and again. Her punishment is very like Rebecca's in the earlier novel when Rebecca suffered murder, vilification and cancer of the womb; Zenia commits suicide – or was she murdered? – she is discredited through the revelation that she was a drug dealer and possibly an arms smuggler, and she is reputed to be suffering from ovarian cancer. As Tony repeats, 'Zenia is history', which does not necessarily mean that she is dead and out of the way but that her story will continue to be retold in different versions and endlessly speculated upon. It is symptomatic that even her funeral urn splits in two and her ashes blow about all over her three mourners. In this Gothic fairy tale retold from a feminist perspective, Zenia is a very disruptive figure for she is the spectacle of desirable femininity, a beautiful façade which hides whatever is behind it. (Is it neurotic insecurity? or nothingness? or frigidity? or is it ruthless egoism?) The final image of Zenia is given by Tony in her ambiguous elegy:

> She's like an ancient statuette dug up from a Minoan palace: there are the large breasts, the tiny waist, the dark eyes, the snaky hair. Tony picks her up and turns her over, probes and questions, but the woman with her glazed pottery face does nothing but smile. (p. 470)

Always an enigma, Zenia is still present or as present as she ever was within her shifting figurations. During the narrative she has taken on all the pains of the twentieth century as the Jewish victim of Nazi persecution and of European wars, as displaced person, as victim of violence and sexual abuse, as suffering from cancer, AIDS and drug addition – just as she has been the ikon of desirable femininity, Robber Bride, Whore of Babylon, and woman warrior. She remains un-dead, a vampiric figure desiring 'a bowl of blood, a bowl of pain, some death' (p. 13) for she derives her life from the insecurities and desires of the living.

The ending of *The Robber Bride* is not an ending but merely 'a lie in which we all agree to conspire' (p. 465). We are reminded of Atwood's voice in *Murder in the Dark* whispering, 'I have designs on you ... by the rules of the game, I must always lie.' Atwood takes

Gothic conventions and turns them inside out, weaving her illusions 'like any magician making us see what she wants us to see', as she transgresses the boundaries between realism and fantasy, between what is acceptable and what is forbidden. Of course these are fictions; *Lady Oracle* and *The Robber Bride* are illusions created by Atwood's narrative art, but they speak to readers in the present as they challenge us to confront our own desires and fears. Atwood, like the old Gothic novelists, like Joan Foster and like Zenia, 'does it with mirrors'.

5

Lost Worlds: *Life Before Man*

An Albertosauras, or – the name Lesje prefers – a Gorgosaurus, pushes through the north wall of the Colonnade and stands there uncertainly, sniffing the unfamiliar smell of human flesh, balancing on its powerful hind legs, its dwarfed front legs with their razor claws held in close to its chest. In a minute William Wasp and Lesje Litvak will be two lumps of gristle. The Gorgosaurus wants, wants. It's a stomach on legs, it would swallow the world if it could. Lesje, who has brought it here, regards it with friendly objectivity.[1]

This is a strange passage to find in a novel which is generally regarded as Atwood's most depressingly realist fiction.[2] Clearly it belongs to another genre altogether, that of science fiction fantasy, for the dinosaur which pushes into the Toronto coffee house on Saturday, 30 October 1976, summoned up by a young woman's imagination, is one of those contingent presences which interrupt the discourses of everyday life, offering an alternative discourse within a radically different time frame of representation which threatens to collapse the conventions of realism. Of course this is Lesje's fantasy, through which she speaks the secret part of herself which is floating around loose outside the limits of the real and the rational, and which at some level relates to her sense of otherness coded into the racial slurs of 'William Wasp' and 'Lesje Litvak' in this first Atwood novel to signal Toronto's multiculturalism. Yet the appearance of this fantasy monster with its ravenous desires intruding into the civilised urban world from the margins of prehistory introduces a principle of heterogeneity into this novel which operates far more radically than the discontinuities signalled by its narrative structure might suggest.

Not only is *Life Before Man* a multivoiced text told from the different perspectives of the three main characters (of whom Lesje is one), but within this structure the novel records a wide range of coexistent and often antagonistic private discourses which have the effect of fracturing the social discourse into multiple individual gestures of resistance and survival. I have adopted here Homi Bhabha's vocabulary of postcolonial difference and cultural displacement which he applies to Third World and 'minority' cultures, transferring it here to talk about heterogeneity within personal relations in an apparently unified urban community, for in both as I see it the implications are inevitably political.[3] We may well ask what kind of story Atwood is telling us in a novel whose title faces both ways, where *Life Before Man* looks backward to prehistory and forward to the future (cf. *Paradise Lost*, 'The World was all *before* them, where to choose – their place of rest and Providence their guide', XII. 646–7).[4] This promise of doubleness is kept throughout in the unsettling shifts between realism and fantasy which characterise the double-voiced discourse of the narrating characters, just as the evolutionary theme suggested by the title balances threats of extinction of the species against evidence of individual survival.

From this perspective, claims about the realism of *Life Before Man* may seem strange indeed, and we may wonder how the reviewer in *The Times* (quoted in Chapter 1) and Marilyn French in the *New York Times Book Review* could say, 'The life of the novel really lies in its texture, in the densely interwoven feelings, memories and insights of the characters'.[5] Yet Atwood herself regards this as her most domestic novel with its triangular plot where a wife takes a lover and later the lover commits suicide, the marriage breaks up, and the husband goes to live with another woman. Atwood is credited with saying that she wrote *Life Before Man* as a homage to George Eliot's *Middlemarch*, which is generally acknowledged to be the classic Victorian realist novel. In response to an interviewer's request to discuss that claim, she replied:

> In *Middlemarch* everything is middle – it's the middle of the nineteenth century, it's middle class, it's the middle of England ... It's about life as lived by the middle and that's what *Life Before Man* is. It's the middle of Toronto, it's somewhat the middle of the twentieth century, the people are middle-aged.   (*Conversations*, p. 226)

Before trying to sort out the puzzles about realism and the relation between Atwood's novel and George Eliot's, I think we should remember that Atwood also refers to *Middlemarch* when speaking about the novel form and the role of convention and innovation, which she calls 'moving the brackets' or 'changing the rules'. It is in the double context of conventions of realism and 'ways of moving beyond the conventions to include things not considered includable' (*Conversations*, p. 194) that connections between *Life Before Man* and *Middlemarch* might be profitably explored.

Conventions of realism in fiction centre on notions of mimesis – that the text is a representation of everyday life, giving the illusion of referentiality through what Roland Barthes called 'solidity of specification'. The action of *Life Before Man* is set in a particular historical moment in a socially and geographically specific location and the characters act in ways with which most readers can readily relate. This is Atwood's 'life as lived by the middle', or as Janice Kulyk Keefer describes it, '*Life Before Man* displays the degree "zero of the way we live now" … Atwood has taken for her subject matter the near-terminal impoverishment of the human, and therefore moral, imagination as applied to contemporary urban life, and she has attempted to situate this impoverishment in its proper devastating context.'[6] Realism tends to be associated with the dreariness and the mundaneity of everyday life as it is here, for it is based on the myth of objectivity which implies that a novelist can see and describe accurately things as they are, a kind of universal validity of observation. Within such definition a realist text would seem to be a 'closed' text productive of only limited meanings, and in the case of *Middlemarch* this closure has been associated with the authority of an omniscient narrator's voice which controls and interprets all the proliferating discourses within the novel. Certainly this is the view of *Middlemarch* as 'classic realist text' which David Lodge argues against in an influential essay of the early 1980s in which he describes George Eliot's methods of evading such reductiveness of meaning.[7] Interestingly, many of the criticisms of *Life Before Man* tend to treat it as a 'classic realist text' despite the fact that Atwood's novel lacks an omniscient narrative voice, presenting instead the multiple shifting perspectives of the three main characters themselves. Against charges of realism we could argue that *Life Before Man* draws attention through its structure to the fact that words are not transparent windows on the world, but that for these characters words become the means of slipping away from the restrictions of real life. *Life Before Man* begins to look like a very slippery text indeed, composed of multiple discourses, some of which conform to realism but many of which do not.

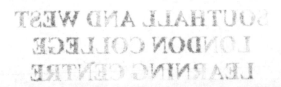

Yet in some ways that homage to *Middlemarch* does frame our reading of *Life Before Man*, and I would like to pursue those questions of similarity further. As far as realism goes, both *Life Before Man* and *Middlemarch* are social chronicles set in a particular historical period and place, tracing a web of invented lives so that the role of the novelist is close to the role of social historian. But there is another dimension to both these novels which makes the comparison more interesting while unsettling many of the criticisms about realism, and that relates to the way in which Atwood and Eliot employ discourses of science – in particular the Darwinian theory of evolution. Charles Darwin's *On the Origin of Species by means of Natural Selection* (1859) and *The Descent of Man* (1871) revolutionised representations of humanity's place and significance in the natural world and raised fundamental questions about the nature of the human species, society, history and religion. George Eliot was standing very close to this radical reassessment, for she and G. H. Lewes read *On the Origins of Species* when it appeared, and she had already read Charles Lyell's *The Principles of Geology* (1830–3). *Middlemarch* might be read as her novelistic response to evolutionary theories, for while she accepted the gradualism of Darwin and Lyell which she incorporated into her conceptualisation of Victorian ideas of social progress, she resisted the vast amoral patterns of determinism in Darwin's biological model, she argued instead for the indeterminacy and unpredictability of individual human lives. Atwood's project a hundred years later seems to me a very similar enterprise, less wide-ranging in its social samplings but vaster in its time projections backwards to prehistory. (It is worth remembering that the early working titles for *Life BeforeMan* were *Notes on the Mesozoic,* and then *Notes from the Lost World.*) Both novels set their enquiry in relation to scientific and social doctrines of evolution, just as they both represent moral and intellectual resistance to any mechanistic concept of determinism. Atwood's scientific frames of reference are natural history, geology and astronomy, with the principal setting for the novel being the Royal Ontario Museum in Toronto where both the female protagonists work. (Lesje is a paleontologist and Elizabeth is in charge of Special Projects and publicity, so that both women are engaged in translating science into popular language for the general public.) It must be said that Atwood's scientific narrative is rather more violent than Eliot's, combining evolution with its correlative of extinction and with catastrophe ('Cosmic Disasters' is the name of the show which Elizabeth goes to see at the Planetarium), no doubt in response to late twentieth-century fears for the destruction of the human race by human beings themselves. However, like Eliot's narrative, Atwood's works against the vast impersonality of the natural world, setting the forces of human intelligence, emotion and imagination within a social narrative of relationships against scientific theories of determinism and natural law.

Atwood's stress falls differently from Eliot's; instead of a late nineteenth-century critique of concepts of progress and reform according to organicist evolutionary models, Atwood focuses on two awkward concepts within evolutionary theory: the struggle for survival and the extinction of the dinosaurs (which unnerves any historical argument for the necessity of progress or even survival through time). However, this is balanced against the more optimistic principle of survival through adaptation to environment. It is the biological concept of adaptation which Atwood translates into the psychological and moral parameters of her novel. Seen from this perspective, *Life Before Man* might actually be read as an argument *for* evolution, though for evolution of a different kind from Darwin's as Atwood sets out possibilities for the moral and social evolution of human beings, an attitude which resonates with Eliot's argument for progress through organic social interdependence. All three major characters have survived by the end of the novel, and their perceptions as well as their circumstances have changed. As Atwood says of Elizabeth:

> The last scene in the Museum looking at the Chinese art show, indicates that Elizabeth is able to formulate a vision beyond the personal (which has obsessed her till now) and though she may not believe in the existence of this vision (a social world in which true interaction and support is possible) the fact that she is able to think of this at all indicates a possible direction for her ... outwards, if not upwards. She's come to the end of merely personal and sexual concerns.[8]

Similar shifts are experienced by the other two main characters, as I shall show. Of course there are no cataclysmic changes in life, for only death is associated with cataclysm in this novel.

It is perhaps worth pointing out a few other similarities and differences between *Middlemarch* and *Life Before Man* in their use of scientific discourse. The opening of *Middlemarch* is clearly a response to Victorian scientific method for Eliot presents her fiction as a series of 'experiments' designed to study the 'history of man, and how the mysterious mixture behaves under the varying experiments of Time'.[9] While this signals her resistance to deterministic conclusions, it also emphasises the gap between mechanical processes of natural law and individual human responses in all their diversity. *Middlemarch* presents no single key or unified meaning but suggests infinite possibilities for variation within the web of social circumstance. Certainly there are parallels between *Middlemarch* and *Life Before Man* in terms of diversity of discourse, and in neither novel is there any attempt to weave them together into one story; instead they both construct a fabric of multiple discourses through dynamic images of lives in process. There are however differences in their uses of science, which might be summarised by the contrast between Eliot's use of the microscope and Atwood's use of the telescope. The first section of *Life Before Man* opens out into the vast spaces of the universe while the third section sweeps back via Lesje's imagination into the primeval forests of the dinosaurs, occupying dimensions of fantasy not envisaged by Eliot's narrative.

Both novels share the same metalanguage, offering versions of determinism which are challenged by the indeterminacy of multiple individual narrative perspectives. It is perhaps a case of there being no new stories to tell, for as Peter Brooks argues, any story is a repetition of other stories, with actions and sequences told according to narrative conventions which have already been written and according to which we read any new text.[10] Atwood's novel combines the story of evolution with the story of a domestic triangle and the fabulous story of discovering an unknown world. (This story too has already been written by Sir Arthur Conan Doyle, as Lesje's references to *The Lost World* amply acknowledge.) The novelistic awareness that every story is a recycling of existing narrative elements parallels the scientific assertion that all the molecules now in circulation were already present at the creation of the earth, a view expressed by Lesje as she sits in the kitchen of her married lover's house at the beginning of their affair:

> These molecular materials have merely combined, disintegrated, recombined. Although a few molecules and atoms have escaped into space, nothing has been added.
> Lesje contemplates this fact, which she finds soothing. (p. 169)

Against that background the problem is to tell any story which will sound new. As Atwood asked on one occasion, 'How am I to know what kind of stories you wish to hear?'[11] – especially, one might add, when there are multiple stories already in circulation from three dif-

ferent characters' points of view. I would argue that against the background of prehistory and the extinction of species as against a more
recent history of individual deaths, this complex social narrative contains three different narratives of survival. The limits of mortality are
recognised by all of them but they resist those limits in order to go
on living in the present. Taken in simple biological terms, the novel
may be seen to be writing against death, with the evidence of a
forward movement there in the plot: it begins with the report of a
suicide and ends with the anticipation of a birth.

Before pursuing the private plots of individual characters, it is
worth looking at the overall narrative design of the novel. Whereas
Middlemarch was a Victorian multiplot novel, *Life Before Man* is a late
twentieth-century multivoiced novel, though both are constructed
on similar principles with parallel interrelated plots narrated from
the perspectives of characters who are equivalent centres of consciousness, thus giving a panoramic representation of lives over a
period of time. With *Life Before Man* the time period is nearly two
years, though there are frequent flashbacks of memory and the
crucial event of the suicide of Chris Beecham, Elizabeth's lover, one
week before the narrative action begins. Arching over all is the evolutionary narrative as a reminder of a 'transcendent' dimension
(functioning rather like the Odyssey in James Joyce's *Ulysses*), while
on a social scale, but outside the characters' consciousness, the narrative itself constructs significant patterns of correspondence which
bind separate lives together in ways that break down difference in
favour of a shared human condition. The scope of the narrative
enterprise is signalled in the two epigraphs, the first referring to a
fossil as it opens out into the spaces of prehistory, and the second
intimately personal and immediate which opens the way into subjective spaces of emotion and memory:

> Look, I'm smiling at you, I'm smiling in you, I'm smiling through
> you. How can I be dead if I breathe in every quiver of your hand?
> Abram Tertz (Andrei Sinyavsky), *The Icicle*

So the contradictory movement of the novel begins, with its signifiers
of absence in the fossilised tracks and also of spectral presences and
demonic possession.

The temporal and spatial documentation here is very specific,
giving details of date, location and speaker for every section rather
like the form of a diary, and for the first couple of days there is a tight
pattern of triple voices per day where the three protagonists are

named: Elizabeth Schoenhof, her husband Nate, and Lesje Green (whose first name encodes her ethnic origins though her 'unlikely' surname obscures these traces).[12] By the third day the rigid structure begins to break down, with variations in the recurrence of voices and irregular time gaps as relationships between characters shift and memories of the past occupy relatively more narrative space. Within the web of shifting perspectives the narrative follows a consistently forward chronological movement over almost two years from 29 October 1976 to 18 August 1978, during which time circumstances change for all the characters. By the end the domestic plots of Elizabeth and Nate and of Lesje and William have fragmented and reformed into different patterns: Nate and Lesje are now living together and Elizabeth is alone in the family home, no longer a wife but a divorced mother with her two young daughters. There are only two flashback sections, both of them recording Nate's memories of climactic meetings with Chris, once when Chris told him about the affair with Elizabeth and the second over a year later, when Chris appeared uninvited at Nate's house, only to be ejected by Elizabeth herself. (This is the occasion when in a proleptic flash Nate knows that one day, 'at some vague place in the future he himself will need to leave her', p. 236.) The novel is characterised by unsettling shifts of focus, not only in its multi-voiced technique but also because of radical changes of perspective within every section as a character's attention moves between intense preoccupation with present domestic or professional issues and the wide spaces of personal memory, world atrocities or prehistory. Such shifts fracture realistic representation so that the identifiable Toronto world with its stable institutions like the Royal Ontario Museum and the family seems to disperse into a variety of other worlds as strange as Maple White Land in *The Lost World*. Toronto is represented in this text as the site of heterogeneous discourses, where remoteness and alienation are precariously balanced against human efforts to imagine better alternatives to the present. All the characters here yearn to go somewhere they have never been.

In order to demonstrate how this contradictory motion works, I shall look closely at the first three chapters, all ostensibly occupying the same time slot in 1976 and the same Toronto location, two of the characters being inside the same house. The novel opens with Elizabeth's interior monologue:

I don't know how I should live. I don't know how anyone should live. All I know is how I do live. I live like a peeled snail. And that's no way to make money.   (p. 11)

With this desperate outcry of a subject at odds with the real world, overwhelmingly aware of the gap between living and knowing or between describing and prescribing, the human dimension is given priority over the vastness of prehistory signalled in the title. For Elizabeth, as we quickly discover, real time has ceased to exist; everything is construed as being merely post-Chris's suicide. This is the focal point of her attention as she continues in dialogue with his ghost, upbraiding and blaming him, 'so angry I could kill you. If you hadn't already done that for yourself.' The shift from first person monologue to objective description of this woman lying alone fully clothed on her bed and looking up at the cracks in the ceiling (where the stripped-down narrative register and the subjective escape strategies exactly parallel Offred's later in *The Handmaid's Tale*) only serve to insist on the splitting of spatial and temporal dimensions within consciousness. Still within the third person, the narrative returns to indirect interior monologue as Elizabeth feels herself to be not anchored to the bed but drifting in space: 'She is not in. She's somewhere between her body ... and the ceiling with its hairline cracks' which open visions of fracture as wide as the universe. Elizabeth's state of suspension is close to that form of daydreaming which Homi Bhabha describes not as an 'alternative' to the real world but as a 'supplement' to it, occupying a problematical space on the borders of the rational, contiguous with perceptual reality but also discontinuous with it, 'near but different'.[13] It is within such a discontinuous scenario that Elizabeth can 'see' the cracks in the ceiling and at the same time 'know' the 'vacuum on the other side of the ceiling, which is not the same as the third floor where the tenants live' (p. 12). The space that she 'knows' to be there is the fantasy space of non-meaning and absence as figured in the 'black holes' which later appear (invisibly) on the screen at the Planetarium of the Royal Ontario Museum. This is Elizabeth's inner space scenario, imaged as the abyss into which she steadfastly resists falling herself, though sucked towards it by the shock of Chris's suicide. Its menace continues to coexist in Elizabeth's mind with the rituals of domestic life as she listens through her half-open door to her daughters innocently preparing for Hallowe'en and sees her husband bringing her a cup of tea: 'How are you, love?' he says. 'I've brought you some tea' (p. 13). The two worlds are contiguous but there is no way of crossing between the two for someone like Elizabeth who is caught between them.

Nate's narrative on the same day is bound to his wife's by the echo of his own word 'love', though he no longer knows what that word means. It is nothing more than an empty ritual left over from what he nostalgically calls 'the olden days' before Chris when their marriage appeared to have some stability. Nate is floundering around in domestic wreckage, shut out from Elizabeth's bedroom as he is shut out from her life, fixated like her on Chris's death which looms in his memory in grisly detail:

> No head left at all, to speak of. The headless horseman. But recognizable. Chris's expression had never really been in that heavy flat face of his; not like most people's. It had been in his body. (p. 16)

For Nate too Chris continues to exist, occupying the subjective space inside his own head and asserting authority over the intersubjective space between him and Elizabeth where Nate feels himself and Chris to be doubles, 'Nate's other body, joined to him by that tenuous connection, that hole in space controlled by Elizabeth' (pp. 16–17). Nate is as trapped by that suicide as Elizabeth, 'cornered' and at a disadvantage in his own home.

Unlike Elizabeth Nate is not given to flights of fantasy, though on rare occasions he imagines what it might be like to be elsewhere. However, his subjective position in this narrative is worth considering in some detail for it is ambiguous and increasingly erratic. Shut away in 'his own room ... as if to keep him in there' Nate does not remain fixed but wanders between the kitchen and his workroom in the cellar with periodic forays to Elizabeth's door, still at her beck and call as her messenger and deputy in the house. As if on a leash (for Elizabeth knows all about it) he also cycles over to visit Martha his former mistress, a place where he no longer belongs or wishes to be. Nate is becoming a displaced person, speaking in outworn clichés to Elizabeth, Martha, his mother and his children. Worse still he finds he is deprived of speech altogether in his attempts to break out of the trap by making a series of silent phone calls to Lesje, a young woman whom he has met at the Museum and whose image floats like a promise of new romance in his mind. He is always in restless motion – running in circles as he jogs around Queen's Park, cycling furiously between houses owned by the four women in his life while not belonging in any of these houses himself, switching between jobs as he moves from his work in Legal Aid at a Toronto lawyer's office to become a toymaker in the basement of his house, then back to the law firm again. Nate seems engaged in a continuous process of reinventing himself, shaving off his beard so that he looks like another person ('His hands have decided it's time for him to be someone else'; p. 43), as he occupies multiple identities as husband and father (later separated and then divorced), as lover, son, and finally father again to Lesje's child without knowing it. Nate does not completely fit into any of these social identities, and while there is a dimension of unsatisfactoriness about his position it must be said that he remains a resisting subject who remains open to new possibilities. Atwood described him as a political idealist and an 'optimist at heart, but he doesn't want to admit it' (*Conversations*, p. 123), also as a man facing a moral dilemma about 'whether to leave the kids because the marriage is rotten, or whether to stay with the marriage for the sake of the kids ... he's actually the nicest person in the book' (*Conversations*, p. 145). Whether we agree with this authorial assessment or not, the language of his narrative suggests some measure of progress and a cautious optimism for the final words of his last entry suggest an end to his wandering. As he thinks about meeting Lesje after work on the steps of the Museum, something he did for years with Elizabeth, Nate considers: 'They will either go for a drink or not. In any case, they will go home' (p. 314).

To return to the opening trilogy, the third voice is Lesje Green's, asocial and isolated, for her imagination inhabits the wide spaces of the Upper Jurassic period where dinosaurs roam free:

> Lesje is wandering in prehistory. Under a sun more orange than her own has ever been, in the middle of a swampy plain lush with thick-stalked plants and oversized ferns, a group of bony-plated stegosaurs is grazing.   (p. 18)

Lesje's position up in the top of one of these trees and watching through binoculars is one of 'blissful uninvolvement' for here her human form is her disguise. Her otherness is so incomprehensible to the dinosaurs that they will not even notice her, which 'is the next best thing to being invisible'. Of course such fantasising is escapist (as Janice Kulyk Keefer and Linda Hutcheon have pointed out),[14] fantasy being 'predicated on the category of the real' and defined in negative terms, where 'invisible' is one in a range of descriptions of fantasy which include '*im*possible', '*un*real', '*un*known', and *un*said'.[15] However, Lesje's fantasy with its violations of 'whatever official version of paleontological reality she chooses' (p. 18) is also creative and recreational, opening up spaces where she feels at home in a way she never does in the real world. Like the 'delicate camptosaurs' Lesje too is 'cautious, nervous, and sensitive to danger, for she is a casualty of her multicultural upbringing across three cultures – those of her Ukrainian and Jewish grandmothers and the Canadian culture of her birth – and among which she has no certainty of self-location. Marked by her ethnicity and her scientific interests as irremediably 'other' in Toronto, Lesje in early childhood discovered her 'true nationality' in the Royal Ontario Museum to which she was regularly taken by one or other of her grandmothers. Not surprisingly, she chose to become a paleontologist and to work in that Museum: 'This is the only membership she values' (p. 307). Lesje's fantasy is that of a professional scientist whose job is to classify fossils and to educate the public 'on matters pertaining to Vertebrate Paleontology', though her passion for her subject is so intense that she has dreamed of reversing the course of history to make the dinosaurs live: 'strange flesh would grow again, cover the bones, the badlands would flower' (pp. 80–1). Like Elizabeth's black holes, this imagined territory is the place where she negotiates the gaps between real life and desire, though like any supplementary state it remains in constant subterranean dialogue with the voice of reason. Lesje knows for instance that her dinosaur scenario is a regressive fantasy, but 'thinking about men has become too unrewarding', by which she means her relationship with William, a young environmental engineer. This is the first signal that their domestic plot has no future, or as Lesje phrases it to herself, 'what they have in common is an interest in extinction. She confines it to dinosaurs, however. William applies it to everything' (p. 126). Whereas Lesje exists with confidence in her imagined world, it is the everyday world whose social codes she cannot fathom. She jumps every time the telephone rings and at work she commits the *faux pas* of mentioning a series of silent phone calls she has been receiving, only to discover when Elizabeth Schoenhof walks out that her lover had been doing the same thing to her for a month before he committed suicide – something Lesje would have known if she had ever listened to office gossip. In this oblique and silent fashion the first significant connection in the plot is made, for Lesje's mysterious caller as we discover later was Elizabeth's husband Nate whose behaviour pattern is a repetition of Chris's as Nate acts through his 'other body' with its speaking silences.

Certainly Lesje's self-division is no more strange than Nate's or indeed Elizabeth's but her fantasies are more exotic, for though she may be a scientist, she is also, like Joan Foster in *Lady Oracle*, an 'escape artist'. How the prehistoric jungle offers her a place of refuge from the embarrassments of social life is amply demonstrated

at the dinner party to which Elizabeth invites her and William, for
Elizabeth already suspects that her husband is falling in love with
Lesje. Awkward and ill at ease, Lesje knocks over her coffee cup and
flees to the bathroom, where locking herself in she escapes to the
lost wilderness:

> Is she really this graceless, this worthless? From her treetop she
> watches an Ornithomimus, large-eyed, birdlike, run through the
> scrub, chasing a small protomammal ... Surely these things are
> important. (p. 157)

Back 'in her field' once again, Lesje realises that though she can see
when she is looking far back into prehistory, she can see nothing
clearly up close:

> It's like being farsighted, the distant lake and its beaches and
> smooth-backed basking sauropods clear-edged in the moonlight,
> her own hand a blur. She does not know, for instance, why she is
> crying. (p. 157)

As a subject Lesje is under continual threat of erasure, preferring
to be invisible and certainly sexless as she runs through the Upper
Jurassic out of her living room 'wearing her Adidas and a navy-blue
sweatshirt that says SMALL IS BEAUTIFUL on it in red' (p. 264). If fantasy
suggests the trajectory of a character's consciousness then we can
trace the subterranean shifts in Lesje's internal dialogue through the
changing scenarios of her lost worlds. Just as her antagonism to
William projected the image of the ravenous Gorgosaurus in the
Colonnade, so at the lowest ebb in her relationship with Nate all her
fantasies become visions of extinction:

> Such visions are still possible, but they don't last long. Inevitably
> she sees a later phase: the stench of dying seas, dead fish on the
> mud-covered shores, the huge flocks dwindling, stranded, their
> time done. All of a sudden, Utah. (p. 238)

This fantasy is, incidentally, an echo of Nate's similar anxieties about
their relationship, suggesting the strongly poetic metalanguage of
image clusters which binds this novel together: 'It's this, this desert,
this growing fiasco, that has driven him, finally, into Elizabeth's
mushroom-coloured parlor' (p. 258). In her state of desperation,
Lesje finally perceives an affinity between herself and Elizabeth's

dead lover in their comparable roles and their possibly comparable fates: 'Chris hadn't died for love. He wanted to be an event, and he's been one' (p. 293). Reinscribing Chris yet again within the narrative action, Lesje first thinks of following his example but suddenly rejects this and switches plots: 'If children were the key, if having them were the only way she could stop being invisible, then she would goddam well have some herself' (p. 293).

As a 'pregnant paleontologist' in the final section of her narrative, Lesje discovers that not only has her perspective on life changed but also her perspective on prehistory, though she is still capable of wryly looking at her own act of vengeful conception from an objective scientific point of view: 'And what will Nate do, what will she do? ... Though the past is the sediment from such acts, billions, trillions of them' (p. 308). Instead of an absence, Lesje's plot now has a centre; at last she has become significant to herself and suddenly visible to her dinosaurs. With that knowledge comes the destruction of her fantasy as she realises not only that they are long since dead but if they were alive, 'they'd run away or tear her apart.' Even her favourite fantasy of the dinosaur dance fades:

> They'd dance stumpily down the stairs of the Museum and out the front door. Eight-foot horsetails would sprout in Queen's Park, the sun would turn orange. She'd throw in some giant dragonflies, some white and yellow flowers, a lake. She'd move among the foliage, at home, an expedition of one.   (p. 310)

But her dinosaur fantasy dies exhausted as the private biological narrative of her own pregnancy takes priority: 'In the foreground, pushing in whether she wants it to or not, is what Marianne would call her life' (p. 311). With the intrusion of real life comes a new quality of compassion less familiar to Lesje than her dinosaurs but opening out her narrative on to hitherto undreamed of possibilities: 'Forgiveness ... She would prefer instead to forgive, someone, somehow, for something; but she isn't sure where to begin' (p. 311). Like Atwood's other female protagonists, Lesje finds that her perceptions have changed, and she is left facing tentatively towards the future.

To double back briefly into Lesje's Jurassic Park fantasy, we should note that this country of the mind is not only nor indeed primarily the product of her scientific imagination. Its topography has already been laid out by Sir Arthur Conan Doyle in *The Lost World* (1912), his scientific romance about an exciting mission to an uncharted South

American plateau where Darwinian evolution has failed to happen. This is Lesje's favourite novel which she first read as a schoolgirl at the age of ten: 'She can't remember which came first, her passion for fossils or this book; she thinks it was the book' (p. 45). With many narratives of origin the original cannot be traced, though in this novel it would seem that the Ur-text is readily available. As is clear in many of the passages from Lesje's fantasy world which I have quoted, her heroic exploring adventures, the wilderness landscape with its lake (Conan Doyle's Lake Gladys and his Maple White Land, renamed by her as 'Lesjeland') and the behaviour of the prehistoric creatures themselves all derive from *The Lost World* – even to the dinosaurs' dance out into the modern city which is already written in Conan Doyle's account of the pterodactyl which escaped from Professor Challenger's scientific lecture in the Albert Hall and flew away over Edwardian London, only to vanish in the Atlantic. We are also reminded of Joan Foster's words at the end of *Lady Oracle*: 'Maybe I'll try some science fiction. The future doesn't appeal as much to me as the past, but I'm sure it's better for you' (p. 345). In *Life Before Man* Atwood writes a pastiche of science fiction while also suggesting that the future may possibly be better for you, but only if science fiction is abandoned. Incidentally, David Ketterer in his masterly study of Canadian science fiction cites two Canadian examples of the scientific romance dealing with the long evolutionary perspective exploited by Conan Doyle: Sir Charles G. D. Roberts's *In the Morning of Time* (1919) and E. J. Pratt's *The Great Feud (A Dream of the Pliocene Armageddon)* (1926), remarking that 'prehistoric creatures occur with sufficient regularity in early Canadian SF to constitute a trend'.[16] The first chapter of Roberts's novel is entitled 'The World Without Man' which conforms to Lesje's version of Life Before Man, so maybe once again the story of origins blurs with the possibility that *Life Before Man* is also the inheritor of its Canadian precursors.

To add a further twist, it is possible to see revisionary elements in Lesje's fantasy which might be interpreted as a resistance to Conan Doyle's imperialist values, where the challenge of the unknown for his white British all-male exploring party was as much cultural as scientific, and where the confrontation was not only with dinosaurs but also with ape men and cave dwellers in an emblematic representation of the whole Darwinian evolutionary scale. Needless to say, 'civilised' values prevail after a bloody combat where the white men have all the rifles, and the territory is marked down as ripe for colonial exploitation. Lesje's relation to the Lost World ('Lesjeland', Herland) is quite different. Not only is she an observer rather than an invader in an unpeopled land, but the distinction between 'civilised' and 'savage' blurs when her prehistoric fantasy brushes up against real life. Given the behaviour of William and Elizabeth, not to mention the documentation of atrocities in Nate's mother's Amnesty International bulletins, primitive violence is not alien to late twentieth-century human beings. Lesje's opinion of the human race is low:

> Does she care whether the human race survives or not? She doesn't know. The dinosaurs didn't survive and it wasn't the end of the world. In her bleaker moments, of which, she realizes, this is one, she feels the human race has it coming. (p. 27)

Her fantasy, far from being merely escapist or recreational, is a continuous reminder of the origins of the human species and of the possibility of savagery latent within the conventions of civilised life. Within the evolutionary story there is as much evidence of instability and regression as there is of progress, so that Lesje's narrative with its juxtaposition of prehistory and the present might be read as illustrative of a continuity of irrationality and violence rather than of the moral evolution of the human race.

However, hers is only one voice in this multivoiced novel, and as we have seen, this bleakness does not characterise Lesje's mood at the end, nor Nate's as he faces their shared future with a shadowed optimism. Neither is it an adequate description of Elizabeth's mood in the final section of the novel as she stands in the empty Museum after closing time looking at the Chinese Peasant Art exhibition which she has been responsible for arranging. In the struggle for social and psychological survival which has been narrated she too has succeeded, though not in the ways she had hoped. Hers is not the dominating discourse of the novel but only one among three in a structure of mutually responsive and frequently antagonistic discourses. Within her roles of wife, lover, mother and neice, she has survived Chris's suicide, separation and divorce from Nate, and the death of her Auntie Muriel (realising finally that 'Dorothy was not jubilant when the witch turned into a puddle of brown sugar. She was terrified' (p. 279). She has come very close to being sucked into the black vacuum by her ghosts and witches, where her collapse at her aunt's funeral is represented through spatial imagery of falling into the abyss of outer space – though at the same time it is ironically interpreted as appropriate social behaviour for the occasion; as far as Auntie Muriel's friends are concerned 'this is exactly what she should have done' (p. 301). Elizabeth returns from that dark fantasy world while remaining aware that those forces continue to rage just beyond the borders of sanity: 'She has no difficulty seeing the visible world as a transparent veil and a whirlwind. The miracle is to make it solid' (p. 302). Elizabeth's vocabulary may be different from Lesje's but she shares with her a similar apprehension about borderlines, though each remains unknown to the other and known only to the reader.

Finally Elizabeth stands alone ('not lonely, but single, alone' (p. 316) in a moment of aesthetic contemplation:

> Elizabeth stands looking at a picture. The picture is framed and glassed. Behind the glass, bright green leaves spread with the harmonious asymmetry of a Chinese floral rug; purple fruits glow among them. Three women, two with baskets, are picking. Their teeth shine within their smiles, their cheeks are plump and rosy as a doll's. *A Fine Crop of Eggplants*, the caption says, in Chinese, English and French.   (p. 315)

Though there is no doubt that Elizabeth remains located in real life, aware that she is meshed into social codes of family and professional responsibility, this picture represents an imagined space outside the limits of the everyday, offering her an image of otherness which is quite separate from the 'black holes' and strikes a correspondence with the spaces of contemplation contained by Kayo's bowls in her living room ('empty bowls, pure grace'; p. 302). These paintings occupy the same dimensions of Oriental space as the bowls though with the difference that the space is no longer empty but filled with images, which Elizabeth apprehends not as representations of real life but as the figures of desire or political idealism:

> China is not paradise; paradise does not exist. Even the Chinese know it, they must know it, they live there. Like cavemen, they paint not what they see but what they want.   (p. 316)

This perception of Elizabeth's is not unlike Atwood's comment on the task of the novelist: 'What kind of world shall you describe for your readers? The one you can see around you, or the better one you can imagine? It is only by the better world we imagine that we judge the world we have.'[17] Though she returns to the parameters of the everyday, remembering that she has to go to the supermarket on the way home, yet Elizabeth has her vision of a better place 'elsewhere' within the impossible space opened up by the picture on the wall: 'China does not exist. Nevertheless she longs to be there' (p. 317). So the novel ends with Elizabeth poised on the borderline between realism and fantasy in the double knowledge that the paintings represent optimistic illusions and that such illusions are necessary for survival. Her moment of suspension is one we have come to recognise as characteristic of Atwood's endings where a way forward is 'seen as a possibility, finally, whereas initially it is not' (*Conversations*, p. 17). This was Atwood's description of the endings of *Survival* and of *Surfacing*, and survival is still a key word in her thematic vocabulary.

Elizabeth's story, like Nate's and Lesje's, is remarkably resistant to threats of closure just as it resists the grand narratives of science with their patterns of determinism based on natural law, which one interviewer commented on when *Life Before Man* first appeared:

> ALAN TWIGG: What's radical about *Life Before Man* is that it's the first Canadian novel I know of that seriously conveys an awareness that the human race can become extinct. Was that a conscious theme while writing the book?
> ATWOOD: Yes. That's why the novel is set in the Royal Ontario Museum. And why Lesje is a paleontologist who studies dinosaurs.
>
> (*Conversations*, p. 121)

Certainly the arguments from prehistory are no more reassuring than the arguments from contemporary history as guarantees for the survival of the human race, but we should not forget that the Chinese Art exhibit as well as the dinosaur skeletons are housed in the Royal Ontario Museum. Both Lesje's and Elizabeth's narratives end there as well, opening out into spaces of the imaginary which exceed the actual dimensions of the Museum, just as the novel exceeds the limits of the classic realist text. This multivoiced narrative contains many more voices than three if we include the discourses of social realism and science as well as of science fiction, fantasy and moral idealism. Similarly, the Royal Ontario Museum itself shimmers with multiple meanings. Of course it offers a specific point of reference on a map of Toronto and a definite location, but what else does it represent in this fiction? Rather like the Mesozoic when viewed from Lesje's deconstructive angle, its definite outlines tend to disperse when viewed subjectively from the inside:

> Sometimes she thinks of the Museum as a repository of knowl-
> edge, the resort of scholars, a palace built in the pursuit of truth
> ... At other times it's a bandits' cave: the past has been vandalized
> and this is where the loot is stored.   (p. 308)

Like everything else in the novel, the Royal Ontario Museum has a
double existence within the contiguous discourses of realism and of
fantasy, a solid edifice which may at any moment disappear into
scenarios of Jurassic swamps or idealised Chinese landscapes. Such
slippages open the way out of the Museum and beyond the deterministic narratives of prehistory contained there so that we may hear
the heterogeneous voices of human survivors in the present – in
'mid-history' as Atwood described it (*Conversations*, p. 123), as the
'before' of the title reverses its direction to point not backwards to
the distant past but forwards to the future.

6
Power Politics: *Bodily Harm*

What art does is, it takes what society deals out and makes it visible, right? So you can see it.

Bodily Harm, p. 208.[1]

This comment by a male porn artist in *Bodily Harm* connects with Atwood's own comments on the social function of the novel made in an interview five years later:

I do see the novel as a vehicle for looking at society – an interface between language and what we choose to call reality, although even that is a very malleable substance.   (*Conversations*, p. 246)

Atwood's formulation is more sophisticated than her visual artist's, taking in both the space of fictional representation and the social myths and fantasies through which people construct their images of reality – all of which might serve as a warning (if as readers of Atwood we still needed it) against reading *Bodily Harm* as straight realistic fiction. On the contrary, *Bodily Harm* is another version of Atwoodian Gothic, full of sinister games like Murder in the Dark; here it is the detective game of Cluedo, where every player can be a possible murder suspect or murder victim and their positions keep changing. Again Atwood 'does it with mirrors' – in this case mirror sunglasses, for this is Gothic in the tropics – and the narrative which moves between Toronto and the Caribbean is populated by characters who keep splitting or dissolving into their doubles or shadow selves in a series of endless substitutions and replications. The Gothic genre with its elements of fear and menace combines here

105

with other popular genres like the murder mystery, the female romance and the spy thriller ('I was writing a spy story from the point of view of one of the ignorant peripherally involved women'[2]) so that the novel becomes an exercise in deciphering clues, not only for the protagonist Rennie Wilford, a Toronto journalist, but for the reader as well, for Rennie's activity is mirrored in our own attempts to make sense of this fragmented narrative. Reality is a very malleable substance here. When it is refracted through Rennie's perspective it becomes a melodrama or an 'exceptionally tacky movie' (p. 159) from which there is no exit. But is reality inside or outside the protagonist, and how much is external reality reshaped through the subjectivity of the viewer? *Bodily Harm* is another version of writing the female body, this time from the point of view of a woman whose own body is already damaged by cancer and a mastectomy. From this 'post-operative' angle she scrutinises social myths of femininity, medical discourse on breast cancer and, most significantly, the rhetoric of pornography; this novel is emphatically not about bodily pleasures but about bodily harm.

As a journalist, Rennie is another of Atwood's women writers like the novelist and poet Joan Foster in *Lady Oracle* or Antonia Fremont the female historian in *The Robber Bride*, so this novel also explores the question of the woman writer's task and possible subjects for women's writing. Rennie is forced to move beyond female romance plots and her 'lifestyle' journalism in Toronto when her escape fantasy to a tropical island opens out into a scenario of political violence in a newly independent Caribbean republic. In many ways this novel may appear to be the least Canadian of Atwood's fictions, but this is true only in the most literal geographical sense; actually it is very much concerned with Canadian attitudes to international relations in its satire on the dangerous naiveté of the 'sweet Canadians':

> I wanted to take somebody [like Rennie] from our society where the forefront preoccupations are your appearance, your furniture, your job, your boyfriend, your health, and the rest of the world is quite a lot further back ... I wanted to take somebody from our society and put her into *that*, cause a resonance there. (*Conversations*, p. 227)

Through the web of connections established by the narrative, Rennie is forced to see how the personal and the political cannot be separated. This is emblematised in the phrase 'massive involvement' where the meaning shifts from a specific medical terminology about cancer to becoming a description of Rennie's moral position as a socially responsible member of the body politic:

> In any case she is a subversive. She was not one once but now she is. A reporter. She will pick her time; then she will report. For the first time in her life, she can't think of a title.   (p. 301)

Rennie has finally found 'something legitimate to say' (p. 66) though the irony is that trapped in her present situation inside the prison of a revolutionary regime, her political commentary is in danger of remaining confined to the private spaces of her imagination.

Bodily Harm is such a complex and enigmatic structure that I am tempted to adopt the approach of the female historian in *The Robber Bride* who decides to 'pick any strand and snip, and history comes unravelled' (p. 3). I shall begin my unravelling attempt as literary critic by referring back to the fascinating mass of manuscript materials for this novel in the Atwood Collection at the University of Toronto Library[3] and in particular to the wide range of epigraphs through which Atwood evidently rehearsed different emphases for her narrative. In the first holograph version (Box 33: 1), entitled 'The Robber Bridegroom' there are no epigraphs at all, though the draft typescripts with titles varying from 'The Robber Bridegroom' to 'Rope Quartet' to 'Bodily Harm' play with a range of 16 different prefatory quotations arranged in six patterns. Given the original title, it is not surprising that the first quotation from Grimm's Fairy Tales recurs quite frequently (in four of the different epigraph listings):

> Then said the bridegroom to the bride, 'Come, my darling, do you know nothing? Relate something to us like the rest.' She replied, 'Then I will relate a dream.'   (33: 2, 33: 4, 33: 6)

This initial emphasis on female storytelling with its revelations of men's crimes against women is second only in frequency of recurrence to the quotation from John Berger's *Ways of Seeing*, which is the only epigraph to appear in the published version:

> A man's presence suggests what he is capable of doing to you or for you. By contrast, a woman's presence ... defines what can and cannot be done to her.   (33: 2, 33: 4, 33: 6)

This statement with its focus on sexual power politics and female victims recurs as a constant in every version after the first draft, indicating what is probably the major focus of the narrative.[4] Yet, interestingly, it is not the exclusive focus, as is proved by the panoply of quotations emphasising the role of fiction as social and moral witness which insistently occur among the epigraphs. Sources are as varied as the perspectives which are presented. Some of them emphasise the uncompromising nature of storytelling, like the ones from Flannery O'Connor and Pablo Neruda:

> The truth does not change according to our ability to stomach it emotionally.   (Flannery O'Connor, *Letters*, 33: 2)

and

> This story is horrifying; if you have suffered from it, forgive me, but I'm not sorry.   (Pablo Neruda, *The Heroes*, 33: 2)

Others pay more attention to reader response, arguing the need for stories when all public access to truth fails:

> What do I do when I am told a lie about events that have happened in my lifetime? I listen for stories.   (Miguel Algarin, 33: 4)

or, more ironically,

> What you are willing to swallow depends on how hungry you are.
>   (Peruvian proverb, 33: 4)

The epigraphs fan out from this awareness of narrative just as they extend beyond sexual power politics to indicate the wide range of topics which are woven into the novel. Certainly there is an emphasis on power with its fascination and its brutality as well as its insidious influence, where the following quotation might serve as summary of Atwood's own project:

> We have to see how issues of power invade every aspect of every relationship in a society that worships it.   (Hugh Drummond, *Diagnosing Marriage, Mother Jones*, July 1979, 33: 4)

The second quotation focuses on what is perhaps the dominating force in Atwood's consumer society, where the coerciveness of social conventions is masked by the seemingly innocent codes of the fashion industry:

> Fashion for those who live within its empire is a force of tremendous and incalculable power. Fierce, and at times ruthless in its operation, it governs our behaviour, informs our sexual appetites, colours our erotic imagination, makes possible but also distorts, our conception of history.   (Quentin Bell, 33: 4)

There are also two epigraphs which hint at Rennie's mastectomy, though they point not towards the theme of bodily harm but to the contradictory nature of the surgeon's art:

> To search for some meaning in the ritual of surgery, which is at once murderous, painful, healing, and full of love.   (Richard Selzer, *Mortal Lessons*, 33: 4)

There is another from the same book:

> Medicine, as is well known, is an offshoot of religion.   (33: 4)

These recur under the novel's second title 'Rope Quartet', which in itself hints at the connections between all the men in Rennie's life: Jake, Daniel, Paul, and most eerily the faceless stranger who left the coiled rope lying on her bed. Such blurring of identities would suggest however an 'inner space' fiction closer to psychodrama than to the published text we have, where the continual to and fro shiftings between inside and outside produce the peculiarly unsettling dynamics of this novel.

Just as the mystery of healing serves to undermine the coercive discourses of power politics, so there is another strand in the epigraphs (one of them again from Selzer and referring back to hospitals, surgery, life and death) which hints at the enigma of sexual love in all its incompleteness and urgency:

> A three-by-five card lies on the floor of the emergency ward ... I pick it up. All at once, it seems as though I have turned over in my sleep and awakened.
> I LOVE YOU MORE THAN I SAY.
> I CAN'T
> (Richard Selzer, *Confessions of a Knife*, 33: 4)

Like that missed message (was it intended to be sent or to be received?) so the sense of otherness and necessary connections in the following epigraph, which occurs twice at a very late stage in the evolution of the drafts and points to Atwood's insistent inquiry into the mysteries of male-female relations:

> Men and women are two locked caskets, each bearing within it the key to the other.   (Isak Dinesen, 33: 4, 33: 6)

While recognising sexual difference, such a perception dissolves any politics of domination and invites a more subtly inflected view than the discourses of pornography and violence within the novel.

The last epigraph I shall mention (though it is not the last in the series and occurs only once) relates the concerns of *Bodily Harm* to *True Stories*, Atwood's collection of poems which appeared the same year. These poems treat many of the same topics, while several of them such as 'Bluejays' and 'Variations on the Word Love', hold out promises as open-ended and tentative as the ending of the novel itself. It is this tenacity of the human spirit speaking its double-voiced discourse under the threat of oppression and death which comes though in the following:

> I hope you are not innocent enough to believe that
> everything I say is true.
> I hope you are not innocent enough to believe that
> nothing I say is true.
> I hope you are not innocent.
> Enough to believe.
> I hope.
>
> (Eleanora Alcuin, *Parables*, 33: 4)

Rennie's voice, speaking with muffled indirectness through her prison narrative, resonates with the same contradictory optimism:

> She will never be rescued. She has already been rescued. She is not exempt. Instead she is lucky, suddenly, finally, she's overflowing with luck, it's this luck holding her up.   (p. 301)

To examine these epigraphs which appear and disappear in the typescript is rather like studying a palimpsest where one word or passage of text is written over another. These multiple layers and revisions suggest not only the range of Atwood's thematic preoccupations

and the shifting emphases of the writing process but also set up resonances behind the single Berger quotation which was her final choice.
However, such drafts are of course the 'raw materials' or the shadow
body of the novel and all they do is to indicate possible directions for
the narrative while it is being made. They are not explicit about many
of its distinctive features like the discourse of pornography (though we
may see it as being implicit in the Berger epigraph) nor the topic of
postcolonial violence (though again the many comments on abuses of
power might seem to suggest this). Moreover, the epigraphs do not
give any indication of the fragmented structure of this novel nor of the
dislocated female subject through whom the story is focused. They
merely serve as another set of clues, outlining the range of discourses
through which reality might be reconstructed as narrative.

The novel opens with the promise of a very specific narrative location and a distinctive narrative voice: 'This is how I got here, says
Rennie' (p. 11), who proceeds to tell her life story. It's a story that
begins with a crisis and an enigma, for the protagonist returns
home to find two policemen sitting in her Toronto kitchen waiting
to tell her that an intruder has broken into her flat and has left one
sinister clue, a coiled rope lying on her bed. Taken together with
the title, this could be the beginning of a detective novel whose plot
would be, 'Who is the faceless stranger?' and indeed Rennie thinks
of the game of Cluedo when she sees the rope. Is it 'Miss Wilford,
in the bedroom, with a rope?' (p. 14) or should it be 'Mr X, in the
bedroom, with a rope?' (p. 41). In a sense it is a detective story, but
the narrative sequence soon begins to disintegrate as the focus
shifts from 'I' to 'she' and time and space become dislocated with
the introduction of numerous memory fragments and the protagonist's flight (which is both literal and metaphorical) away from
Toronto to the Caribbean as she tries to sidestep the problems of
her real life. Instead she finds herself in a political situation where
she is really in danger of physical violence. By the end we realise
that this is actually a prison narrative (so, where is 'here'?)[5] but a
sense of awkwardness and unease is there from the opening section.
Sections are separated from one another by large graphic dots
which create the effect of a peculiarly fragmented text. Despite the
shift from first to third person, a technique familiar from *The Edible
Woman*, the reader soon becomes aware that this account of external reality is told not by an omniscient narrator but is being shaped
by Rennie's disturbed consciousness, for this is entirely subjective
narration refracted through her dreams and memory flashbacks,
distorted by her fears, and pervaded by her precarious sense of

unreality. It is the 'Gothic chamber of horrors interior to the heroine's consciousness' which Judith McCombs identified in her essay on Atwood's poetic sequences at the beginning of the 1980s: 'The Gothic terror and the Gothic horror, so divided and redoubled, take place in a hall of mirrors, where reality is constantly evaded and yet reflected, distorted and yet magnified.'[6] Not only the reader but Rennie herself has difficulty in negotiating between what is going on inside and outside her own head as her narrative shifts from one crisis point to another, insistently trying to figure out connections yet baffled by the opacity of surfaces and threats of imminent collapse.

The opening episode is crucial for Rennie's representation of her own position. She is a woman living alone at the end of an affair and under threat, for her private space has been invaded by a 'faceless stranger' and the coiled rope on the bed would seem to signify the possibility of a malevolent sexual attack. She is a victim and yet in the eyes of the Toronto police she is not innocent precisely because she is a woman: 'He wanted it to be my fault.' It is Rennie's resistance to this sexist imputation which makes her reveal the evidence of her mastectomy. These first five pages focus on the crucial points of breakdown in Rennie's image of herself as an independent heterosexual woman, and the narrative represents a tracing and retracing of these new unaccommodated events. It is surely no accident that Rennie begins with the sinister image of the rope, for in its indeterminacy of meaning it provides the perfect connection between her fears of death from cancer and external physical violence, just as it also signals the perversion of sexual love and desire when the male erotic gaze becomes the hostile scrutiny of a rapist or a killer, a scenario to which Rennie is peculiarly vulnerable since her mastectomy and her break-up with Jake. There is a further dimension of which we become subsequently aware through Rennie's flashbacks to her childhood in the small Ontario town of Griswold, 'not so much a background as a subground ... nothing you'd want to go into' (p. 18). Brought up by her lonely mother and her grandmother, Rennie knows about threadbare decency and the hidden casualties of the safe provincial female world where women grow embittered and dream they have lost their hands – 'the ones they feel with' – and where retribution for being an unconventional woman like Rennie is bound to descend sooner or later: 'In Griswold everyone gets what they deserve. In Griswold everyone deserves the worst' (p. 18). Despite her acquired urban sophistication, Rennie remains a small-town girl haunted by those moral codes of outraged decency and malignancy so that the man with the rope, like her breast cancer, would seem to emerge from the shadows of her past.

For all her reinvention of herself, Rennie still operates within a Griswoldian concept of femininity. Her image of her feminine identity is closely bound up with conventional discourses of beauty and romance and with women's complicity in the traditional system of patriarchal values. It is as if Rennie's narrative is really a series of separate stories about herself which coexist in different time frames and from which she chooses certain blocs, juxtaposing them in such a way that they resonate against one another to figure bizarre connections in her own private game of Cluedo. It is Rennie who always occupies the role of victim. As she says of her own sensibility when describing her detective skills as a reader of Dell murder mysteries from the 1940s: 'She's not doing too well with the murderers, but she's eighty percent on the victims' (p. 246).

Rennie is first and most shockingly to herself the victim of her own body's betrayal, and arguably the diagnosis of breast cancer and her subsequent mastectomy is the central trauma of her life:

> The body, sinister twin, taking its revenge for whatever crimes the mind was supposed to have committed on it. Nothing had prepared her for her own outrage, the feeling that she'd been betrayed by a close friend.   (p. 82)

The knowledge of her cancer is a radical assault on her subjective sense of identity which in turn is closely related to the mesh of personal and social myths through which Rennie projects her own image of herself. In her first shock at the news Rennie's concept of her body changes, for she no longer sees it as a unified whole but as something being undermined from within as the blood cells 'whisper and divide in darkness' (p. 100). Yet she fears the operation almost as much as she fears death from cancer, for she has a horror of the violence of surgery and of her body being dismembered. When she wakens after the operation, 'She did not want to look down, see how much of herself was missing' (p. 32). In her discussion of Rennie's condition (which is as much one of psychological as of physical trauma) Sonia Mycak calls this 'the horrible corporeal sense of fragmentation and dissolution,' referring to Julia Kristeva's psychoanalytical concept of 'abjection' to explain the processes of Rennie's dislocation and decentring.[7] Rennie no longer trusts herself inside her own skin, as her imaginary representations of her body would suggest. At times she fears that her scar will come unzipped like a purse whose contents will spill out all over the place, and sometimes she fears that her body is 'infested' and that monsters will crawl out of the stitched-up wound:

> The creature looks far too much like the kind of thing she's been having bad dreams about: the scar on her breast splits open like a diseased fruit and something like this crawls out. (p. 60)

It is this irrational fear of splitting open and of collapsing boundaries between inside and outside which haunts Rennie in her dreams and in her waking life, transforming even the sight of Lora's bitten fingernails into a site of psychological horror:

> She wouldn't want to touch this gnawed hand, or have it touch her. She doesn't like the sight of ravage, damage, the edge between inside and outside blurred like that. (p. 86)

Rennie is a woman on the edge of collapse, for huge gaps have opened up in her imaginative topography of self and personal relations as she faces the breakdown of all her fictions of femininity and romance. She can no longer contemplate her sexual fantasy games with Jake where she had willingly displayed her body as object for his pleasure and her own, to be admired and fantasised about. Disgusted with her damaged body, Rennie gets to the point where she cannot bear to be touched by Jake though she yearns for the 'healing touch' of Dr Daniel Luoma, her surgeon, whose hands Rennie tries to see as loving hands which have rescued her from death. However, the ambiguity of Rennie's attitude to surgery is suggested in the way that Daniel's hands are remembered in multiple combinations, sometimes juxtaposed with her grandmother's lost hands or the miraculous healing hands of the old Caribbean woman or even with the hand of the mute beggar wishing her luck. She becomes obsessed with dismembered female bodies, seeing herself as partially dismembered by the surgeon's hands (for Daniel is also 'the man with a knife' like the intruder in her room in the Sunset Inn at St Antoine, who slits open the parcel with the gun inside, another implement of death hidden beneath the smooth packaging). It is no wonder that Rennie 'no longer trusts surfaces'. These shifting associations around hands – alternately as agents of violence and of miraculous healing – provides an excellent figure for the contradictory and overlapping patterns which characterise this highly subjective narrative.

Rennie is a woman divided against herself, needing desperately to revise the old fictions of femininity and romance but obsessed with loss and damage and as yet unable to imagine the second part of her life as promised by Daniel:

> It would be different from the first part, she would no longer be able to take things for granted, but perhaps this was a plus because she would see her life as a gift and appreciate it more.   (p. 84)

Rennie's rehabilitation takes the whole time of the novel, and only at the end does she learn to see her individual pain in a wider human perspective:

> The scar prods at her, a reminder, a silent voice counting, a count-down. Zero is waiting somewhere, whoever said there was life ever-lasting; so why feel grateful? She doesn't have much time left, for anything. But neither does anyone else. She's paying attention, that's all.   (p. 301)

Rennie's traumatised sense of her own body inevitably affects her account of her relationships with men in the novel. Jake the Toronto interior designer, Daniel the Finnish-Canadian surgeon and Paul the American drug dealer and gun-runner in the Caribbean (described by Rennie both as 'the X factor' and as 'the connection') are all her lovers at different times in her painful progress through the failure of old romance patterns to which she clings. As a further twist, one of the draft titles, 'Rope Quartet', suggests a more sinister connec-tion between these three and the 'faceless stranger' within the scenarios of Rennie's psychodrama about female victims and male power games. In her highly subjectivised account it is difficult to see these men as individuals, for each of them appears in multiple focus through Rennie's stories of their real lives and their fantasy lives as well as their relation to her fantasy life, where they occupy a shifting series of roles – as lovers, rescuers, tormentors and betrayers. The stories of all three overlap as they shift in and out of focus, appear-ing and disappearing at different stages of the narrative almost as functions of Rennie's desire and need, though of course they have all vanished by the time Rennie tells this story. Oddly, Jake's exist-ence is first signalled by his absence: ('It was the day after Jake left'; p. 11) and their love affair is recapitulated through a series of vividly remembered fragments – Jake's rape fantasies, his soft porn art photographs and his 'lunchtime quickies' – all belonging to

Rennie's carefree Toronto period of invented lifestyles and carniva-
lesque sexual pleasures. These are now recalled with a pained sense
of severance from that past and an overwhelming sense of failure,
'Failure, of a larger order than they would once have thought possible' (p. 236), for that relationship was one of the casualties of her
mastectomy. Trapped inside her victim scenario Rennie cannot
acknowledge that Jake leaves only because she has rejected him and
that neither of them is capable of imagining a new structure for a
loving relationship.

Rennie's failures of imagination are again evident in her brief
affairs with Daniel and Paul, both of whom she tries to coerce into
her fantasy scripts of romance, though in both cases the plots switch
in ways for which she is not prepared. As she admits, it is difficult to
have an affair with her doctor. Not only is he too busy but his
decency and his professionalism cause him to behave within a different series of codes from those of the trendy lifestyle of open options
which Rennie has adopted:

> Daniel spent one whole lunch explaining, earnestly and unhap-
> pily, why he couldn't go to bed with her.
>   It would be unethical, he said. I'd be taking advantage of you.
> You're in an emotional state.   (p. 143)

The affair with Daniel really is Rennie's invention though the ending
does not conform to her fantasies of rescue. It is just the opposite, in
fact, for when she finally does persuade Daniel to go to bed with her
what she discovers is that they have changed places:

> The fact was that he had needed something from her, which she
> could neither believe nor forgive. She'd been counting on him
> not to: she was supposed to be the needy one, but it was the other
> way around ... She felt like a straw that had been clutched ... She
> felt raped.   (p. 238)

Whereas Jake and Daniel are figures out of a familiar social
context, it is Paul, the American whom she meets in the Caribbean,
who remains an enigma. Occupying multiple roles in relation to
Rennie, he too is one of her guides and rescuers, but he is also the
confidence trickster who helps to set her up to collect a suspect
package at the airport. (Much later, Rennie sees the same box,
though not the gun, under Paul's bed. This is one of the minor
unsolved mysteries of the novel.) Paul would seem to represent the

mysterious stranger in the ideal holiday romance, 'the biggest cliché in the book', as Rennie is the first to recognise:

> Love or sex? Jocasta would ask, and this time Rennie knows. Love is tangled, sex is straight. High-quality though, she'd say. Don't knock it. (p. 223)

However, as the narrative shows, the plot with Paul becomes very tangled and it is through her affair with him that Rennie finds herself involved in the revolutionary coup and thrown into prison. Yet she feels grateful to Paul, for it is he who restores her lost confidence in her sexuality – by his gaze as much as by his lovemaking. Her scar when looked at by him ceases to be a disfigurement and becomes simply a mark of human mortality, for Rennie knows that 'he's seen people a lot deader than her':

> He reaches out his hands and Rennie can't remember ever having been touched before. Nobody lives forever, who said you could? This much will have to do, this much is enough. She's open now, she's been opened, she's being drawn back down, she enters her body again and there's a moment of pain, incarnation ... she's grateful, he's touching her, she can still be touched. (p. 204)

The lyricism of this passage finds its echoes in the brief lovemaking episode between Marian and Duncan at the sleazy downtown hotel in *The Edible Woman* and also in the illicit affair between Offred and Nick in *The Handmaid's Tale*, while the painful restoration of feeling harks back through Rennie's memory of her operation all the way to *Surfacing*, when the unnamed narrator feels her body tingling 'like a foot that's been asleep' (*Surfacing*, p. 146). It is one of the ironies of *Bodily Harm* that Rennie is rescued only in time to be thrown into prison and that Paul disappears, 'which could mean anything' (p. 283).

In prison Rennie summons her three ghosts, all of whom appear to be dismembered and incomplete: she can hardly remember what Jake looks like, whereas 'Of Paul, only the too-blue eyes remain' (p. 283) and Daniel moves through the day at an immense distance from her, 'enclosed in a glass bubble' like a mirage. Though Rennie does not know it, she is saying her farewells and for the first time seeing these men as separate from herself, though necessary illusions. They are also part of her fantasy life as they have always been, slipping in and out of her dreams in an endless series of shifting identities:

Rennie is dreaming about the man with the rope, again, again. He is the only man who is with her now, he's followed her, he was here all along, he was waiting for her. Sometimes she thinks it's Jake ... sometimes she thinks it's Daniel ... But it's not either of them, it's not Paul ...he's only a shadow, anonymous, familiar, with silver eyes that twin and reflect her own.   (p. 287)

Rennie is back in her Gothic chamber of horrors enclosed within her own subjective space like a heroine in one of Ann Radcliffe's novels, 'who does not gaze outward for clues capable of solving the mysteries of her situation, but inward, to the topography of dreams, to the pleasurably horrifying spectral'.[8]

Rennie's subjective reconstruction of reality shapes the narrative, but her story is always breaking down as she is forced to take into account unexpected events and other discourses which represent reality from perspectives other than her own. As a woman writer who specialises in lifestyle journalism inventing fake fashion trends and doing pieces on personality makeovers and fast food outlets, Rennie would seem to have chosen a carefully calculated apolitical stance where her social comment is confined to the trivial: 'I see into the present, that's all. Surfaces. There's not a whole lot to it' (p. 26). Yet from this deliberately marginalised position ('Rennie saw herself as off to the side. She preferred it there'; p. 26) the novel develops a passionately committed moral stance towards political issues relating to gender and colonial oppression, which is epitomised in the title *Bodily Harm.* Searching for clues to this mysterious change, again we need to direct our gaze inwards where I would suggest that the crisis point for Rennie is the article she is asked to write on pornography for the men's magazine *Visor,* which she researches but then refuses to write. Embedded in the text in Section 5, this episode provides an interesting crux for a woman's novel of the early 1980s written in the wake of vigorous American feminist anti-pornography campaigns which began in the late 1970s. I want to trace this issue of pornography in *Bodily Harm,* focusing on Rennie's responses but casting my net more widely as an inquiry into Atwood's position on the sexual/textual politics of fiction at this time. I think we shall arrive at some very interesting insights into the significance of Atwood's remarks at the beginning of this chapter, where she situated the novel not at an aesthetic distance from life but at the 'interface' between language and reality, implying that the novel is not morally disengaged from the social and political issues on which it speculates. Indeed, I would go further to assert that though Rennie cannot write that article on pornography from the woman's angle Atwood's narrative does it for her, so that the ground of my inquiry becomes the way in which Atwood uses the rhetoric of pornography to explore the connections between discourses of sexuality on the one hand and discourses of political power on the other.

Rennie's journalistic assignment to write about pornography as an art form is contextualised in two ways: first in relation to Jake's rape fantasies and his dangerous games ('Danger turns you on, he said. Admit it', p. 207) and then in the context of late 1970s feminism ('There had already been a number of anti-porno pieces in the more radical women's magazines, but Keith thought they were kind of heavy and humourless'). Both Jake and her editor emphasise the playfulness of sexual fantasy, though as Rennie points out, this is a very male perspective: 'Rennie said she thought the subject might have more to do with men's fantasy lives, but Keith said he wanted the woman's angle' (p. 207). Her research leads Rennie first to the studio of a male porn artist who makes chairs and tables out of female mannequins locked into attitudes of submission, and whose comment on art as social representation I quoted at the beginning of this chapter. It is a comment paralleled in the remark made by Rennie's friend Jocasta, proprietor of the junk punk dress shop called Ripped Off: 'Of course it's gross, said Jocasta. But so's the world, you know what I mean? Me, I'm relaxed' (p. 24). Rennie would like to be able to emulate this moral insouciance, as she tries to do in her article on drain-chain jewellery and slave girl fictions, just as she would like to feel less uneasy about Jake's violent games and the soft-porn art photographs he has hanging in their apartment; but the old Griswold morality is always niggling away behind her seemingly cheerful complicity in the pornographic culture. As long as she can stay on the surface Rennie can survive, but the breaking point comes when she has to confront the unmediated evidence of hard-core pornography, known in the trade as the 'raw material'. Rennie's visit with Jocasta to the Metropolitan Police Department's pornography collection reveals terrifying visual evidence of male sadistic fantasies of power and violence against women; there are images of female bodies bound and mutilated and, most shocking of all, the film clip of the black woman's pelvis with a live rat poking its head out of her vagina (p. 210). The peculiar horror of this image lies in its double representation of male and female sexual fantasies where women's fears of violation work in counterpoint to male fantasies of invading the mystery of the female body in order to see what it is impossible to see. In Luce Irigaray's formulation of woman's

position in the male 'dominant scopic economy', 'her sex organ represents the horror of having nothing to see. In this [male] system of
representation and desire, the vagina is a flaw, a hole in the representation's scoptophilic objective',[9] a challenge that may only be met
by dismemberment or violation of the female body. After watching
the film clip Rennie is immediately sick all over the policeman's
shoes and withdraws from the assignment. To recall the words of
Mary Ann Caws in this context, 'How could we possibly think that a
seeing woman writing about women [and pornography] would have
an "objective" point of view? ... She, we are bound to think and say,
is implicated heavily.'[10] Neither Jocasta nor Jake will contemplate the
implications of this image for even a moment; Jocasta angrily
upbraids the policeman with the remark, 'You need your head
repaired' (p. 211) and when Rennie tells Jake he replies, 'Come on,
don't confuse me with that sick stuff' (p. 212). Yet their reasons for
refusing to look are different from Rennie's, for where they resist
taking up any moral position, she cannot separate fantasy from
moral issues in this way – any more easily than she can say 'fuck'
unselfconsciously: 'Swearing was one of the social graces Rennie
hadn't learned early in life, she'd had to teach herself' (p. 117).
Troubled as she is by glimmerings of a connection between rape
games and male violence against women, she can no longer take
pleasure in playing the victim in Jake's fantasies for 'she now felt that
in some way that had never been spelled out between them he
thought of her as the enemy', while she starts thinking of herself as
'raw material' (p. 212).

Within the iconography of porn as presented in this novel – either
hard core or the soft core of Jake's art photos – there is an underly-
ing rhetoric of representation which relates directly to discourses of
patriarchal power. None of the images Rennie has seen pays any
attention to women as subjects, but projects them only as objects of
male fantasies of desire and domination. Female bodies are all
passive, distorted, dismembered or coerced, witnesses to the sexual
power politics of the Berger epigraph. To define pornography as 'a
coincidence of sexual phantasy, genre and culture in an erotic
organisation of visibility' as film critic Beverley Brown did in 1981[11]
may be an objective definition of a cultural phenomenon, but it
leaves out the issue of the gendered gaze which is crucial to
Atwood's treatment of the topic in relation to a power politics of
sexual domination.

As I have already suggested, *Bodily Harm* begins with a very crude
representation of sexual power politics, the rope on the bed and

Jake's rape fantasies being very close to the early 1980s feminist anti-pornography position which asserted strong links between pornography as misogynist power fantasy and male violence against women. No doubt the 'heavy' anti-pornography feminist pieces which the *Visor* editor had in mind would have referred to Andrea Dworkin's *Pornography: Men Possessing Women* (1979), Susan Griffin's *Pornography and Silence: Culture's Revenge against Nature* (1981), and Laura Lederer's influential collection of essays *Take Back the Night: Women on Pornography* (1980). Maybe he had even seen Robin Morgan's essay in Lederer's collection with its ultimate feminist condemnation of pornography as a genre which threatens to become another lifestyle: 'Pornography is the theory and rape is the practice.'[12] This position assumes that not only is violence inherent in male sexual fantasies about women but that there is a dangerous blurring of borders between fantasy and real life, where the fundamental issue is always power and where pain and fear are its visible proofs ('With lovers like men, who needs torturers?'[13]). Within such an interpretation of our contemporary 'pornographic culture' women like Rennie, Jocasta and Lora would all be seen as collaborators and willing victims of sadistic male power fantasies. (This extreme view has been recently reiterated by Andrea Dworkin in *Intercourse* (1987) and Catherine MacKinnon in *Only Words* (1994).)

However – and it is one of Atwood's most skilful narrative manipulations – by the time Rennie is telling her story, her perspective and her situation have entirely changed. For all its illusion of presentness, the whole novel is about the *past*, post her mastectomy and post her experience of revolutionary violence and the brutality of the police, and spoken from within her prison cell – all of which offers a subtly inflected view of the feminist scenario about pornography and violence. In many ways Rennie's critique has strong similarities with Linda Williams's critical remarks ten years later on Robin Morgan's slogan where Williams asserts, ' "Pornography is the theory and rape is the practice" is a woefully inadequate explanation of the causes of violence against women'[14] – and of violence against men as well, if we consider the particular Caribbean context of this novel. Rennie has learned that violence is not confined to visual representation but that it pervades the relations between the sexes at every level of social and aesthetic activity – in pornographic art and advertising, prostitution, child abuse and wife beating, as in the threat of the man with the rope ('It was also a message; it was someone's twisted idea of love'; p. 41), all of which would endorse the feminist anti-porn position. Where Atwood dissents from that position is in her

recognition that while pornography as patriarchal discourse may be
focused on sexual difference, its rhetoric of domination extends
beyond sexual difference to the wider political scenario which is displayed here in the exercise of patriarchal power and violence against
a whole community during the first general elections to be held in a
former British Caribbean colony, now an independent republic.

Looking back, Rennie perceives that her escape to the Caribbean
islands lands her in a truly unfamiliar place where everything seems
vaguely mad and threatening. Alighting from the plane at St
Antoine, Rennie finds herself in a landscape full of oddly undecod-
able messages like the airport advertisement, 'THE BIONIC COCK: IT
GIVES YOU SPURS' (p. 38) or the woman whom Rennie assumes to be a
religious maniac because she is wearing a T-shirt with the slogan
'PRINCE OF PEACE' on it – though she turns out to be the doughty old
woman Elva, mother of one of the election candidates (whose name
is Prince) and the possessor of miraculously healing hands. It is
evident that Rennie's view of the Caribbean has all the fragmentari-
ness and distortion of an outsider's perspective where everything
looks as unreal and stereotypical as a television film because she has
no idea what is going on. Her condition, described by Paul as 'alien
reaction paranoia' (p. 76), feels like living in a nightmare for the
person inside it. The decisive point of Rennie's breakthrough into a
new (or rather, out of an old) cultural awareness occurs during her
affair with Paul, though this time the resonance is not at all personal
but entirely political and productive of nothing less than a radical
scepticism of all the western social myths on which her constructions
of reality have so uncritically depended. Speaking of his time in
Vietnam and Cambodia, Paul announces:

> Democracy and freedom and the whole bag of tricks. Those
> gadgets don't work too well in a lot of places and nobody's too
> sure what does. There's no good guys and bad guys, nothing you
> can count on, none of it's permanent any more, there's a lot of
> improvisation. Issues are just an excuse.   (p. 240)

Amid the confusion and danger of the revolt when the newly elected
prime minister is shot in the back of the head and Rennie is thrown
into prison on charges of 'suspicion' (Paul volunteers that she is
thought to be a spy), Rennie experiences an erosion of confidence
in civil order and her own safety. Although she has not been harmed
herself, she has been forced to witness within her cell the brutal
bashing up of her friend Lora, and through the window the naked

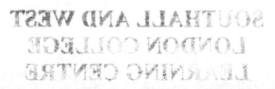

exercise of police power in the prison yard. The violence is not against women this time but against other men, though the discourse partakes of the same sadistic performance elements as the representations of pornography:

> The courtyard is oddly silent, the noon beats down, everything is bright, the men's faces glisten with sweat, fear, the effort of keeping in the hatred, the policemen's faces glisten too, they're holding themselves back, they love this, it's a ceremony ... The man with the bayonet stuffs the handful of hair into the bag and wipes his hand on his shirt. He's an addict, this is a hard drug. Soon he will need more.   (p. 289)

Atwood has taken the rhetoric of pornography but here she has drained out the sexual dimension, leaving on view only the vulnerability of human bodies, male or female. Rennie's sudden flash of insight as she looks out at events in the prison yard fuses the discourses of pornography and power politics together:

> It's indecent, it's not done with ketchup, nothing is inconceivable here, no rats in the vagina but only because they haven't thought of it yet ... She's afraid of men and it's simple, it's rational, she's afraid of men because men are frightening.   (p. 290)

Atwood does not elide the sexual differences emphasised by pornography though she does point to the features that all male and female bodies share and to those ways in which both sexes can be abused and victimised.

Working against those brutal assertions of male power, a further permutation on violence more personal to Rennie would be that it may sometimes be benign and necessary – like her mastectomy. (She imagines Daniel 'holding the hand of a blonde woman whose breasts he has recently cut off. Who wants to cure, who wants to help, who wants everything to be fine', p. 283.) Lurking one stage further back as in a hall of mirrors is Rennie's cancer which inflicts unseen violence on her body from within. The narrative of pornography turns out to be as multifaceted as the shifting faces and roles of Rennie's lovers or any of the other elusive double clues in this text, as Atwood turns the topic inside out till there is no longer 'a *here* and a *there*' and 'nobody is exempt from anything' (p. 290). Narrative scrutiny reveals the topic of pornography to be infinitely more psychologically and socially complex than the simple slogans of the early 1980s

feminists would allow. Any slogan or image when scrutinised critical-
ly is likely to reveal its opposite, as Rennie demonstrates when she
looks at the male porn artist's representation of a kneeling woman
with a Handy Andy container in her mouth and chained to a toilet
seat; the sculpture is entitled 'Task Sharing'. She comments, 'If a
woman did that, they'd call it strident feminism' (p. 208). It all
depends on the viewer's perspective, as Alain Robbe Grillet reminds
us: '*La pornographie c'est l'érotisme des autres.*'[15] By a similar movement
of demonstration, it is by no means clear that the connections
between rape fantasies and actual rape are direct, though Rennie
does not entirely rule out the possibility:

> What would Jake make of it, the sight of one of his playful fan-
> tasies walking around out there, growling and on all fours? He
> knew the difference between a game and the real thing, he said: a
> desire and a need. She was the confused one.   (p. 236)

Yet from another perspective Rennie's confusion may be said to be
rational, for the trouble with dangerous games is the danger
of overlap between fantasy and reality when boundaries are
transgressed.

Rennie's narrative comes from that borderline territory between
fantasy and reality as she sits in the prison cell beside the brutally
battered body of a dead woman, realising finally that she is powerless
and alone. Spoken from that interior space, her narrative is a reconstruction and a reinterpretation as she laboriously tries to fit together the fragments of her life, seeking connections across the facts of
Lora's damaged body and her own mastectomy, as between the overt
violence which she has seen in the Caribbean and the hidden violence which she has not seen in Toronto but which she knows is
there. The plot which she constructs might be said to hinge on discovering the identity of the 'faceless stranger' at the end of the rope.
Rennie thinks she has solved the riddle when she sees the brutality
of the policemen in the prison yard ('She's seen the man with the
rope'; p. 290), but just as in the game of Cluedo the player's positions change, so the identity of the faceless stranger turns out to be
plural. Paul when she first meets him wearing his sunglasses is a faceless stranger 'without his eyes' (p. 99), and Rennie also dreams that
she sees her own face mirrored in the sunglasses, 'those silver eyes
that twin and reflect her own' (p. 287). Finally, the faceless stranger
is Lora when she has been battered out of all recognition. In an
unfamiliar gesture of compassion Rennie reaches out her hand to

touch the face of this now anonymous Other, and so learns a different meaning for faceless stranger: 'It's the face of Lora after all, there's no such thing as a faceless stranger, every face is someone's, it has a name' (p. 299).

Rennie's effort to tell the story is, like her effort to save Lora, an exercise of the moral imagination, being both reportage and invention. She is finally fulfilling the requests of two of her ghosts, Lora and Dr Minnow, both of whom had urged her to 'tell somebody what happened' (p. 282). As she is a reporter she determines to 'report', offering her interpretation of contemporary lifestyles in two different countries but now with an edge of moral engagement which had been lacking since her student days when she earnestly desired to find 'something legitimate to say' (p. 66). Daniel's advice to her echoes here infused with new meanings: 'Do what you want to, he said. What you really want to' (p. 85). Rennie does more than report; she tries to imagine things differently and better than they are, taking up the now vacant position of the most fervently idealistic character in the novel:

> Dr Minnow pauses ... They cannot imagine things being different. It is my duty to imagine, and they know that for even one person to imagine is very dangerous to them, my friend. You understand? (p. 229)

Rennie does understand at last about the moral function of writing, which does more than 'take what society deals out and make it visible'. She has begun to imagine a future which will be different from the present, just as from her prison cell she manages to see herself at the end as 'overflowing with luck' and in flight: 'It's this luck holding her up' (p. 301).

7

Science Fiction in the Feminine: *The Handmaid's Tale*

My room, then. There has to be some space, finally, that I claim as mine, even in this time.

The Handmaid's Tale, p. 60[1]

These words spoken by Atwood's Handmaid, deprived of her own name and citizenship and known simply by the patronymic 'Offred', might be taken as emblematic of a woman's survival narrative told within the confines of a patriarchal system represented by the distopia known as Gilead. Restricted to private domestic spaces and relegated to the margins of a political structure which denies her existence as an individual, nevertheless Offred asserts her right to tell her story. By doing so, she reclaims her own private spaces of memory and desire and manages to rehabilitate the traditionally 'feminine' space assigned to women in Gilead. Atwood's narrative focuses on possibilities for constructing a form of discourse in which to accommodate women's representations of their own gendered identity while still acknowledging 'the power of the (male 'universal') space in which they cannot avoid, to some extent, operating'.[2] Like *Bodily Harm,* this is another eye-witness account by another 'ignorant, peripherally involved woman', this time interpolated within the grand patriarchal narratives of the Bible and of history, just as Offred's Tale is enclosed within an elaborate structure of prefatory materials and concluding Historical Notes. However, her treasonable act of speaking out in a society where women are forbidden to read or write or to speak freely effects a significant shift from 'history' to 'herstory'. Offred's Tale claims a space, a large autobiographical space, within the novel and so relegates the grand narratives to the margins as mere framework for her story which is the main focus of interest. Storytelling is this woman's only possible gesture of resistance to imprisonment in silence, just as it becomes the primary means for her psychological survival. In process of reconstructing herself as an individual, Offred becomes the most important historian of Gilead.

The Handmaid's Tale is Atwood's most popular novel, which is perhaps surprising given its bleak futuristic scenario. It has won many prizes and it has been made into a film directed by Volker Schlondorff and starring Natasha Richardson, Faye Dunaway and Robert Duvall.[3] A great deal of critical attention has been paid to it as distopian science fiction and as a novel of feminist protest.[4] Certainly Atwood's abiding social and political concerns are evident here in her scrutiny of structures of oppression within public and private life as well as her concerns with the environment, and her nationalist engagement with Canadian–American relations. Yet the novel exceeds definitions of political correctness and has provoked much unease in its critique of second wave North American feminism. It is not exactly science fiction, 'if by that you mean Martians, teleportation, or life on Venus. Nor is it a sort of travelogue of the future. It's the story of one woman under this regime, told in a very personal way, and part of the challenge for me was the creation of her voice and viewpoint.'[5] A critical reading which focuses attention on the female narrator's position, on her language, and on the structural features of her narrative might allow us to see how *The Handmaid's Tale* eludes classification, just as Offred's storytelling allows her to escape the prescriptive definitions of Gilead.

Nevertheless, the political dimensions of the distopian model need to be considered in order to gauge the purpose of the fiction, bearing in mind Atwood's definition of what 'politics' means: 'What we mean is how people relate to a power structure and vice versa' (*Conversations*, p. 185). Set in a futuristic United States at the beginning of the twenty-first century after a military coup has wiped out the President and the Congress, Gilead is a totalitarian regime run on patriarchal lines derived from the Old Testament and seventeenth-century American Puritanism plus a strong infusion of the American New Right ideology of the 1980s. Individual freedom of choice has been outlawed and everyone has been drafted into the service of the state, classified according to prescribed roles: Commanders, Wives, Aunts, Handmaids, Eyes, down to Guardians and Econowives. There is strict censorship and border control, as Offred reminds us in her recurrent nightmare memory of her failed escape to Canada with her husband and daughter, which has resulted in her being conscripted as a Gileadean Handmaid. The novel is an exposure of power politics at their most basic: 'Who can do what to whom.' Women are worst off because they are valued only as child-breeders in a society threatened with extinction where, because of pollution, AIDS and natural disasters, the national birthrate has fallen to a catastrophically low level. This essentialist definition of women as 'two-legged wombs' works entirely in the interests of a patriarchal elite, denying women any freedom of sexual choice or of lifestyle. Atwood's feminist concerns are plain here but so too are her concerns for basic human rights. Most men are oppressed in this society: there are male bodies hanging every day on the Wall, while homosexuals, Roman Catholic priests and Quakers of both sexes are regularly executed, and male sexual activity is severely restricted as well. A more comprehensive reading of the novel would suggest that it is closer to the new feminist scholarship which has moved beyond exclusively female concerns to a recognition of the complexities of social gender construction. Offred's tale challenges essentialist definitions whether patriarchal or feminist, showing how state sexual regulation not only criminalises male violence against women and suppresses women's sexuality but how it also militates against basic human desires for intimacy and love. As Offred reminds her Commander, Gilead's policies of social engineering have left out one crucial factor:

> Love, I said.
> Love? said the Commander. What kind of love?
> Falling in love, I said.　　(pp. 231–2)

The novel represents Atwood's version of 'What If' in the most powerful democracy in the world. She describes her distopian project precisely in an unpublished essay:

> It's set in the near future, in a United States which is in the hands of a power-hungry elite who have used their own brand of 'Bible-based' religion as an excuse for the suppression of the majority of the population. It's about what happens at the intersection of several trends, all of which are with us today: the rise of right-wing fundamentalism as a political force, the decline in the Caucasian birth rate in North America and northern Europe, and the rise in

infertility and birth-defect rates, due, some say, to increased chemical-pollutant and radiation levels, as well as to sexually-transmitted diseases.[6]

As Atwood has declared repeatedly, both in interviews and in the novel itself, 'there's nothing in it that we as a species have not done, aren't doing now, or don't have the technological capability to do';[7] 'there was little that was truly original or indigenous to Gilead: its genius was synthesis' (*The Handmaid's Tale*, p. 319). When she began thinking about the novel in the early 1980s she kept a clippings file (now in the Atwood Papers, University of Toronto Library) of items from newspapers and magazines which fed directly into her writing. These show her wide-ranging historical and humanitarian interests, where pamphlets from Friends of the Earth and Greenpeace sit beside reports of atrocities in Latin America, Iran and the Philippines, together with items of information on new reproductive technologies, surrogate motherhood, and forms of institutionalised birth control from Nazi Germany to Ceausescu's Romania. It is to be noted that Gilead has a specifically American location, for Offred lives in the heartland of Gilead in a city that was formerly Cambridge, Massachusetts, and Harvard Campus (where Atwood was herself a student) has become the site for the Rachel and Leah Women's Re-education Centre, the setting for public rituals like Prayvaganzas and Particicutions, and Gilead's Secret Service head-quarters. When asked why she had not set her novel in Canada, Atwood replied:

> The States are more extreme in everything … Canadians don't swing much to the left or the right, they stay safely in the middle … It's also true that everyone watches the States to see what the country is doing and might be doing ten or fifteen years from now. (*Conversations*, p. 223)

When we consider that the American 'New Right', as it was called in the 1980s (it is now called the 'Extreme Right', being no longer new), is one of Atwood's prime satiric targets, the location takes on a particular significance. The clippings file contains a lot of material on the New Right with its warnings about the 'Birth Dearth', its anti-feminism, its anti-homosexuality, its racism and its strong religious underpinnings in the Bible Belt.[8] Perhaps by coincidence one of the best known New Right studies is the collection of seminar papers *The New Right at Harvard*, edited by Howard Phillips[9] which includes

papers on family issues, abortion and pornography. These refer to
the desirability of building a coalition, 'a small dedicated corps' to
'resist the Liberal democracy' with its 'libertarian positions', so that
the militaristic rhetoric of Gilead could already be heard at Harvard
three years before *The Handmaid's Tale* was published. It is possible
to read the novel as an oblique form of Canada–US dialogue where a
Canadian writer warns Americans about their possible future.

If this is a political fable with nationalist implications, then
Canadians are implicated in other ways as well. *The Handmaid's Tale*
opens out not only into the future (and there are two futuristic
scenarios here, one set in America and one in Canada) but also into
the space of Canadian prehistory, for 'those nagging Puritans really
are my ancestors ... The mind-set of Gilead is really close to that of
the seventeenth-century Puritans' (*Conversations*, p. 223). Atwood's
interest in Puritan New England is signalled from the start in her
dedication of the novel to Mary Webster and Perry Miller. Mary
Webster was her own favourite ancestor, who was hanged as a witch
in New England in 1683 but who survived her hanging and went
free. Recounting this anecdote in a talk on 'Witches' at Harvard in
1980, Atwood commented, 'If there's one thing I hope I've inherited
from her, it's her neck ... One needs a neck like that if one is determined to be a writer, especially a woman writer.'[10] Professor Perry
Miller who was Atwood's Director of American Studies at Harvard
has written two very influential books, *The New England Mind: The
Seventeenth Century* (1939) and *The New England Mind: From Colony to
Province* (1953). Much of the rhetoric and many of the cultural practices of Gilead are to be found in Miller's histories, such as the
Founding Fathers' references to women as 'handmaids of the Lord'
or Cotton Mather's description of a dissenting woman as 'an
American Jezebel'. Gilead also employs many of the Puritan practices associated with childbirth, like the Birthing Stool and the provi-
sion of refreshments at a birth which were known as 'groaning beer'
and 'groaning cakes'.[11] While paying tribute to Miller's scholarship,
Atwood shifts the emphasis to reinvent those discordant women's
voices which ran counter to patriarchal Puritan voices in a fiction
which is presented as historical reconstruction of a future already
inscribed in the policies of the New Right. It is at this point that
Atwood's fable shimmers with the possibility of a nationalist reading,
for behind the threat of totalitarianism lurks an insistent preoccupation with Canada's relations to the United States. A scenario from
Canadian prehistory is used to predict the bleak possibility of
an Americanised future, where the space to be claimed for a belea-

guered Canadianness is delineated within a dissenting Handmaid's tale.

Not only does Atwood satirise the New Right and its Puritan inheritance, but she also takes a critical look at North American feminism since the 1960s. As a feminist with a deep distrust of ideological hardlines, she refuses to simplify the gender debate or to swallow slogans whole, for slogans always run the risk of being taken over as instruments of oppression, like the late 1970s feminist phrase 'a women's culture' which Gilead has appropriated for its own purposes. It is significant that Gilead is a society 'in transition' where all the women are survivors of the time before, and their voices represent a range of feminine and feminist positions dating back to the Women's Liberation Movement of the late 1960s. Offred's mother belongs to that early activist group with its campaigns for women's sexual freedom, their abortion rallies, and their 'Take Back the Night' marches. Thanks to the feminist movement in the United States women gained an enormously widened range of life choices when equal rights and legalised abortion were endorsed by Congress in the early 1970s, despite the opposition of Pro-Life campaigners and fundamentalist Christians. These voices are represented by the Commanders' Wives and the terrible Aunts. Among the Handmaids (who were women of childbearing age who must have grown up in the 1980s and early 1990s) positions are equally varied, ranging from the classic female victim figure of Janine (later Ofwarren), to radical feminists like Moira the lesbian separatist, to Offred herself who highlights the paradoxes and dilemmas of contemporary feminism. Offred, aged 33 at the time she tells her story, must have been born in the early 1970s, a date which would fit with her mother's feminist activities and the film about the Nazi's mistress which she sees at the age of eight; she would have been at university with Moira in the late 1980s. Just as there are many different kinds of women, so there is no simple gender division between masculine and feminine qualities: if men are capable of violence then so are women – even the Handmaids themselves at the Particicution – and Aunt Lydia with her coyly feminine manner is probably the most sadistic character in the novel. *The Handmaid's Tale* may be a critique of feminism but it is a double-edged one which rejects binary oppositions, just as Offred's double vision allows her to evaluate both Gilead and her own lost late twentieth-century America: that was not entirely good, but Gilead is undoubtedly worse. Atwood insists that women have never marched under a single banner: 'As for Woman, Capital W, we got stuck with that for centuries. Eternal woman. But really, Woman is the sum total of women. It doesn't exist apart from that, except as an abstracted idea' (*Conversations*, p. 201). It is Offred, the witty hetero-sexual woman who cares about men, about mother–daughter rela-tionships and about her female friends, whose storytelling voice survives long after Gilead has been relegated to past history.

Offred's narrative forms the bulk of the novel, refiguring the space which she can claim as her own within a very restrictive social system. In Gilead woman's place is in the home, though for a Handmaid the home is never her own but that of her Commanders and their Wives. *The Handmaid's Tale* is inner-space fiction, or perhaps space-time fiction, for it deals with the continuities of memory and those persistent traces of social history which survive to undermine the authority of even the most repressive regime. Though trapped within a system where there would seem to be no room for individual freedom, Offred claims her own private space by her refusals; she refuses to forget the past, she refuses to believe in the absolute authority of Gilead, just as she refuses to give up hope:

> Deliver us from evil.
>   Then there's Kingdom, power, and glory. It takes a lot to believe in those right now. But I'll try it anyway. *In Hope,* as they say on the gravestones ...
>   Oh God. It's no joke. Oh God oh God. How can I keep on living?   (p. 205)

Crucially Offred refuses to be silenced, as in unpropitious circum-stances she speaks out with the voice of late twentieth-century femi-nist individualism resisting the cultural identity imposed on her. She manages to lay claim to a surprising number of things which the system forbids: 'my own time' (p. 47), 'my room' (p. 60), 'my own territory' (p. 83), and even 'my name' (p. 94). She guards her lost name as the secret sign of her own identity and as guarantee of her hopes for a different future:

> I keep the knowledge of this name like something hidden, some treasure I'll come back to dig up, one day. I think of this name as buried ... the name floats there behind my eyes, not quite within reach, shining in the dark.   (p. 94)

Incidentally, this name is one of the secrets which Offred keeps from the reader though she does trust her lover Nick with it, and at the end the name does seem to act as guarantee of a future beyond

Gilead. One Canadian critic argues that Offred's real name is hidden in the text, there to be deduced from the one missing name in the whispered list of Handmaids' names at the end of the first chapter: 'Alma. Janine. Dolores. Moira. June' (p. 14).[12]

Offred's assertion about the 'space I claim as mine' directly addresses questions about the feminine subject's position within a rigidly patriarchal system and a woman's possible strategies of resistance. Appropriating her temporary room in the Commander's house as her own, Offred transforms it from prison cell into a point of stability from which she can escape at will into the spaces of memory and desire:

> I lie, then, inside the room ... and step sideways out of my own time. Out of time. Though this is time, nor am I out of it.
>
> But the night is my time out. Where should I go?
>
> Somewhere good.   (p. 47)

There is a surprising amount of mobility in the narrative as Offred moves out and away into her private imaginative spaces. Her story induces a kind of double vision in the reader as well, for she is always facing both ways as she shifts between her present life and her past or sometimes looks longingly towards the future.

In the face of state repression and domestic tyranny Offred manages to tell her wittily dissident tale about private lives, not only her own story but the stories of other women as well. Appropriating their remembered turns of phrase in her telling, Offred's voice doubles and multiplies to become the voices of 'women' rather than the voice of a single narrator. There is the story of Moira the rebel who spectacularly defies the power of the Aunts and escapes from the rehabilitation centre, only to reappear in the brothel scene at Jezebel's where she satirises male sexual fantasies by looking totally ridiculous as a Bunny Girl with a floppy ear and a draggly tail. There is also the story of Offred's unnamed predecessor at the Commander's house, who scratched a secret message in the wardrobe before hanging herself from the light fitting in the room Offred now occupies:

> Above, on the white ceiling, a relief ornament in the shape of a wreath, and in the centre of it a blank space, plastered over, like the place in a face where the eye has been taken out. There must have been a chandelier, once. They've removed anything you could tie a rope to.   (p. 17)

Offred comes to regard that absent woman as her own dark double. She also tells the stories of older women like her mother, the old-fashioned Women's Libber, condemned by the Gileadean regime as an Unwoman and sent to the Colonies to die but who refuses to stay dead. Instead she reappears to Offred and to Moira, preserved on film at the rehabilitation centre, and haunts her daughter's memory. Through time Offred gradually learns to appreciate the heroism of her mother who in life had been such a source of embarrassment, just as she begins to understand the dimensions of her own loss: 'I've mourned for her already. But I will do it again, and again' (p. 265). By contrast, there is the story of the Commander's Wife whom Offred remembers from the time before as 'Serena Joy' a popular gospel television show personality but who now finds herself trapped within that New Right ideology which she had helped to promote: 'She stays in her home, but it doesn't seem to agree with her. How furious she must be, now that she's been taken at her word' (p. 56). Sitting in her beautiful enclosed garden in her blue gown, Serena appears to Offred like an ageing parody of the Virgin Mary, child-less, arthritic and snipping vengefully at her flowers. All these women are casualties of the system though perhaps the saddest figure of all is Janine, a female victim in both her lives. Gang-raped in the time before Gilead, she becomes the Handmaid Ofwarren who produces the required baby, only to see it condemned to death as a 'shredder'. When Offred sees Janine for the last time after the Particicution she has become a madwoman, a 'woman in free fall' drifting around grasping a clump of the murdered man's blood-stained blond hair. Combined with fragments of gossip overheard from the Wives and the Marthas, Offred's story presents a mosaic of alternative female worlds which undermine Gilead's patriarchal myth of women's submissiveness and silence.

Offred describes her narrative as 'this limping and mutilated story', referring both to its structure and to the violent social condi-tions out of which it is told:

> I'm sorry there is so much pain in this story. I'm sorry it's in frag-ments, like a body caught in crossfire or pulled apart by force. But there is nothing I can do to change it.   (p. 279)

Composed of isolated scenic units with gaps and blanks in between where 'episodes separate themselves from the flow of time in which they're embedded' (*Conversations,* p. 216), the fragmented narrative also represents the mental processes of someone in Offred's isolated situation as her mind jumps between vividly realised present details and flashbacks to the past. Indeed, these are the characteristics of any story reconstructed from memory. As Offred asks herself, why does she need to tell this story? At the time, she tells it in her head in order to survive by seeing beyond the present moment where she does not wish to be and also because she needs to believe there is still someone outside Gilead who is listening to her: 'Because I'm telling you this story, I will your existence. I tell, therefore you are' (p. 279). As an ironic revision of Descartes's famous sentence in his *Discourse on Method* (1637), 'I think, therefore I am', Offred's comment shifts the emphasis away from the isolated thinking subject to the speaking subject whose storytelling becomes a substitute for dialogue. In fact Offred's story is a double reconstruction, as we discover at the end when she tells it again in a second retrospective version, like a letter addressed to '*Dear You* ... *You* can mean thousands' (p. 50). It takes a long time for her letter to be delivered, though as one critic has pointed out, the cassette tapes on which her message is recorded are found in a metal foot locker 'sealed with tape of the kind once used on packages to be sent by post' (p. 313) and Offred's is one of the missed messages which finally reaches its destination.[13] Though the male historians in Cambridge, England, get it first and rename it 'in homage to the great Geoffrey Chaucer' (p. 313), it finally comes to us the readers when Professor Pieixoto delivers his paper to the Twelfth Symposium on Gileadean Studies. The reader's own position in time is ambiguous, for we are reading in a fictive future which bears an uncomfortable resemblance to our present society.

Offred's story is incomplete and her account of life in Gilead is overlaid by Professor Pieixoto's academic reconstruction at the end, yet it is her voice coming through the transcribed tapes which gives the narrative its interest and continuity. This is history written in the feminine gender:

> I wish this story were different ... I wish it were about love, or about sudden realizations important to one's life, or even about sunsets, birds, rainstorms, or snow.
>   Maybe it is about those things, in a sense; but in the meantime there is so much else getting in the way.   (p. 279)

Offred's insistence on her preference for traditionally feminine subject matter would seem to suggest that equally traditional equation between 'woman/nature' as opposed to 'man/culture' and

given the literary tradition out of which Atwood comes, we may
wonder if Offred's tale is another version of Canadian women's
wilderness writing.[14] The answer of course is not simple; Offred is
actually very far from the wilderness, being situated in a city and
living in a house with a walled garden in a neat tree-lined street. Her
husband and daughter have been lost to her in the bush of the bor-
derland territory between Gilead and Canada, so that any wilderness
that exists for her would be merely within the inner realm of imaginative possibility. Yet there is, as we have seen with *Surfacing* and
Survival and *Wilderness Tips,* a distinctive linguistic system relating to
wilderness experience, with its signifiers of the unexplored natural
world and the quest for freedom with its accompanying emotional
and physical revitalisation. It is within this territory of imagination
and metaphor that Offred claims the space to write about her body,
her memories and her womanly desires, and so manages to elude
the confines of Gilead. Her tale is as profoundly subversive as
Hélène Cixous's French feminist text of the mid 1970s, 'The Laugh
of the Medusa', with which it has much in common as a project to
inscribe the complex dimensions of female being.[15] Atwood's novel
enacts in practice what Cixous's essay proposes as theory, for Offred
is Cixous's woman 'confined to the narrow room' and 'given a
deadly brainwashing' but who becomes the 'I-woman, escapee'
'breaking out of the snare of silence' to 'write herself'. (The vocabulary here is entirely taken from 'Medusa'.) Offred's situation might
be read as a literal translation of Cixous's highly metaphorical text,
except that Atwood is sceptical of any Utopian vision of woman's
glorious liberation from the shackles of patriarchy. Offred is not a
revolutionary; she refuses to join the Mayday resistance movement in
Gilead and she does not want to adopt Moira's separatist feminist
space, though she admires her friend's recklessness and swashbuck-
ling heroism. Her own position is much closer to the traditionally
feminine role of woman as social mediator, for though she resists
the brutal imposition of male power in Gilead she also remembers
the delights of heterosexual love and yearns to fall in love again. Her
story *is* about love with a strong traditional female romance component and Offred does the very traditional thing of becoming pregnant through her lovemaking with Nick though not through
state-regulated sex with the Commander. It is symptomatic of
Offred's non-confrontational role that though she finally defeats the
Commander's assurance of male superiority, she herself is not in a
commanding position at the end (unlike the film version where she

murders the Commander and escapes). Led out of his house as a prisoner and feeling guilty at having let down the household, she has no idea whether she is going to her death or towards a new life of freedom when she steps up into the Black Van. Offred never makes Cixous's 'shattering entry into history'; on the contrary, she never finishes her story and her voice is almost drowned out by the voice of a male historian.

However, Offred's story is a 'reconstruction' in more senses than one, for not only is it her narrative of memory but it is also the means by which she manages to rehabilitate herself as an individual in Gilead. Though she begins her tale as a nameless woman traumatised by loss and speaking in whispers, Offred refuses to believe that she is nothing but a Handmaid, 'a two-legged womb': 'I am alive, I live, I breathe, I put my hand out, unfolded, into the sunlight' (p. 18). She insists on chronicling her subjective life from within her own skin, offering her own personal history of physical sensations and the impact of emotion on her body, together with those imaginative transformations through which body space opens out into fantasy landscape. According to Cixous's prescription, 'By writing herself [or in Offred's case "speaking herself"] woman will return to the body which has been more than confiscated from her, which has been turned into the uncanny stranger on display' ('Medusa' p. 250). This is for Offred the uncanny shape of the red-robed Handmaid. Indeed, it is from within this role that Offred finds her strength to resist, for just as Gilead is obsessed with the female body and its reproductive system so this is where Offred turns her attention, though in terms significantly different from patriarchal prescriptions and closer to feminist polemics: 'Write yourself. Your body must be heard ... This emancipation of the marvellous text of her self which she must urgently learn to speak' (ibid.).

The language through which Offred writes her body has significant affinities with Cixous's, for the female body is the 'dark continent' which both claim as their own. Cixous asserts that 'the dark continent is neither dark nor unexplorable', and Offred answers that challenge, using similar images of immense bodily territories, volcanic upheavals and the Medusa's own subversive laughter. There are, however, some interesting cultural differences, one of them being Atwood's use of wilderness imagery. On the evening of the monthly Ceremony of sexual intercourse with the Commander (a time when her body would seem least of all to be her own) Offred becomes the explorer of her own dark inner space:

I sink down into my body as into a swamp, fenland, where only I know the footing. Treacherous ground, my own territory. I become the earth I set my ear against, for rumours of the future. Each twinge, each murmur of slight pain, ripples of sloughed-off matter, swellings and diminishings of tissue, the droolings of the flesh, these are signs, these are the things I need to know about. Each month I watch for blood, fearfully, for when it comes it means failure. I have failed once again to fulfil the expectations of others, which have become my own.

I used to think of my body as an instrument, of pleasure, or a means of transportation, or an implement for the accomplishment of my will ... single, solid, one with me.

Now the flesh arranges itself differently. I'm a cloud, congealed around a central object, the shape of a pear, which is hard and more real than I am and glows red within its translucent wrapping. (pp. 83–4)

With her minute attention to physical details, Offred chronicles her bodily awareness and her shifts of perspective under the influence of cultural doctrines which have effected a change in her imaginative conceptualisation of her self. No longer a 'solid object, one with me', her body has become a 'cloud' surrounding the dark inner space of her womb, whose dimensions expand till it becomes Cixous's 'immense astral space' or Atwood's cosmic wilderness, 'huge as the sky at night and dark and curved like that, though black-red, rather than black'. Her intense meditation offers a kind of imaginative transcendence though without Cixous's promise of erotic pleasure, for Offred knows that she is nothing more in Gilead than a breeding machine serving the state. Though it is not rape ('Nothing is going on here that I haven't signed up for'; p. 105), intercourse with the Commander 'has nothing to do with passion or love or romance or any of those other notions we used to titillate ourselves with. It has nothing to do with sexual desire, at least for me' (p. 105). What Offred experiences is a sense of dissolution within her body as every month its only issue is menstrual blood: 'To feel that empty again, again. I listen to my heart, wave upon wave, salty and red, continuing on and on, marking time' (p. 84). This is the hidden female space where time is kept by the body: 'I tell time by the moon. Lunar, not solar' (p. 209), though 'marking time' also reminds Offred that time is running out and she will be sent to the Colonies if she does not soon produce a child. Offred's condition is one of compromised resistance, where she regrets not becoming pregnant as the system requires of her ('Give me children, else I die'), while at the same time she resists Gilead's imposition of patriarchal control over her. In her mind her body remains unconquered territory which will be forever beyond the Commander's reach, despite the monthly Ceremony:

> Intent on his inner journey, that place he is hurrying towards, which recedes as in a dream at the same speed with which he approaches it.   (p. 105)

Offred's body is capable too of seismic upheavals in what is her most ebullient gesture of resistance to the Commander, her secret outburst of laughter after their first forbidden game of Scrabble. The game provides her with the welcome opportunity to play with words, and her image of the Scrabble counters as candies which she would like to put into her mouth makes a beautifully literal equivalent for Cixous's metaphor of women's seizing language 'to make it hers, containing it, taking it into her mouth' ('Medusa', p. 257). That game and the Commander's forlorn request for her to kiss him as if she meant it is followed by Offred's paroxysm, her own Medusa laughter:

> Then I hear something, inside my body. I've broken, something has cracked, that must be it. Noise is coming up, coming out, of the broken place, in my face ... If I let the noise get out into the air it will be laughter, too loud, too much of it.   (p. 156)

In order to laugh, Offred goes into the one hidden place in her room, the cupboard scrawled with her nameless predecessor's secret message, '*Nolite te bastardes carborundorum*'. As she asks later: 'How could I have believed I was alone in here? There were always two of us' (p. 305). There in the cupboard with its spectral witness to female solidarity, Offred laughs her defiance:

> My ribs hurt with holding back, I shake, I heave, seismic, volcanic, I'll burst. Red all over the cupboard, mirth rhymes with birth, oh to die of laughter.   (p.156)

From such private inner spaces Offred's narrative of feeling opens out into the spaces of desire as her irrepressible energy impels her towards life rather than death. Though still enclosed within domestic spaces and decorums, Offred revels in the summer sunshine of the Commander's Wife's garden, a space which is of course not her own but which she appropriates imaginatively. She always refers to it as 'our' garden. This garden is not a wilderness, though it is a place of organic natural forces which establishes a correspondence with Offred's remembered past life: 'I once had a garden. I can remember the smell of the turned earth' (p. 22). Now she turns to the garden as a welcome release from her loveless isolation:

> I wish this story were different ... I've tried to put some of the good things in as well. Flowers, for instance, because where would we be without them?   (p. 279)

One of the most lyrical passages in the novel is her celebration of the garden in full bloom, a place of fertility and sensuous delights combined with the subtly sexual suggestiveness of the bleeding hearts 'so female in shape' and the phallic irises so cool on their tall stalks:

> There is something subversive about this garden of Serena's, a sense of buried things bursting upwards, wordlessly, into the light, as if to point, to say: Whatever is silenced will clamour to be heard, though silently.   (p. 161)

The garden provides a sublimated image of Offred's own repressed desires, but more than that it becomes suddenly and overwhelmingly the space of romantic fantasy, a 'Tennyson garden, heavy with scent, languid; the return of the word *swoon*' (p. 161), where traditional images of femininity breathe through Offred's prose as the garden itself 'breathes, in the warmth, breathing itself in. To walk through it in these days, of peonies, of pinks and carnations, makes my head swim.' In this eroticised feminine space conjured by Offred in her state of heightened sensitivity everything signifies romance, temptation and desire:

> The willow is in full plumage and is no help, with its insinuating whispers, *Rendezvous*, it says, *terraces*: the sibilants run up my spine, a shiver as if in fever. The summer dress rustles against the flesh of my thighs, the grass grows underfoot, at the edges of my eyes there are movements, in the branches; feathers, flittings, grace notes, tree into bird, metamorphosis run wild. Goddesses are possible now and the air suffuses with desire. Even the bricks of the house are softening, becoming tactile; if I leaned against them they'd be warm and yielding. It's amazing what denial can do.   (pp. 161–2)

In this passage Offred is aware of herself as both female and feminine, an element of 'nature' in her bodily responses and an element of 'culture' as her riot of feelings is filtered through her literary imagination. No wilderness place, this is both a real garden and a place of myth where 'goddesses are possible', a pagan fantasy landscape metamorphosed into Offred's rhapsody of the flesh. Of course it is characteristic that she should see round her fantasy even while revelling in it, wryly recognising that such excess is at least in part a sublimation of her sexual frustrations where longing generates its own scenarios. Yet it is the very intensity of her desire which allows Offred for a moment to transcend her human limits and to enter into the life of the pulsating organic world around her:

> Winter is not so dangerous. I need hardness, cold, rigidity; not this heaviness, as if I'm a melon on a stem, this liquid ripeness. (p. 162)

Offred has become that speaking subject whom Cixous describes in her '*écriture feminine*':

> I am spacious, singing flesh, on which is grafted no one knows which I, more or less human, but alive because of transformation. Write! And your self-seeking text will know itself better than flesh and blood, rising ... with sonorous, perfumed ingredients, a lively combination of flying colors, leaves, and rivers plunging into the sea we feed. ('Medusa', p. 260)

Cixous's text here runs in harmony with Offred's where images of desire deriving from the human body and the natural world constitute a 'feminine' alternative language which resists Gilead's polluted technological nightmare and its compromised 'biblico-capitalist rhetoric' ('Medusa', p. 257).

Offred's text is truly self-seeking as she tries to win back 'her womanly being, her goods and her pleasures' ('Medusa', p. 250) which have been stolen from her. Even within the restrictive circumstances of Gilead Offred yearns to fall in love again, and she does – not with the Commander whose image is irretrievably tainted with patriarchal authority – but with his chauffeur Nick. Their love story follows the pattern of traditional female romance with its strong undercurrent of sexual magnetism which leads the heroine into dangerous forbidden territory and finally results in her rescue by the hero. There are, however, significant differences from the traditional script, for falling in love flouts all the rules of sexual conduct in puritanical Gilead and Offred knows that she and Nick would be shot if they were discovered in bed together. Their love story is fraught with so many difficulties that Offred has trouble in telling it at all, yet it runs as secret subtext beneath the deprivations of her daily life as a Handmaid. Offred's response to Nick is overpoweringly sexual, for the first time his boot touches her shoe when they are sitting decorously in the Commander's Wife's sitting room, ironically enough on the first night of the monthly Ceremony, she says, 'I feel my shoe soften, blood flows into it, it grows warm, it becomes a skin' (p. 91). Though Offred moves her foot away, the sudden sensation of coming to life again under Nick's touch is the first signal of the strong physical attraction between them. We are reminded of Atwood's poem, 'Nothing like love to put blood in the language'[16] as Offred attempts to tell the story of her reawakening sexuality and the burgeoning of her romantic fantasies. It is a fragmented narrative filled with obstacles and marked by brief illicit encounters where urgent desire is figured as mutual irrational hunger for the other:

> I want to reach up, taste his skin. He makes me hungry. His fingers move, feeling my arm under the nightgown sleeve, as if his hand won't listen to reason. It's so good, to be touched by someone, to be felt so greedily, to feel so greedy. Luke [addressing the ghost of her lost husband] you'd know, you'd understand. It's you here, in another body.
> Bullshit.   (pp. 109–10)

Offred is too honest to substitute one man for another even in her fantasy; after all, that would be to repeat Gilead's own methods. ('Each one remains unique. There is no way of joining them together. They cannot be exchanged one for the other', pp. 201–2.) Yet there is a complex process of doubling and substitution going on here between her lost husband Luke, the Commander and Nick, in parallel to the doublings between Wives and Handmaids, or in this particular case between Offred and Serena Joy, who together set up the liaison with Nick: 'I see the two of us, a blue shape, a red shape in the brief glass eye of the mirror as we descend. Myself, my obverse' (p. 271). A similar process of doubling happens in Offred's account of her first sexual encounter with Nick, which she tells in two different versions before admitting that neither of them is true. The first version (pp. 272–3) is a minimalist wordless encounter, while the second version (pp. 273–5) follows the script of a tough-talking Hollywood movie of the 1950s. Yet both these fictitious versions are undermined by Offred's sudden outbursts of overpowering sexual joy (Version 1):

> His mouth is on me, his hands, I can't wait and he's moving, already, love, it's been so long, I'm alive in my skin, again, arms around him, falling and water softly everywhere, never-ending. I knew it might only be once.   (p. 273)

This vibrantly charged '*écriture feminine*' stands in contrast to the second version, which is starker and more elemental (Version 2):

> There wasn't any thunder though, I added that in. To cover up the sounds, which I am ashamed of making.   (p. 275)

Offred's assertions, denials and revisions suggest erotically charged experience which can only be gestured towards in language but which can never be accurately written down, for love happens in the gaps between words: 'All I can hope for is a reconstruction: the way love feels is always only approximate' (p. 275).

Despite the difficulties, Offred tries to write her loving desire in her confessional narrative towards the end, when we realise that her relation with Nick has been going on beneath the text for quite a long time:

> I went back to Nick. Time after time, on my own, without Serena knowing. It wasn't called for, there was no excuse. I did not do it for him, but for myself entirely.   (p. 280)

Her clear-eyed account offers fascinating glimpses into a woman's sexual feelings which are occluded in love stories told from a male perspective. There is no feminine coyness here, for now it is Offred who is the reckless seeker knocking on the door of Nick's bedroom with 'a beggar's knock', yet there is a kind of diffidence and vulnerability within her daring. She always dreads rejection and so is perpetually overwhelmed with gratitude as everything brims to excess:

> We make love each time as if we know beyond a shadow of a doubt that there will never be any more ... And then when there is, that too is always a surprise, extra, a gift.   (p. 281)

What Offred emphasises (and the reason why she says 'I did it for myself entirely') is the transforming power of sexual desire, as under

Nick's touch and gaze she feels released into the 'marvellous text of herself':

> He seems indifferent to most of what I have to say, alive only to the possibilities of my body, though he watches me while I'm speaking. He watches my face.   (p. 282)

Though neither of them says the word 'love' Offred represents herself in very traditional terms as a woman in love, 'daydreaming, smiling at nothing, touching my face lightly' (p. 283). At the same time, she and Nick have crossed over into wilderness territory of passion and instinct as the imagery suggests, finding there a place of security where like primitive cave-dwellers they cling together in their shared private space – though Offred also knows that this is nothing more than the state of mind of two people in love:

> Being here with him is safety, it's a cave, where we huddle together while the storm goes on outside. This is a delusion, of course. This room is one of the most dangerous places I could be. (p. 281)

Her account is written in the double-voiced discourse so characteristic of women, partaking both of 'nature' (as Offred according to the female biological rhythm becomes pregnant through her lovemaking with Nick) and of 'culture' (as she sees herself like a Canadian settler's wife, making a life for herself in the wilderness with the man she loves: 'The fact is that I no longer want to leave, escape, cross the border to freedom. I want to be here, with Nick, where I can get at him', p. 283).

However, this is a love story which is cut short and lacks the conventional happy ending (an ending, which incidentally, Volker Schlondorff's film version provides). The romance plot is put to a crucial test when one day Nick bursts into Offred's room accompanied by a party of Eyes (secret police) to take her away in the dreaded Black Van reserved for dissidents. Is this a betrayal or a rescue? Offred does not have the faintest idea and she realises that she knows so little about Nick that 'trust' is, ironically, all that she is left with: 'Trust me, he says, which in itself has never been a talisman, carries no guarantee', p. 306). Her narrative ends with Offred laying herself open to all risks and all possibilities as she departs from the Commander's house like a criminal under guard and climbs into the van:

I have given myself over into the hands of strangers, because it can't be helped.

And so I step up, into the darkness within; or else the light. (p. 307)

So Offred enters Cixous's moving open transitional space of becoming ('Medusa', p. 264) at the same moment as her voice ceases. This is no Utopian ending but a radical disruption, and we never find out what becomes of her. From the discovery of her tapes there is a strong assumption that she was indeed rescued by Nick, but there is no evidence of what happened after that. (The film version seems more certain of the outcome than Atwood's narrative.) The final frame of the novel is provided by the Historical Notes which introduce several crucial shifts in perspective. They offer an interpretative view of Offred's tale which has truly been 'given over into the hands of strangers', and it can't be helped because Offred is long since dead. Two hundred years later Gilead has become ancient history and knowledge of it is buried in the past, so that only traces of its failed social experiment remain in the form of archaeological fragments, scattered diaries and letters, among which are Offred's cassette tapes. These Notes are a transcript of a lecture given by a Cambridge Professor, Darcy Pieixoto, at an academic symposium on Gileadean Studies held in the year 2195. It is this professor who together with a colleague is responsible for the transcription and editing of the story we have just finished reading, or what he describes pedantically as the '*soi-disant* manuscript ... which goes by the title of *The Handmaid's Tale*' (p. 312). Already the voice of the male academic threatens to drown out the voice of Offred and the significance of this woman's autobiography.

Before pursuing the implications of this shift in voice, it is necessary to consider that other shift in time and place which occurs in these Notes. The novel actually rehearses two different futuristic scenarios: Offred's Gilead set in a nightmarish polluted and fundamentalist United States whose population is threatened with extinction; and there is the second one (post-Gilead) which is set in Arctic Canada (post-Canada as we know it?). This territory is clearly unpolluted, for the conference participants are invited to go on a Nature Walk, having enjoyed a dinner of fish from the sea the evening before. The conference session is chaired by a woman professor, Maryann Crescent Moon, whose name indicates that she is a Native Person (as is Professor Running Dog). The most crucial evidence for the Canadian location is the place name, for the conference is held at the University of Denay, Nunavit. The Dené are the Native People who live in northern Alberta, while 'Nunavut' is the name of a huge area in the eastern Arctic which will become in the last year of the twentieth century the first aboriginal self-governing territory in Canada. Of course 'Denay, Nunavit' is also a pun, a piece of authorial advice to the reader to believe Offred's story, no matter what interpretations or misinterpretations might be offered in the Historical Notes.

Indeed, misinterpretations are offered in what turns out to be a ferocious satiric thrust at male academic historians; sexist attitudes have not disappeared, as we gather from the professor's sexist jokes about 'tails' and 'frailroads' and in his reading of the Tale itself. He is not concerned with Offred as an individual; instead he is preoccupied with establishing the authenticity of her text and its value as objective historical evidence, while sidestepping the crucial moral issues raised by her account: 'Our job is not to censure but to understand' (at which, to their discredit, the assembled academics applaud). He blames Offred for not keeping a piece of the Commander's computer printout as evidence of the way the Gileadean system of government worked. His reconstruction effects a radical shift from 'herstory' to 'history' as he attempts to discredit Offred's narrative by accusing her of not paying attention to significant things. In response, the reader may feel that it is the professor who is paying attention to the wrong things, for Atwood highlights perspective rather than knowledge or truth as the main feature of any historical narrative. Pieixoto's account obliterates Offred as a person; he never tells what happened to her because he does not know and he is not interested. In fact, he does exactly what Offred feared history would do to the Handmaids: 'From the point of view of future history, we'll be invisible' (p. 240).

The abrupt shift from Offred's voice to the historian's voice challenges the reader on questions of interpretation. We have to remember that *The Handmaid's Tale* was Offred's transcribed speech, reassembled and edited by male historians and not by her. Really the tale is their structure, which may account for some of the disruptions in the narrative. Her tale has been appropriated by an academic who seems to forget that his reconstruction is open to questions of interpretation too. He is abusing Offred as Gilead abused her, removing her authority over her own life story and renaming it in a gesture which parallels Gilead's patriarchal suppression of a woman's identity in the Handmaid's role. No wonder the professor claims to have lost Offred, as like Eurydice's ghost 'she slips from our grasp and flees' (p. 324), though he is quite wrong to accuse her of not answering him when he has refused to listen to what she has been saying. The challenge of interpretation is finally directed out to the readers, who have heard it all. Finally, I would suggest that just as Offred's story has shown up the limits of Gilead's autocratic power to control the subjective lives of at least two of its inhabitants, so it defies Pieixoto's appropriation 200 years later. This may look like a case of the 'disappearing author', though that is a postmodern position that Atwood vigorously resists (Deny None of It) in the interests of our shared moral responsibility. By putting herself into the text, Offred has put herself 'into the world and into history', challenging readers to connect her world with our own in the present in the hope of averting a nightmare like Gilead for our own future.

8

Atwood's Retrospective Art: *Cat's Eye*

What's the difference between vision and a vision? The former relates to something it's assumed you've seen, the latter to something it's assumed you haven't. Language is not always dependable either.

Margaret Atwood, 'Instructions for the Third Eye'[1]

The light that we see from distant galaxies left them millions of years ago, and in the case of the most distant object that we have seen, the light left some 8,000 million years ago. Thus, when we look at the universe, we are seeing it as it was in the past.

Stephen Hawking, *A Brief History of Time*[2]

These two passages, one from a prose poem questioning the reliability of modes of visual perception and the other from a book of popular physics describing how we see back through the present to the distant past, might together serve as preface to *Cat's Eye*, for this is a novel which combines the discourses of fiction and autobiography, science and painting in its attempt to represent the female subject in the text. Arguably *Cat's Eye* could be read as Atwood's own retrospective glance back at the imaginative territory of her earlier fictions. There is a female artist who is more successful than the nameless woman in *Surfacing* and the same parent and brother figures as in that novel; the same childhood tormentors and traumatic experiences in the Toronto ravine have appeared in *Lady Oracle* and in some of the poems in *The Circle Game*; 'the eyes of cats, fixed for the pounce' have been referred to in *The Handmaid's Tale*, to name but a few of the intertextual references here. There are figures and events and modes of imagery which chime with resonances from Atwood's earlier works, but I do not want to pursue those explorations here, fascinating as they are.[3] Instead I shall focus on the crucial importance of retrospective art in the female protagonist's construction of her self, for *Cat's Eye* is Atwood's most developed version of life-writing in the feminine, where her middle-aged protagonist Elaine Risley struggles to define herself through figuring out her life story in different versions, a process analogous to the narrative structuring of *Lady Oracle* and *The Robber Bride*. Who is Elaine Risley? And what is the significance of the *Cat's Eye* of the title? Elaine is a painter; the story is littered with references to her pictures and culminates in her first retrospective exhibition in Toronto. It is her return to her home town for this exhibition which provides the stimulus for her curiously doubled narrative with its 'discursive' memoir version and its 'figural' version presented through her paintings.[4] Indeed, it is this double figuration of the self, projected through the relationship between the discursive and the figural as forms of autobiography, that is the site of my inquiry. I shall pay particular attention to Elaine's paintings and the retrospective exhibition in order to highlight Atwood's distinctive contribution to the problematical construction of female subjectivity in fiction.[5]

The retrospective exhibition positioned at the end of the novel (or almost) might be taken as Elaine's final statement, a *summa* of all the elements of her life already contained in the narrative. The exhibition is presented as a chronicle, with its brief views of earlier paintings and detailed descriptions of five later paintings (the last one with the promising title 'Unified Field Theory'), together with a few less-than-helpful interpretations from the catalogue supplemented by/contradicted by Elaine's comments. As readers we have the advantage over the compiler of the catalogue because we already know the private references which are coded into the paintings, whereas she does not. What we also know (if we remember back 318 pages) is that this retrospective statement is not an authoritative one, for Elaine has left the arrangement of the paintings to the gallery's director (p. 87). Her own position at the opening is that of a visitor:

> I walk slowly around the gallery, sipping at my glass of wine, permitting myself to look at the show, for the first time really. What is here, and what is not.   (p. 404)[6]

Actually the exhibition has the same kind of provisionality as *The Handmaid's Tale*, where Offred's narrative transcribed from her tapes is presented as the editor's version rather than as her own. In both cases, the recording subject remains elusive; she cannot be defined by the statements made on her behalf. Yet a retrospective exhibition (not the one described at the end) is the informing principle of the novel, for it has already been constructed on the Contents page, where the chapter titles are all given the names of paintings mentioned in the text. (That is, all except for the first one, 'Iron Lung', which Elaine cannot paint because she is still inside it for as long as she lives, 'being breathed' by time. In the Atwood papers there are two versions of the 'Iron Lung' painting, both deleted from the published novel, and both are striking for what the artist realises much later in time. One version is particularly interesting, for the exhibition catalogue entry suggests that the 'mandala-shaped object' reflects the 'influence of Op Art' on Risley's work, whereas the artist's own comment contradicts this: 'It isn't a mandala, or Op Art. The smaller points are rivets, the larger circle is an iron lung, as seen from the bottom end. I painted it that way because I didn't know whose head to put, sticking out the top end. I would know now'; MS Collection 200, Box 102, Folder 2.) Throughout the narrative, individual paintings offer a disruptive commentary figuring events from a different angle to the memoir, so that it is only appropriate that they should be collected and shown in a gallery named 'Sub-Versions'. The doubled retrospective device[7] creates a complex patterning where painted surfaces present a riddling version of the truth. These visual artefacts (always of course mediated through/invented by language) represent the relation between 'vision' and 'a vision' (what it's assumed you've seen and what it's assumed you haven't), where socially accepted codes of seeing are challenged by the eye of the artist. As Elaine looks through the lens of the Cat's Eye, her Third Eye, 'the single eye that sees more than anyone else looking' (p. 327), she sees more because she sees differently.

However, for all her insight Elaine remains a slippery subject, difficult to get into focus. Even now at the age of nearly 50 she is a 'blur' to herself when she looks in the mirror:

> Even when I've got the distance adjusted, I vary. I am transitional; some days I look like a worn-out thirty-five, others like a sprightly fifty. So much depends on the light, and the way you squint. (p. 5)

And again, 'There is never only one, of anyone' (p. 6). It is surely significant that the first and only complete picture of her face is the photograph on the poster near the gallery where her exhibition is to be held: 'The name is mine and so is the face, more or less. It's the photo I sent the gallery. Except that now I have a moustache' (p. 20). Her view of her own face 'defaced' is surrounded by images of multiple identities, disguises ('I could be a businesswoman ... a bank manager ... a housewife, a tourist, someone window-shopping'; p. 19), and by a reference to her double, Cordelia – all of which underline Elaine's indeterminacy and multiplicity as a subject.

In order to 'read' Elaine's autobiography we could not do better than turn to the theoretical essay by Paul de Man, 'Autobiography as De-facement', which would seem to be signalled by the grotesque visual self-image on the poster. Atwood's project in this novel bears a fascinating resemblance to de Man's deconstructive critique:

> Are we so certain that autobiography depends on reference, as a photograph depends on its subject or a (realistic) picture on its model? We assume that life produces the autobiography as an act produces its consequences, but can we not suggest, with equal justice, that the autobiographical project may itself produce and determine the life and that whatever the writer *does* is in fact governed by the technical demands of self-portraiture and thus determined, in all its aspects, by the resources of his [her] medium?[8]

This construction of subjecthood would seem to be confirmed by Elaine's response to the poster, which, may be, as she says, a feeling of wonder, but which also may be read as a self-reflexive comment on her autobiography: 'A public face, a face worth defacing. This is an accomplishment. I have made something of myself, something or other, after all' (p. 20). Elaine's confrontation with her own face defaced, like her return to Toronto, constitutes that 'specular moment' which de Man identifies as the autobiographical impulse with its sudden alignment between present and past selves that opens up multiple possibilities for 'mutual reflexive substitution', displacements and doublings. These are for him the 'defacements' endemic to the autobiographical project, which 'deals with the giving and taking away of faces, with face and deface, figure, figuration and disfiguration'.[9] *Cat's Eye* would seem to provide the perfect exemplars of such 'defacements' – wittily in the comic-book story of the two sisters, 'a pretty one and one who has a burn covering half her face' who comes back from the dead to get 'into the pretty one's body' (p. 211); and more seriously, in Elaine's portrait of Cordelia which is called 'Half a Face' (p. 227). It is Cordelia, her childhood

companion and tormentor, for whom Elaine searches incessantly on
her return to Toronto, Cordelia who belongs to that city which 'still
has power; like a mirror that shows you only the ruined half of your
face' (p. 410). Lacking her dark double trapped in an earlier period
of time, Elaine remains unfixed, incomplete: 'We are like the twins
in old fables, each of whom has been given half a key' (p. 411).
Cordelia as the absent Other would also confirm de Man's theory of
autobiography as a double project of self-representation, moving
towards self-restoration at the same moment as it marks otherness
and deprivation: 'Autobiography deprives and disfigures to the
precise extent that it restores.'[10]

Returning for a moment to an earlier stage of de Man's critique, I
should like to highlight his question about figures and figuration:

> Does the referent determine the figure, or is it the other way
> round: is the illusion of reference not a correlation of the struc-
> ture of the figure, that is to say no longer clearly and simply a
> referent at all but something more akin to a fiction, which
> then, however, in its own turn, acquires a degree of referential
> productivity?[11]

The notion that it is the mode of figuration which produces the ref-
erent is crucial to Atwood's subject-constructing project where two
modes of figuration are used. While Elaine's discursive narrative
remains incomplete, her paintings offer a different figuration, acting
as a kind of corrective to the distortions and suppressions of memory
and offering the possibility of theoretical solutions. Not that autobiography can ever attain completeness:

> The interest of autobiography, then, is not that it reveals reliable
> self-knowledge – it does not – but that it demonstrates in a striking
> way the impossibility of closure and totalization (that is the impos-
> sibility of coming into being) of all textual systems made up of
> tropological substitutions.[12]

Though de Man's discussion focuses exclusively on linguistic
signifiers here, and Elaine's autobiography offers the variant of (ver-
balised) visual images, the result is the same. As seeing eye or discursive recorder, she tells her own private history, together with
fragments of Cordelia's story, her brother Stephen's story, the stories
of her parents and of Josef, Jon and Ben the men in her life, and the
story of Mrs Smeath. She also presents a historical documentary

account of Toronto in the 1940s and 1950s from the perspective of an English-speaking Canadian girl, together with a cultural critique of feminism in Canada in the 1970s and 1980s. Arguably, Elaine succeeds in establishing her position as a speaking/painting subject, but she herself always exceeds her carefully constructed parameters of vision: 'I'm what's left over'(p. 409).

Atwood's novel adds one important dimension to de Man's theory of autobiography, and that is the dimension of time. Curiously, he neglects this, possibly because he is more interested in the opposition between life and death implied by life-writing, but Atwood does not. As she said in her *Cat's Eye* discussion at the National Theatre, London, in April 1989, 'The thing I sweated over in that novel was Time', for Elaine's story covers a period of nearly 50 years from the early 1940s to the late 1980s. This is a 'space-time' novel (a phrase with precise scientific connotations here) where the narrator tries to establish her position by using the three spatial co-ordinates plus the temporal co-ordinate, only to discover that back in Toronto, though her space might be defined, she is living in at least two time dimensions at once as she remembers the past: 'There are, apparently, a great many more dimensions than four' (p. 332). Here Elaine transcribes the words of her dead brother Stephen, who grows up to become a theoretical physicist and is later killed by terrorists in an aircraft hijack incident. As so often happens in life-writing, her story is also a memorial to the dead. The narrative begins with a speculation on time: 'Time is not a line but a dimension, like the dimension of space ... It was my brother Stephen who told me that' (p. 3). It is filled with echoes of Stephen's voice in allusions to his theories about space-time, curved space, the expanding universe, light, black holes, string theory and the uncertainty principle.[13] In significant ways Stephen's scientific enthusiasms have shaped Elaine's imagination, so that her paintings and his theories come to occupy the same area of speculation on the mysterious laws which govern the universe. They are both engaged in trying to reconstruct the past, he through physics and mathematics and she through memory and imaginative vision. His discourse from theoretical physics provides the conceptual framework for her paintings, for Elaine is 'painting time': 'These pictures of her, like everything else, are drenched in time' (p. 151), and finally at the retrospective, 'I walk the room, surrounded by the time I've made' (p. 409). Recording her brother's death, she recalls his anecdote about identical twins and the high-speed rocket, part of his youthful disquisitions on the theory of relativity and its effect on the behaviour of time:

What I thought about then was the space twin, the one who went on an interplanetary journey and returned in a week to find his brother ten years older.

Now I will get older, I thought. And he will not.   (p. 392)

Perhaps the most important single memorial to her brother's influence is her last painting, 'Unified Field Theory', to which I shall return in my discussion of the retrospective exhibition.

We should remember that Elaine trained not as a painter but as a biologist, like her father, producing slide drawings of planaria worms that looked like 'stained glass windows under the microscope' (p. 247), and that her instructor Dr Banerji appears in one of her late paintings dressed like a magus holding a round object figured with bright pink objects ('They are in fact spruce budworm eggs, in section; but I would not expect anyone but a biologist to recognize them', p. 406). The boundaries between science and art are dissolved here in what might be seen as an act of gendered transgression, where Elaine's paintings and drawings show one way in which a woman deals with the master discourse of science, transforming it through another medium or 'another mode of figuration'.[14]

Whether as a trainee biologist or a painter, or as the sister of a budding astronomer, Elaine's primary activity is 'seeing'. Eyes are important, but so are microscopes and telescopes, and so are lenses, with their ability to magnify and to focus more powerfully than the naked eye. It is in this context that we might consider the significance of the Cat's Eye of the title. Certainly the cat's eye marble exists as a referential object in the text, introduced first in the childhood games in the schoolyard with 'puries, bowlies, and cat's eyes' ('my favourites'; p. 62), where it is strongly associated with her brother's superior skill.[15] It recurs many times in an almost casual way, as something to be fingered in Elaine's pocket as a secret defence against her tormentors when she is nine years old (p. 141); later, as something she has grown out of, like her red plastic purse (p. 203); and later still, as an object to be rediscovered among the debris in the cellar:

The red plastic [purse] is split at the sides, where the sewing is. I pick it up, push at it to make it go back into shape. Something rattles. I open it up and take out my blue cat's eye ... I look into it, and see my life entire.   (p. 398)

Suddenly the cat's eye marble is transformed into the lens of imaginative vision, becoming that Third Eye[16] through which 'each brick, each leaf of each tree, your own body, will be glowing from within, lit up, so bright you can hardly look. You will reach out in any direction and you will touch the light itself'.

But is it a sudden transformation? Hardly that, for the cat's eye marble has always had a duplicitous existence: 'The cat's eyes really are like eyes, but not the eyes of cats. They're the eyes of something that isn't known but exists anyway ... like the eyes of aliens from a distant planet. My favourite one is blue' (pp. 62–3). Invested by the nine-year-old girl with supernatural powers to protect her, it becomes for her a talismanic object and the sign of her own difference: 'She doesn't know what power this cat's eye has, to protect me. Sometimes when I have it with me I can see the way it sees ... I am alive in my eyes only' (p. 141).

Cat's eyes, planets and stars swirl together in Elaine's power dream, when the cat's eye enters her body:

It's falling down out of the sky, straight towards my head, brilliant and glassy. It hits me, passes right into me, but without hurting, except that it's cold. The cold wakes me up. My blankets are on the floor.   (p. 145)

It functions as the nexus for all those contradictory feelings of fear and longing, love hatred and resistance that she feels towards Cordelia, Grace Smeath and Carol Campbell 'in that endless time when Cordelia had power over me' (p. 113). Indeed, it is already functioning beyond her consciousness as her Third Eye when, deserted by her friends and lying in the snow in the dark, she has her vision of the Virgin Mary, 'Our Lady of Perpetual Help', floating over the footbridge in the Toronto ravine. Elaine's reassumption of her own independence after this agony is marked by the sign of the cat's eye: 'I am indifferent to them. There's something hard in me, crystalline, a kernel of glass. I cross the street and continue along, eating my licorice' (p. 193): much later Elaine will recognise it as the sign of the artist's powers of vision, and it will appear again and again in her paintings as her signature (the pier-glass, the globe, the cat's eye marble). She will use it to figure curved space where 'Nothing goes away'.

The cat's eyes disappears entirely from her discursive memoir narrative of her adolescence and early adulthood in a complex process of repression:

I've forgotten things, I've forgotten that I've forgotten them ... I find these references to bad times vaguely threatening, vaguely

insulting: I am not the sort of girl who has bad times.
(pp. 200–1)

However, in the double mode of figuration employed in this novel,
the discontinuous narrative constructed by Elaine's paintings tells a
different story about Elaine as subject. She may feel like 'nothing' but
a 'seeing eye', though her paintings display an excess of signification
that goes beyond the discursive narrative produced by her conscious
mind. They are truly 'sub-versions', uncovering that highly complex
network of conflicting energies, conscious and unconscious, which
make up the human 'subject' in its psychoanalytical definition.[17] The
presence of the cat's eye is signalled in Elaine's fascination with the
effects of glass when she is studying the history of visual styles, and a
little drama of substitution is played out for the reader (though not
for her) in her particular concern with the pier-glass in Van Eyck's
picture 'The Arnolfini Marriage', where the 'round mirror is like an
eye' (p. 327). The cat's eye is there, multiplied, in some of her early
still lifes, though scarcely visible; 'far back, in the dense tangle of the
glossy leaves, are the eyes of cats' (p. 337). Arguably, it is through
that alien lens that Elaine paints her savage exposures of Mrs Smeath:
'One picture of Mrs Smeath leads to another. She multiplies on the
wall like bacteria, standing, sitting, flying, with clothes, without
clothes, following me around with her many eyes' (p. 338). This is a
form of revenge that her conscious mind fails to understand, either at
the time of painting or when her pictures are attacked by the ink-
throwing woman at the feminist art show in Toronto: 'It is still a
mystery to me, why I hate her so much' (p. 352). The answer hovers
in the reader's mind as the words of Atwood's prose poem whisper,
'The third eye can be merciless, especially when wounded'.[18]

What is never explained in either the discursive or the figural narrative are Elaine's moments of revelation: her childhood vision of
the Virgin Mary or that moment when she looks through the lens of
the cat's eye marble and sees her 'life entire' (p. 398). Yet these are
perhaps the crucial moments which determine her life as an artist
and they both figure together in her final painting, where the Virgin
Mary holds 'an oversized cat's eye marble, with a blue centre'
(p. 408). ('Vision ... a vision: something it's assumed you've seen ...
something it's assumed you haven't.') Through the logic of the
image Elaine's paintings present 'a vision' as 'vision', so that as we
follow the verbal descriptions of the paintings, reading changes to
gazing. We 'see' through Elaine's mediating eye, which dissolves the
boundaries between the visionary and the visible.

The retrospective exhibition occurs in the chapter 'Unified Field Theory', which, with its echoes of Stephen's lecture 'The First Picoseconds and the Quest for a Unified Field Theory: Some Minor Speculations' (p. 331), places it in a relational context and also signals its function in this autobiographical narrative. Within the parameters of theoretical physics Elaine traces her figural interpretation of her life-story, which offers a significantly different series of projections from her discursive memoir. By way of explanation for such differences, we might consider briefly Norman Bryson's emphasis on the double nature of painting, which he calls 'the divided loyalty of the image'.[19] This seems a useful analogy to describe the fissure within Elaine's remembering process, between her conscious mind's discursive narrative and the figural narrative of her imagination. From physics comes the definition of a 'field':

> In physics a field can only be perceived by inference from the relationships of the particles it contains; the existence of the field is, however, entirely separate from that of the particles; though it may be detected through them, it is not defined by them.[20]

Unified field theory itself (the attempt to formulate a comprehensive theory of the laws that govern the universe) belongs to the discourse of theoretical physics; to a non-physicist like Elaine, her brother's lecture sounds as close to metaphysics as to physics.[21] At the end of it, after his speculation on picoseconds, space-time and matter-energy, Stephen does, however, give her a sentence which is crucial to her project of self-representation: 'But there is something that must have existed before. That something is the theoretical framework, the parameters within which the laws of energy must operate' (p. 332). It is this relationship between the cosmic and the humanly particular that Elaine figures in her paintings, none of which offer a totalised representation of her 'self', though maybe that 'self' is the 'field' that might be inferred from the constructions of her pictures.

At the retrospective, we are invited to 'read' the pictures in sequence as we are led by Elaine past the 'early things' and the 'middle period' (all of which we have already 'seen'), to her five most recent paintings which she has never shown before. These are described in detail, and we realise first that these paintings have a double significance as representations. There is a personal rationale behind the collocation of images in each picture which Elaine interprets for us, for these are plain statements in her own private

narrative of crises, revelations and memories. However, as the
wickedly satirical extracts from the catalogue commentary suggest,
they also have a public life as paintings in an exhibition, available to
the viewer's interpretation, so that plain statements become riddles
provoking other people's narrative solutions: 'I can no longer
control these paintings or tell them what to mean. Whatever energy
they have came out of me. I'm what's left over' (p. 409).

The second thing we notice is that these late paintings share a
common structural feature: they all introduce further dimensions of
meaning into the figural image by their pier-glass motifs or their
triptych designs, which initiate shifts in perspective. A host of possible meanings are generated through different spatial patternings,
different time dimensions, executed in different painterly techniques. As each painting contains several styles of representation, so
the referentiality of any single image is undercut. These multiplici-
ties are quite simply illustrated in Elaine's self portrait, 'Cat's Eye'
('There is never only one, of anyone', and anyway her portrait, like
the one she painted of Cordelia, is only 'Half a Face'), while more
complex representations of space-time and vision are developed in
'Unified Field Theory'. The structural feature of the convex lens also
highlights artifice, for these paintings reveal themselves as construc-
tions/reconstructions, where realistic images are used to map a
psychic landscape in Elaine's project of painting time.

It is important in the double mode of figuration of this novel to
note that the paintings effect quite significant revisions in Elaine's
retrospective narrative, for they encode insights that she herself only
later realises when she looks at the paintings. Now she reads the Mrs
Smeath paintings differently, understanding at last not only 'Why I
hated her so much' but also how vengeful she was, and how her
earlier self lacked the compassionate recognition which she had
actually painted into Mrs Smeath's eyes:

> It's the eyes I look at now. I used to think these were self-
> righteous eyes, piggy and smug inside their wire frames; and
> they are. But they are also defeated eyes, uncertain and melan-
> choly, heavy with unloved duty. The eyes of someone for whom
> God was a sadistic old man; the eyes of a small-town threadbare
> decency. Mrs Smeath was a transplant to the city, from somewhere
> a lot smaller. A displaced person; as I was.   (p. 405)

This process of moving from the blindness of consciousness to the
insight of imaginative seeing occurs in Elaine's reading of all her late

paintings, with her questioning of the reliability of memory in 'Picoseconds', her awareness of mutual limits of understanding in 'Three Muses', her ignorance of her brother's last moments in 'One Wing', and her recognition of what her childhood torments were and how they were crucial to the development of her artistic powers.

It is the last painting, 'Unified Field Theory', which effects the most significant revision of all in its effort at synthesis. Elaine's figuration of her vision of the Virgin Mary holding the cat's eye marble and floating above the bridge of her childhood traumas combines with her brother's cosmic imagery ('Star upon star, red, blue, yellow and white, swirling nebulae, galaxy upon galaxy'). This representation of the night sky could also be read as a black hole under the ground, as the secret place of her brother's buried treasure, or as 'the land of the dead people', one of the many terrors of her childhood. Here the figural presents oppositions as co-existing on the same plane: the past and the present, 'a vision' and 'vision', the sacred and the profane, science and art, the universal and the particular. This is Elaine's attempt to present her 'life entire' in an impersonal vision of wholeness, painting the forces which govern the laws of her being. All this is carefully spelled out by Elaine (there is no comment from the catalogue this time) and as readers we probably believe her interpretation because it gathers up so many anecdotes from her memoir text, offering a possible site for accommodating the Virgin Mary vision. The meanings also work forwards as well as backwards to enhance Elaine's discursive narrative when she will record her last 'vision' of Cordelia, in language which sets up parallels and echoes with the account of the first vision. However, the painting might also work another way, to problematise further her memoir narrative by highlighting its gaps and omissions. In a universe where 'Nothing goes away' (p. 3), 'What have I forgotten?' (p. 334) always remains an open question.

Of course, the last painting, like the retrospective, like the memoir, offers only a theoretical framework for the definition of Elaine's self, providing an illusion of completeness which is dispelled by the final chapter entitled 'Bridge', where the narrative takes up once again the quest for Cordelia and Elaine's registration of lack and loss. Our view of Elaine herself remains partial and provisional; though we have learned to see through her eyes, we have only ever seen half her face or her face 'defaced'. Apparently the human subject is as mysterious as the universe: 'The universe is hard to pin down; it changes when you look at it, as if it resists being known' (p. 388).

In this version of life-writing in the feminine with its double project for constructing female subjectivity through the discursive and the figural modes, the emphasis on displacements, doublings and 'defacements' underlines the inherent instability of the narrating subject at the same time as it 'undoes the model [of autobiography as a genre] as soon as it is established'.[22] Though we may be persuaded that Elaine succeeds in locating her distinctive 'position' as a subject in her figural constructions of space-time, the discursive narrative as a 'textual system made up of tropological substitutions'[23] will always register some incompleteness in the construction of 'subjecthood', a lack that is confirmed at the thematic level by Elaine's failure to find Cordelia and her recognition that she is by herself. A manuscript note clarifies this point while amplifying it in interesting ways: 'Cordelia is gone, this is empty landscape. Or not empty. Full of whatever is there without our hatreds and desires' (MS Collection 200, Box 99, Folder 8). Elaine is left stranded in the present, surrounded by the wash of time:

> This is what I miss, Cordelia: not something that's gone, but something that will never happen. Two old women giggling over their tea.   (p. 421)

Through the multiple modes of narrative representation Elaine, like Offred or Cordelia, 'slips from our grasp and flees'. By telling the reader so much, Atwood has paradoxically exposed the limits of autobiography and its artifice of reconstruction. The best Elaine Risley or Margaret Atwood can offer is a Unified Field Theory from which inferences about the subject may be made, but the subject herself is always outside, in excess, beyond the figurations of language. The 'I' remains behind the 'eye'. At the end, Elaine recedes back into her seeing eye, voided of personality, as her narrative dissolves into light:

> Now it's full night, clear, moonless and filled with stars, which are not eternal as was once thought, which are not where we think they are. If they were sounds, they would be echoes, of something that happened millions of years ago: a word made of numbers. Echoes of light, shining out of the midst of nothing.
> It's old light, and there's not much of it. But it's enough to see by.   (p. 421)[24]

Conclusion

She gets up from her chair and pours herself a glass of water; then, on top of Europe in the thirteenth century, she spreads out a street map, a map of downtown Toronto ... Here is McClung Hall, and, to the north, Tony's own house, with West in it, upstairs in bed, groaning gently in his sleep; with the cellar in it, with the sand-table in it, with the map on it, with the city in it, with the house in it, with the cellar in it, with the map in it. Maps, thinks Tony, contain the ground that contains them. Somewhere in this infinitely receding headspace, Zenia continues to exist.

The Robber Bride, p. 464

I want to take advantage of the pause while Atwood's invented character Antonia Fremont, Canadian female military historian, shifts her attention for a moment, to conclude this open-ended account of Atwood's fiction. It seems an appropriate place for us to pause as well, at the end of her latest novel before she too, like Tony, turns her attention to something else with refocused concentration. What that something else will be we can only guess at, for over her 25 years of writing fiction Canada's most famous novelist has shown a talent for endlessly surprising her readers with her ongoing experimentalism and her radical challenge to contemporary social myths and fashionable ideologies. Yet I think we can make an informed guess at the likely range of topics which Atwood will treat in her next novel(s) as a result of our retrospective glance back over the imaginative territory of her fiction, where we see strong continuities in areas of concern endlessly refigured and revised from one novel to the next. To write a critical study like this is the equivalent of mounting the kind of retrospective exhibition that the Sub-Versions gallery did for the middle-aged painter Elaine Risley (though I hope I have avoided some of Charna's more obviously fatuous interpretations). Like Elaine Risley's paintings, so Atwood's novels would seem to be constructing a 'Unified Field Theory' which represents the dynamics

of her fictional world. 'Like Tony', 'like Elaine' – the points of correspondence between Atwood and her female narrators are numerous,
for she is also like the popular Gothic novelist Joan Foster in *Lady
Oracle* or like Zenia the supreme plotter in *The Robber Bride*, or like
Rennie Wilford the lifestyle journalist in *Bodily Harm* who comes to
an awareness of political engagement, or like Offred the Handmaid
whose futuristic tale challenges official histories of the past while
warning readers about consequences in the present, or even like the
anonymous narrator of *Surfacing* who manages to find a 'dialect of
her own' to speak of her identity as a Canadian and a woman.
' "Like" and "like" and "like" – but what is the thing that lies beneath
the semblance of the thing?' as one of Virginia Woolf's narrators
bursts out in *The Waves*,[1] the 'thing' itself here being Margaret
Atwood the person who remains infinitely elusive behind her multiple personas and shifting narrative perspectives. 'There's never only
one, of anyone' of course, as Elaine Risley is aware, just as there is
never only one point of view or one true story:

> The true story lies
> among the other stories ...
>
> The true story is vicious
> and multiple and untrue
>
> after all. Why do you
> need it? Don't ever
>
> ask for the true story.[2]

Atwood's novels, situated 'at the interface between language and
what we choose to call reality,' highlight nothing so much as the
artifice of representation, where the real world is transformed and
reinvented within the imaginative spaces of fiction. Yet within this
seemingly infinite variety there is a recognisably Atwoodian voice,
witty, self ironical, politically and morally engaged as her worldly
texts respond to what is actually going on in her own place and time,
speaking her double vision of how things look on the surface and
what else is happening at the same time inside, underneath or elsewhere. There are also those distinctively Atwoodian topics which I
have traced in this study, where it would seem that the most 'capa-
cious topic' is Atwood's concern with the operations of power politics at every level, from national and international relations to

sexual politics within social institutions filtering down to the most intimate levels of personal relationships. These parameters might be said to contain all Atwood's other topics which are interwoven in a web of interrelated discourses, for her fiction canvasses such questions as Canadian national identity, Canada's relations with the United States and with Europe, human rights issues, environmental issues which initially focussed on Canadian wilderness but which have branched out in increasingly urgent warnings against the dangers of global pollution with its threat to human survival. There are the feminist issues (or perhaps more accurately gender issues, for Atwood, the best-known feminist writer in English, has always been critical of its ideological definitions in her chronicling of North American feminism as a social movement since the late 1960s) which include her scrutiny of social myths of femininity; male and female fantasies about women; representations of women's bodies in art, fiction, popular culture and pornography; women's social and economic exploitation; as well as women's relations with each other, not to mention their relations with men. This list of Atwood's 'topical topics' eddies in a seemingly endless proliferation, for 'everything needs a preface: a preface, a postscript, a chart of simultaneous events', as Tony reminds us. There are however 'definitive moments' in history, so that 'We can look at these events and we can say that after them things were never the same again' (*The Robber Bride*, p. 4) – just as for us there are Atwood's eight novels which are our fixed points of reference.

I would like to return to the passage I quoted at the beginning of this chapter, for it seems emblematic of Atwood's fictional project and of her own position as a writer. Tony is a historian, not a novelist but a storytelling academic who reconstructs the past from the facts available to her, and who represents the wide perspective of European history as a map on a sand-tray in her basement where she continually reshuffles the pieces in her effort to make sense of the riddles of human behaviour in battles which she has never seen. She is also a Canadian woman living in Toronto in the 1990s who can at any time overlay her scene of historical reconstruction with a map of her home city – which she does – so that her perspective shifts radically to the specific topographical details of home while the map of Europe is still there underneath as a reminder of the international context within which her Canadian place is located. To make explicit one of the correspondences between Tony as historian and map maker with Atwood as cultural historian and novelist, we notice that both the preface and the postscript to that most Toronto-

centred fiction *The Robber Bride* contain references to what is going
on in the world outside the city in October 1990 and November
1991: 'The Soviet bloc is crumbling, the old maps are dissolving ...
There's trouble in the Gulf' (p. 4) and a year later: 'Famine is rolling
over Africa; in what was once Yugoslavia there is ethnic feuding.
Atrocities multiply, leaderships teeter, car factories grind to a halt.
The war in the Gulf is over and the desert sands are spackled with
bombs' (p. 465). To return to Tony as she studies her street map,
which we as readers are also invited to do with her, the focus gets
narrower and narrower as it shifts ever inwards into her own house
and into the details of her own private life, so that places marked on
the map become markers for the inner spaces of psychological landscape. In a characteristically Atwoodian shift of perspective precise
topographical description takes on the double aspect of personal
memory marker, as with McClung Hall at the University of Toronto,
the building where Tony works and where she once lodged as a
student when it was still a women's hall of residence – and where
she first met her husband West and also Zenia the 'Robber Bride'.
Just as the map figures space for Tony so it also figures time, both
historical time and her own subjective time as a thinking, feeling,
remembering woman – academic, wife and friend. In Tony's
memory Zenia though she is dead 'continues to exist' for 'She's in
there somewhere, that other one', as Elaine Risley remarked (*Cat's
Eye*, p. 399), and 'nothing goes away'. Tony occupies multiple positions, seeing differently and remembering differently as the spaces
keep shifting when viewed from different perspectives. Yet beneath
all the changes, the nursery rhyme litany of 'The House That Jack
Built' enacts a process of infinite repetition from a specific point of
location, rather like the convex mirror in Van Eyck's painting of
'The Arnolfini Marriage' which so fascinated Elaine. The specific
point of location here is of course Tony in her house in Toronto
down in the cellar at midnight, in whose mind, 'that infinitely receding headspace', these multiple refigurings take place. They are then
represented in Atwood's fiction so that the novel itself becomes a
reconstruction for the reader, rather like a map which accommodates multiple stories and shifting perspectives, all different but all
coexisting within the one fictional space of the text.

So, nothing goes away though perspectives change over time and
revisionary readings are always possible. Indeed, Atwood's own perspectives have changed over the period of 25 years since her first novel
was published, in response to her widening international audience
and changes in cultural politics on the international globalised

scenario as well as to shifts in Canadian social and political attitudes. The key term remains for Atwood (as it has always been) 'survival' in a context of environmental change which is both ecological and ideological. As I have tried to show in my discussion of her changing representations of wilderness, Atwood's view of prospects of survival for the human race has grown bleaker even as her position has changed from her early Canadian nationalist stance to her growing transnational engagement with issues of environmental pollution in the 1990s. The word 'wilderness' is still there, acknowledging the Canadian tradition out of which she continues to write, but whereas back in the early 1970s wilderness represented a distinctively Canadian national space, by the 1990s wilderness has become destabilised as the traditional marker of Canadian cultural identity in Atwood's fiction. The forests are under threat and the New World wilderness myth has come under increasing ideological pressure in postcolonial multicultural Canada, where traditional narratives of national identity are being revised. Atwood pushes her narratives to the verge of collapse and disaster, then shifts the perspective to a wider historical context which holds out hope for the future for 'nothing has happened, really, that hasn't happened before' ('Wilderness Tips', p. 221). Her narratives open out space for the transformation of attitudes and policies before it is too late. As with the stories in *Wilderness Tips*, so it is in *The Handmaid's Tale* with its double visions of the future which sweep back to the past, only to land readers squarely in the present at the end with the final challenge, 'Are there any questions?' (p. 324). Atwood's fictional mode in these texts belongs to traditions of eighteenth century English satire, resembling nothing so much as the ending of Alexander Pope's *The Dunciad* where his 'Universal Darkness' which 'buries all' is a staged scenario of prophecy and warning.

I have attempted to trace similar shifts of emphasis in Atwood's representations of femininity and the female body over nearly 25 years, and in her use of Gothic narrative conventions where there is a discernible shift from Joan Foster's wide-eyed Canadian responses to Europe as romantically Gothic and 'Other', through the duplicitous games of Murder in the Dark and Cluedo, to *The Robber Bride* where European Gothic comes to Canada and lodges right in Toronto in the person of Zenia, the Robber Bride of Grimm's fairy tale. No longer can Canada be viewed as peculiarly safe and separate from the international community, for Atwood uses a Canadian location here as one more example of contemporary crisis where 'something ordinary but horrifying is taking place' (*The Robber Bride*, p. 3). It could be anywhere, for 'nobody is exempt from anything' as

Rennie Wilford realises in her prison cell on the Caribbean island of St Antoine, but the place happens to be Toronto in Atwood's novel.

'Revision', 'retrospection' and 'reconstruction' are related impulses of mind and artistic creativity. Just as Elaine Risley in middle age has reached a new stage and status in her profession with her first retrospective exhibition, so we notice that Atwood's fictions are becoming increasingly retrospective themselves. Elaine realises that she is painting time: 'I walk the room, surrounded by the time I've made' (*Cat's Eye*, p. 409); Atwood is writing time as she is writing women, writing Canada, mapping cultural shifts and changing fashions. In that novel she is also casting a retrospective glance over the territory of her earlier fictions, constructing a private documentary as well as a historical account of post-war Toronto in the 1940s and 1950s as remembered in the mid 1980s, all within one woman's fictive autobiography. The revisionary narratives of the stories in *Wilderness Tips* depend on processes of retrospection and revaluation, and *The Robber Bride* continues that retrospective process with its documentation of the last 30 years of Toronto's social history through the life stories of three Canadian women; they are of course always shadowed by the missing figure of Zenia, who 'continues to exist' in their stories. Arguably all Atwood's novels are retrospectives in the sense that they are narrative reconstructions of women's lives, with all the provisionality that comes with the recognition of the duplicitous tricks that memory can play and where gaps in the remembering subject's own history parallel gaps in official records – as Offred and Tony both notice. However, there is a difference which is first signalled in *The Handmaid's Tale* with what we might call Offred's conscious awareness of being a cultural historian, for she is not only unofficial chronicler of Gilead but of the North American feminist movement since the 1960s. It is this documentary historicising impulse which has become increasingly evident in Atwood's novels since the mid-1980s.

There is one further issue which has been implicit throughout this study and which I would like to make a little more explicit, and that is Atwood's figuring of women artists – writing women and painting women with the woman as subject, the 'I-witness'. Interestingly Atwood's early women artists like the anonymous narrator of *Surfacing* or even Joan Foster in *Lady Oracle* are women who face crises of confidence in their own creative powers. The 'surfacer' is a failed painter who never trusts her own vision and as a narrator she struggles through inherited patriarchal discourses to find a language of her own. Yet she is also aware of the power locked inside herself, symbolised I believe in her clenched fist as she sits alone and silent on the other side of the wall listening to her group of friends talking together: 'It was there in me, the evidence, only needing to be deciphered' (p. 76). Certainly, by the end her visionary experiences have released the power to heal herself, though she has not yet found a voice to answer Joe's call: '"Are you here?" Echo: here, here?' (p. 192). For Joan Foster, writer of popular Gothic romances, wordlessness is not the problem, though she is still struggling to find her own voice even as she takes enormous pains to disguise it through her slavish adherence to clichéistic Gothic conventions and her automatic writing. At the end she is still seeking an appropriate language and subject matter: 'But maybe I'll try some science fiction ... I keep thinking I should learn some lesson from all of this, as my mother would have said' (*Lady Oracle*, p. 345). Rennie Wilford is not in a much better position than Joan really, for she only manages to break through the false representations of her lifestyle journalism and to find her own voice when there is nobody to hear it, and she realises that she cannot think of a title for her story. In a similarly incarcerated situation, Offred in *The Handmaid's Tale* does manage to reclaim her own lost identity and to tell her story but only in secret, and her history only becomes available long after she is dead; even then her recorded voice is in danger of being drowned out by the voice of a male historian. All these narratives represent the processes by which women write their attempts to speak (or to write or to paint), just as they also write in their difficulties and failures and silencings. It is only with *Cat's Eye* and the *Robber Bride* that the female artist or the female historian, now middle-aged, gains confidence in her vision and her powers of interpretation. As Elaine looks at the world through her cat's eye talisman, she 'sees more than anyone else looking' (p. 327) and she dares to paint a picture with the title 'Unified Field Theory', taking on the discourse of her brother's theoretical physics and reinterpreting it through her private vision of human particularity. For all that, she remains an elusive subject and at the end she flies off to the other side of Canada, leaving her life energy in her paintings: 'I'm what's left over' (p. 409). So we come back once again to Tony, sitting over her maps in the basement of her own house. She is the first of Atwood's female narrators who is willing to assume full responsibility as a storyteller. Taking up the fragments of Zenia's story (that arch-plotter who abused her superb narrative skills: 'Zenia wouldn't answer. Or she would lie ... She has before', p. 3), Tony tries to make a story for her/out of her, with an appropriate ending. For once, a female narrator revels in her power to make meaning:

> She will only be history if Tony chooses to shape her into history.
> At the moment she is formless, a broken mosaic; the fragments of
> her are in Tony's hands, because she is dead, and all of the dead
> are in the hands of the living.   (p. 461)

Certainly Tony ends up devising a different ending from the one she
had planned for Zenia but she does manage an ending – though it
must be said that in the process she learns to move beyond otherness
and difference towards likeness, which could open the way to a new
narrative: 'Was she in any way like us? thinks Tony. Or, to put it the
other way around: Are we in any way like her?' (p. 470). Tony finds
herself in a significantly different position from any other of
Atwood's narrators at the end: instead of being alone she is at home
and the member of a community, so that she can choose finally to
come in from outside and join her friends when she has finished
telling her story: 'Then she opens the door, and goes in to join the
others' (p. 470).

I should like to end with Atwood's voice as a poet, questioning not
social myths this time but poetic conventions as false representations
of reality. Though the genre is different, the poem, like the novels,
shares the characteristic Atwoodian textual space which accommodates both the vastness of the cosmos and social space on a human
scale, just as the poetic voice situates her distinctly humanist exhor-
tation within the traditional rhetoric of spirituality. However, she
does not supplicate for divine revelation but for the power to see
without distortion of vision, while urging the need for clarity of mind
in order to know our position in the universe. This poem might be
read as one kind of answer to Atwood's original and ongoing search
to find a definition of what it means to be 'human', though the
poem is also a prayer which inscribes incompleteness and an ending
which is always provisional:

> What idiocy could transform the moon, that old sea-overgrown
> skull seen from above, to a goddess of mercy?
>   ...
> Let the other moons pray to the moon. O Goddess of Mercy,
> you who are not the moon, or anything we can see clearly,
>
> we need to know each other's names and what we are asking.
> Do not be any thing. Be the light we see by.[3]

Notes

Chapter 1   Fact File and Significant Characteristics

1. Patrick Parrinder, 'Making Poison', *London Review of Books*, 20 March 1986, pp. 20–2.
2. *Margaret Atwood: Conversations*, ed. Earl G. Ingersoll (London: Virago, 1992), p. 108. All other references to *Conversations* will be included in the text.
3. Philip Howard, *The Times*, 13 March 1980, p. 14.
4. See Margaret Atwood, *Second Words: Selected Critical Prose* (Toronto: Anansi, 1982), p. 430.
5. Ibid., p. 111.
6. 1967 marked the 100th anniversary of Canadian Confederation (1867) when Canada became a Dominion within the British Empire. In 1982 the Patriation of the Constitution established Canada as an independent nation within the British Commonwealth.
7. Philip Howard, Introduction to *Margaret Atwood: Conversations*, p. vii.
8. Jeremy Brooks, *The Sunday Times*, 27 May 1973.
9. Peter Prescott, *Newsweek*, 4 October 1976.
10. Marilyn French, *The New York Times Book Review*, 3 February 1980.
11. Philip Howard, *The Times*, 13 March 1980, and Lorna Sage, *The Times Literary Supplement*, 14 March 1980.
12. Atwood, *Second Words*, p. 14.
13. *Independent*, 6 February 1987.
14. Margaret Atwood, *Cat's Eye* (London: Virago, 1990), p. 20.
15. Linda Hutcheon, *The Canadian Postmodern: A Study of Contemporary English-Canadian Fiction* (Toronto: Oxford University Press, 1988) p. 21.
16. Adrienne Rich, 'When We Dead Awaken' (1971), in *On Lies, Secrets and Silence: Selected Critical Prose, 1966–1978* (London: Virago, 1980) pp. 33–50. Atwood reviewed Rich's work frequently during the 1970s.
17. Maggie Humm, *Border Traffic: Strategies of Contemporary Women Writers* (Manchester and New York: Manchester University Press, 1991) pp. 123–59.
18. Currently concepts of the literary canon and nationhood are under attack, reflecting pressures of bilingualism and multiculturalism. See Robert Lecker (ed.), *Canadian Canons: Essays in Literary Value* (1991)

and Frank Davey, *Post-National Arguments: The Politics of the Anglophone-Canadian Novel* (1993), both published Toronto: University of Toronto Press.

19. Northrop Frye, *The Bush Garden* (Toronto: Anansi, 1971). See also Sandra Djwa, 'The Where of Here: Margaret Atwood and a Canadian Tradition', in *The Art of Margaret Atwood: Essays in Criticism*, ed. Arnold and Cathy Davidson (Toronto: Anansi, 1981) pp. 15–34.
20. Atwood, *Second Words*, p. 190.
21. M. Fulford (ed.), *The Canadian Women's Movement, 1960–1990: A Guide to Archival Resources* (Toronto: ECW, 1992); R. R. Pierson, M. G. Cohen, P. Bourne and P. Masters, *Canadian Women's Issues: Strong Voices*, vol. 1 (Toronto: James Lorimer, 1993).
22. Betty Friedan, *The Feminine Mystique* (1963) (London: Gollancz, 1965).
23. Brief accounts of the history of second wave feminism are available in Toril Moi, *Sexual/Textual Politics* (London: Routledge, 1985) and Maggie Humm (ed.), *Feminisms: A Reader* (New York and London: Harvester Wheatsheaf, 1992).
24. Introduction to Margaret Atwood, *The Edible Woman* (London: Virago, 1979).
25. Hutcheon, *The Canadian Postmodern*, p. 110.
26. Margaret Atwood, *The Robber Bride* (London: Virago, 1994) p. 370

Chapter 2　Atwood's Canadian Signature

1. Jacques Derrida, 'Signature Event Context', repr. in *Margins of Philosophy*, trans. Alan Bass (New York and London: Harvester Wheatsheaf, 1982) pp. 173–8; see also Stephen Scobie, *Signature Event Cantext* (Edmonton: NeWest, 1989).
2. Margaret Atwood, 'Death by Landscape', in *Wilderness Tips* (London: Virago, 1992), pp. 107–29.
3. There are earlier versions of wilderness in the unfinished novel *The Nature Hut* (c. 1966) and the unpublished story 'Transfigured Landscape' (Margaret Atwood Papers Ms Collection 200, Thomas Fisher Rare Book Library, University of Toronto, Boxes 17 and 79.
4. Margaret Atwood, *The Journals of Susanna Moodie* (Toronto: Oxford University Press, 1970) 'Afterword', p. 62.
5. Margaret Atwood, *Surfacing* (London: Virago, 1979) p. 11. All further page references will be to this edition and included in text.
6. Margaret Atwood, *Survival: A Thematic Guide to Canadian Literature* (Toronto: Anansi, 1972) p. 13. All further page references will be included in the text.
7. For fullest accounts of *Surfacing* criticism, see Ildiko De Papp Carrington, 'Margaret Atwood', in *Canadian Writers and Their Works: Fiction Series*, vol. 9, ed. R. Lecker, J. David, E. Quigley (Toronto: ECW, 1987) pp. 25–118; and George Woodcock, *Introducing Margaret Atwood's 'Surfacing': A Reader's Guide* (Toronto: ECW, 1990). The major areas discussed are: (a) quest narrative: Annis Pratt, 'Surfacing and the Rebirth

Journey,' in *The Art of Margaret Atwood: Essays in Criticism*, ed. Arnold and Cathy N. Davidson (Toronto: Anansi, 1981) pp. 139–57; Carol Christ, 'Margaret Atwood: the Surfacing of Women's Spiritual Quest and Vision', *Signs*, vol. 2, no. 2 (Winter 1976) pp. 316–330; (b) shamanism: Rosemary Sullivan, 'Surfacing and Deliverance', *Canadian Literature*, vol. 67 (Winter 1976) pp. 6–20; Kathryn van Spanckeren, 'Shamanism in the Works of Margaret Atwood', in *Margaret Atwood: Vision and Forms*, ed. K. van Spanckeren and J. Garden Castro (Carbondale: Southern Illinois University Press, 1988), pp. 183–204; (c) nationalism: Gloria Onley, 'Surfacing in the Interests of Survival', *West Coast Review*, vol. 7, no. 3 (Jan. 1973) pp. 51–4; (d) feminist issues: Sherrill Grace, 'In Search of Demeter: the Lost, Silent Mother in Surfacing', in *Vision and Forms*, pp. 35–47; Maggie Humm, *Border Traffic* (1991); Barbara Hill Rigney, *Margaret Atwood* (London: Macmillan, 1987); (e) language and narrative structure: Linda Hutcheon, 'From Poetic to Narrative Structure: the Novels of Margaret Atwood', in *Margaret Atwood: Language, Text and System*, ed. S. Grace and L. Weir (Vancouver: UBC, 1983); Frank Davey: *Margaret Atwood: A Feminist Poetics* (Vancouver: Talonbooks, 1984); Robert Cluett, *Canadian Literary Prose: A Preliminary Stylistic Atlas* (Toronto: ECW, 1990); W. J. Keith, *A Sense of Style* (Toronto: ECW, 1989).

8. Kildare Dobbs in the *Toronto Star*, 12 September 1972.
9. Margaret Atwood Interview in G. Gibson, *Eleven Canadian Novelists* (Toronto: Anansi, 1973) pp. 1–31.
10. *North Bay Nugget*, 3 September 1976.
11. Atwood Papers, Box 22: 12, 141-A.
12. Keith, *A Sense of Style*, p. 180.
13. See note 7.
14. Gibson, *Eleven Canadian Novelists*, p. 27.
15. Margaret Atwood, 'Wilderness Tips', in *Wilderness Tips*, p. 207. All further page references will be included in text.
16. Michael Hurley, *The Borders of Nightmare: The Fiction of John Richardson* (Toronto: University of Toronto Press, 1992) p. 4.

Chapter 3 'Feminine, Female, Feminist'

1. Margaret Atwood, *The Edible Woman* (London: Virago, 1980); 'The Female Body' in *Good Bones* (London: Virago, 1994) and *The Robber Bride* (London: Virago, 1994). Page references to these editions will be included in the text.
2. Toril Moi, 'Feminist, Female, Feminine,' repr. in *The Feminist Reader: Essays in Gender and the Politics of Literary Criticism*, ed. C. Belsey and J. Moore (London: Macmillan, 1989) pp. 117–32.
3. Betty Friedan, *The Feminine Mystique* (1963) (London: Gollancz, 1965). Page references will be to this edition and included in the text.
4. This is the territory explored by Rachel Bowlby in *Shopping with Freud* (London: Routledge, 1993). It will be evident that *The Edible Woman* is

not really about shopping in the sense of buying and selling but about packaging and consumer choice.

5. Graeme Gibson, *Eleven Canadian Novelists*, p. 27; repr. in *Margaret Atwood: Conversations*, pp. 16–17.
6. Noelle Caskey, 'Interpreting Anorexia Nervosa', in *The Female Body in Western Culture: Contemporary Perspectives*, ed. Susan Rubin Suleiman (Cambridge, Mass., and London: Harvard University Press, 1985) pp. 175–92.
7. Dennis Cooley, 'Nearer by Far: the Upset 'I' in Margaret Atwood's Poetry', in *Margaret Atwood: Writing and Subjectivity*, ed. Colin Nicholson (London: Macmillan; New York: St Martin's Press, 1994) pp. 68–93.
8. Caskey, 'Interpreting Anorexia Nervosa', p. 181
9. For a fuller account of the psychoanalytic model in feminist criticism, see Chris Weedon, *Feminist Practice and Poststructuralist Theory* (Oxford: Basil Blackwell, 1989), esp. chs 3 and 4.
10. Adrienne Rich, 'When We Dead Awaken', in *On Lies, Secrets and Silence*, p. 42.
11. Gibson, *Eleven Canadian Novelists*, p. 21.
12. For a brief comprehensive discussion of the supernatural in relation to Duncan, see W. J. Keith, *Introducing Margaret Atwood's 'The Edible Woman': A Reader's Guide*, Canadian Fiction Series 3 (Toronto: ECW, 1989) p. 41.
13. Margaret Atwood, 'The Sin Eater', in *Bluebeard's Egg* (Toronto: McClelland & Stewart, 1983) pp. 133–66.
14. Mary Ann Caws, 'Ladies Shot and Painted: Female Embodiment in Surrealist Art', in *The Female Body in Western Culture*, pp. 262–87.
15. Nancy K. Miller, 'Rereading as a Woman: the Body in Practice,' in ibid., pp. 354–62.
16. Atwood, 'The Female Body', pp. 39–46.
17. J. Derrida, 'Structure, Sign and Play in the Discourse of the Human Sciences' (1966), repr. in *Modern Criticism and Theory*, ed. David Lodge (London: Longman, 1988) pp. 108–23.
18. Luce Irigaray, *Ce sexe qui n'en est pas un* [This Sex Which Is Not One], trans. Claudia Reeder, in *New French Feminisms: An Anthology*, ed. E. Marks and I. de Courtivron (Brighton, Sussex: Harvester, 1981) pp. 99–110.
19. Moi, *Sexual/Textual Politics*, p. 130.
20. See Caws, 'Ladies Shot and Painted', for illustrations of Surrealist paintings and photographs.
21. Irigaray, *Ce sexe qui n'en est pas un*, p. 107.
22. Ibid., p. 105.
23. Atwood, *Conversations*, p. 214; see also Carol Gilligan, *In a Different Voice: Psychological Theory and Woman's Development* (Cambridge, Mass., and London: Harvard University Press, 1982) which usefully discusses sexual difference in relation to concepts of identity and moral development.
24. Irigaray, *Ce sexe qui n'en est pas un*, p. 103.
25. Scenarios of male loss are presented by Irigaray and also by Christine Brooke-Rose, 'Woman as a Semiotic Object', in *The Female Body in Western Culture*, pp. 305–16; see also Sandra Gilbert and Susan Gubar's essay

'Sexual Linguistics: Gender, Language, Sexuality', in *The Feminist Reader*, pp. 81–99, which offers speculations on male anxiety about women and 'vagina envy'.
26. Miller, 'Rereading as a Woman', p. 361.
27. Margaret Atwood, 'Alien Territory', in *Good Bones*, p. 80.

Chapter 4 Atwoodian Gothic

1. Margaret Atwood, *Murder in the Dark* (1984) (London: Virago, 1994) pp. 49–50.
2. Eve Kosofsky Sedgwick, *The Coherence of Gothic Conventions* (New York and London: Methuen, 1986) pp. 4–5.
3. For a succinct discussion of the uncanny, see Rosemary Jackson, *Fantasy: The Literature of Subversion* (London: Methuen, 1981) pp. 63–72.
4. Earl Ingersoll (ed.) *Margaret Atwood: Conversations* (London: Virago, 1992) p. 45.
5. See also C A Howells, *Love, Mystery and Misery: Feeling in Goltic Fiction* (London: Athlone Press, 1978); William Patrick Day, *In the Circles of Fear and Desire: A Study of Gothic Fantasy* (Chicago and London: University of Chicago Press, 1985) and Michelle A. Massé, *In the Name of Love: Women, Masochism and the Gothic* (Ithaca, N.Y., and London: Cornell University Press, 1992).
6. Sharon R. Wilson, 'Sexual Politics in Margaret Atwood's Visual Art (With an Eight-Page Color Supplement)', in K. van Spanckeren and J. Garden Castro (eds) *Margaret Atwood: Vision and Forms* (Carbondale: Southern Illinois University Press, 1988) pp. 215–232.
7. *Conversations*, p. 18.
8. C. A. Howells, 'A Question of Inheritance: Canadian Women's Short Stories', in J. Birkett and E. Harvey (eds.), *Determined Women: Studies in the Construction of the Female Subject, 1900-90* (London: Macmillan, 1991) pp. 108–20.
9. Quoted from Atwood's address delivered at a conference 'Imagined Realities in Contemporary Women's Writing', Dyffryn House, Cardiff, October 1982.
10. Margaret Atwood, *Lady Oracle* (1976) (London: Virago, 1993) p. 310.
11. Paul de Man, 'Autobiography as Defacement', *MLN*, vol. 94 (1979) pp. 931–55.
12. For a full account of criticism of *Lady Oracle*, see Margery Fee, *The Fat Lady Dances: Margaret Atwood's Lady Oracle* (Toronto: ECW, 1993).
13. Margaret Atwood Papers, MSS Collection 200, Box 27. See also Marilyn Patton, '*Lady Oracle* and the Politics of the Body', *Ariel*, vol. 22, no. 4 (1991), pp.29–50.
14. Margaret Atwood, *Cat's Eye* (London: Virago, 1989) p. 409.
15. Atwood Papers, letter to Donya Peroff, 16 January 1974 (Box 27).
16. The relation between Gothic romance and the dilemma of domesticity is explored by Kate Ferguson Ellis in *The Contested Castle: Gothic*

Novels and the Subversion of Domestic Ideology (Urbana and Chicago: University of Illinois Press, 1989).

17. Janice Radway, *Reading the Romance: Women, Patriarchy and Popular Literature* (Chapel Hill: University of North Carolina, 1984).

18. See Barbara Godard 'My (m)Other, My Self: Strategies for Subversion in Atwood and Hébert', *ECW*, vol. 26 (1983) pp. 13–44; Marilyn Patton, '*Lady Oracle* and the Politics of the Body', a slightly misleading title, as this valuable essay is concerned with Atwood's feminist revisions of the myth of the White Goddess, analysing with the use of manuscript materials the ways in which this novel exposes socially constructed myths about women. It is interesting also to note in this revisionist context that Adrienne Rich's influential essay on feminist reappropriations of myth, 'When We Dead Awaken: Writing as Re-Vision', first appeared in *College English*, vol. 34, no. 1 (October 1972); reprinted in *On Lies, Secrets and Silence* (London: Virago, 1980).

19. Margaret Atwood, 'Superwoman Drawn and Quartered: the Early Forms of *She*', *Second Words* (Toronto: Anansi, 1982) pp. 35–54.

20. Margaret Atwood, *The Robber Bride* (1993) (London: Virago, 1994) p. 3.

21. Hayden White, 'The Historical Text as Literary Artefact', in *Tropics of Discourse: Essays in Cultural Criticism* (Baltimore, Md, and London: Johns Hopkins University Press, 1978) pp. 81–100.

22. As an interesting historical note which shows how attentive Atwood is to precision of contemporary detail, from 1972–77 there was a Toronto-based feminist collective newspaper called *The Other Woman*. This information is from M. Fulford (ed.), *The Canadian Women's Movement, 1960–1990: A Guide to Archival Resources* (Toronto: ECW, 1992) p. 53.

23. Alison Light, 'Returning to Manderley – Romance Fiction, Sexuality and Class', *Feminist Review*, vol. 16 (1984) pp. 7–25.

Chapter 5   Lost Worlds

1. Margaret Atwood, *Life Before Man* (1979) (London: Virago, 1982) p. 30. All page references will be to this edition and included in the text.

2. Janice Kulyk Keefer, 'Hope against Hopelessness: Margaret Atwood's *Life Before Man*', in C. Nicholson (ed.), *Margaret Atwood: Writing and Subjectivity*, (London: Macmillan; New York: St Martin's Press, 1994) pp. 153–76.

3. Homi K. Bhabha, *The Location of Culture* (London and New York: Routledge, 1994).

4. For other interpretations of the title, see *Margaret Atwood: Conversations*, p. 123.

5. Marilyn French review in *New York Times Book Review*, 3 February 1980.

6. Kulyk Keefer, 'Hope against Hopelessuess', p. 15.

7. David Lodge, '*Middlemarch* and the idea of the classic realist text', in *After Bakhtin: Essays on Fiction and Criticism* (London and New York: Routledge, 1990) pp. 45–56.

8. Margaret Atwood Papers, MS Collection 200, Box 32, Folder 6.
9. George Eliot, *Middlemarch* (1871) (Harmondsworth, Middx: Penguin, 1979) 'Prelude', p. 25.
10. Peter Brooks, *Reading for the Plot: Design and Intention in Narrative* (Oxford: Clarendon Press., 1984) p. 260ff.
11. Margaret Atwood, *Second Words: Selected Critical Prose* (Toronto: Anansi, 1982) p. 334.
12. For discussion of the name 'Lesje', see Irena R. Makaryk, 'Ophelia as Poet: Lesje Ukrainka and the Woman as Artist', *Canadian Review of Comparative Literature/Revue canadienne de la littérature comparée*, vol. 20, nos. 3–4 (1993) pp. 337–54.
13. Bhabha, *The Location of Culture*, p. 181.
14. Kulyk Keefer, 'Hope against Hopelessuess', p. 165; also Linda Hutcheon, *The Canadian Postmodern: A Study of Contemporary English–Canadian Fiction* (London: Oxford University Press, 1988) p. 152.
15. Rosemary Jackson, *Fantasy: The Literature of Subversion* (London: Methuen, 1981) p. 26.
16. David Ketterer, *Canadian Science Fiction and Fantasy* (Bloomington and Indianapolis: Indiana University Press, 1992) pp. 19–22.
17. Atwood, *Second Words*, p. 333.

Chapter 6   Power Politics

1. Margaret Atwood, *Bodily Harm* (1981) (London: Virago, 1983). All references are to this edition and included in the text.
2. Quoted from Atwood's address at a conference held at Dyffryn House, Cardiff, in October 1982 when Atwood received the annual Welsh Writers Prize.
3. MSS Collection 200, Margaret Atwood Papers, Fisher Rare Book Room, Box 33: Folders 2–6; Box 34: Folder 1.
4. For full quotation, see John Berger, *Ways of Seeing* (London: British Broadcasting Commission and Penguin, 1972) pp. 45–6.
5. Lorna Irvine, 'The Here and Now of *Bodily Harm*', in K. Van Spanckeren and J. Garden Castro (eds), *Margaret Atwood: Vision and Forms* (Carbondale: Southern Illinois University Press, 1988) pp. 85–100.
6. Judith McCombs, 'Atwood's Haunted Sequences: *The Circle Game, The Journals of Susanna Moodie* and *Power Politics*', in A. E and C. N. Davidson (eds), *The Art of Margaret Atwood* (Toronto: Anansi, 1981) pp. 35–54.
7. Sonia Mycak, 'Divided and Dismembered: the Decentred Subject in Margaret Atwood's *Bodily Harm*', *Canadian Review of Comparative Literature*, vol. 20, nos 3–4 (1993) pp. 469–78.
8. Robert Miles, *Gothic Writing, 1750–1820: A Genealogy* (London and New York: Routledge, 1993) ch 6: 'Radcliffe and Interiority: Towards the Making of *The Mysteries of Udolpho*', p. 142.
9. Luce Irigaray, 'This Sex Which Is Not One', in E. Marks and Courtivron I. de (eds), *New French Feminisms: An Anthology* (Brighton: Harvester, 1981) p. 101.

10. M. A. Caws, 'Ladies Shot and Painted: Female Embodiment in Surrealist Art', in S. R. Sulieman (ed.), *The Female Body in Western Culture* (Cambridge, Mass., and London: Harvard University Press, 1985) p. 263.

11. Beverley Brown, 'A Feminist Interest in Pornography – Some Modest Proposals' (1981); quoted by Linda Williams, *Hard Core: Power, Pleasure, and the 'Frenzy of the Visible'* (London: Pandora, 1990) p. 269. Williams offers an extremely useful documentation and reinterpretation of the hard-core porn film genre to which I am indebted for information, though my fictional material and interpretations differ in many respects from hers.

12. Ibid., p. 16.

13. Susanne Kappeler, *The Pornography of Representation* (1986), quoted in ibid., p. 18.

14. Ibid., p. 275.

15. Ibid., p. 282.

Chapter 7 Science Fiction in the Feminine

1. Margaret Atwood, *The Handmaid's Tale* (London: Virago, 1987). All further page references will be included in the text.

2. Linda Hutcheon, *The Canadian Postmodern* (London: Oxford University Press, 1988) p. 110.

3. The film of *The Handmaid's Tale*, directed by Volker Schlondorff, produced by Cinecom, Bioskop and Cinetudes, USA and Germany, 1990.

4. For discussions of feminist and distopian elements, see Kate Fullbrook, *Free Women: Ethics and Aesthetics in Twentieth-century Women's Fiction*, (Hemel Hempstead, Herts: Harvester-Wheatsheaf, 1990) ch. 7; Krishan Kumar, *Utopianism* (Milton Keynes: Open University Press, 1991); and Frances Bartowski, *Feminist Utopias* (London and Lincoln, Neb.: University of Nebraska Press, 1989).

5. Margaret Atwood Papers, MS Collection 200, University of Toronto, '*The Handmaid's Tale*: Before and After', November 1986, Box 96, Folder 11.

6. Ibid.

7. Ibid.

8. Zillah R. Eisenstein, 'The Sexual Politics of the New Right: Understanding the "Crisis of Liberalism" for the 1980s', in N. O. Keohane, M. Z. Rosaldo and B. C. Gelpi (eds), *Feminist Theory: A critique of Ideology* (Brighton: Harvester, 1982) pp. 77–98.

9. Howard Phillips (ed.), *The New Right at Harvard* (Virginia: Conservative Caucus Inc. National Headquarters, 1983).

10. Margaret Atwood, 'Witches', reprinted in *Second Words: Selected Critical Prose* (Toronto: Anansi, 1982) pp. 329–33.

11. I am indebted for this information to Mark Evans, 'Versions of History: *The Handmaid's Tale* and its Dedicatees', in Colin Nicholson

(ed.), *Margaret Atwood: Writing and Subjectivity* (London: Macmillan; New York: St Martin's Press, 1994) pp. 177–88.

12. Constance Rooke, 'Interpreting *The Handmaid's Tale*: Offred's Name and "The Arnolfini Marriage"', in *Fear of the Open Heart* (Toronto: Coach House, 1989) pp. 175–96.

13. Jonathan Bignell, 'Lost Messages: "The Handmaid's Tale", Novel and Film', *BJCS*, vol. 8, no. 1 (1993) pp. 71–84.

14. Heather Murray, 'Women in the Wilderness', in S. Newman and S. Kamboureli (eds), *A Mazing Space: Writing Canadian Women Writing* (Edmonton: Longspoon/Newest, 1986) pp. 74–83. In this useful essay, influenced by the American feminist critic Elaine Showalter's 'Feminist Criticism in the Wilderness', Murray comments on women's mediating function between nature and culture as well as on the characteristic features of women's wilderness discourse.

15. Hélène Cixous, 'The Laugh of the Medusa' (1976), trans. Keith and Paula Cohen, repr. in *New French Feminisms: An Anthology*, ed. E. Marks and I. de Courtivron (Brighton: Harvester, 1981) pp. 245–54. All further page references to Cixous's essay will be taken from this edition and included in the text.

16. Margaret Atwood, 'Nothing', from *True Stories, Poems 1976–1986* (London: Virago, 1992) p. 63.

Chapter 8   Retrospective Art

1. Margaret Atwood, 'Instructions for the Third Eye', in *Murder in the Dark* (London: Virago, 1994) p. 108.

2. Stephen Hawking, *A Brief History of Time* (London: Bantam, 1988) p. 28.

3. This point has already been made by Constance Rooke in 'Interpreting *The Handmaid's Tale*: Offred's Name and "The Arnolfini Marriage"', in *Fear of the Open Heart: Essays on Contemporary Writing* (Toronto: Coach House, 1989) pp. 175–96; see also Sherrill Grace, 'Gender as Genre: Atwood's Autobiographical "I"' in Colin Nicholson (ed.), *Margaret Atwood: Writing and Subjectivity* (London: Macmillan, 1994) pp. 189–203.

4. In its use of paintings *Cat's Eye* focuses on a similar area of inquiry to Norman Bryson, *Word and Image: French Painting of the Ancien Régime* (Cambridge: Cambridge University Press, 1981). His discussions about writing and painting have suggested important directions for my inquiry into Atwood's novel.

5. Sharon R. Wilson has commented on Atwood's involvement with the visual arts, discussing photographic images and some early watercolours: 'Camera Images in Margaret Atwood's Novels', in B. Mendez-Egle (ed.), *Margaret Atwood: Reflection and Reality* (Texas: Pan American University Press, 1987) pp. 29–57; and 'Sexual Politics in Margaret Atwood's Visual Art', in K. Van Spanckeren and J. Garden Castro (eds), *Margaret Atwood: Vision and Forms* (Carbondale: Southern Illinois University Press, 1988) pp. 205–14.

6. Margaret Atwood, *Cat's Eye* (1988) (London: Virago, 1990). All page references will be to this edition.
7. There is a third mini-retrospective as well, when Elaine at her mother's house after her father's death finds the cat's eye marble in her old red plastic purse (p. 398).
8. Paul de Man, 'Autobiography as De-facement', *MLN*, vol. 94 (1979) pp. 931–55.
9. Ibid., pp. 926.
10. Ibid., pp. 930.
11. Ibid., pp. 920.
12. Ibid., pp. 922.
13. For definitions of these terms, see Hawking, *A Brief History of Time*, a book to which Atwood draws attention in her Acknowledgements.
14. See Lola Lemire Tostevin's interview with Christopher Dewdney, *Poetry Canada Review*, vol. 3 (1989) pp. 1–3, 29.
15. In my thinking about the way that objects work in texts, I am indebted to Simone Vauthier's exemplary essay, 'Images in Stones, Images in Words', in C. Nicholson (ed.), *Critical Approaches to the Fiction of Margaret Laurence* (London: Macmillan, 1990) pp. 46–70.
16. Atwood, 'Instructions for the Third Eye', pp. 109–10.
17. For a brief discussion of subjectivity, see Toril Moi, *Sexual/Textual Politics* (London: Methuen, 1985) pp. 9–11.
18. Atwood, 'Instructions for the Third Eye', p. 109.
19. Bryson, *Word and Image*, p. 13: 'A sign is always divided into two areas, one which declares its loyalty to the text outside the image, and another which asserts the autonomy of the image: a ratio of the sign which is as important a fact of art history as any of its discoveries about the individual styles that form variables within this overall sign-format – the typical sign-format of painting in the West.'
20. Dennis Lee's definition, quoted by Helen Tiffin, 'Post-Colonial Literature and Counter-Discourse', *Kunapipi*, vol. 9 no. 3 (1987) pp. 17–34.
21. For a glimpse into this territory, see Hawking, *A Brief History of Time*, pp. 155–69.
22. De Man, 'Autobiography as De-facement', p. 922.
23. Ibid.
24. Elaine's final words echo Stephen's (p. 104); see also Hawking, *A Brief History of Time*, p. 28.

Conclusion

1. Virginia Woolf, *The Waves* (1931), repr. in *Collected Novels of Virginia Woolf*, ed. Stella McNichol (London: Macmillan, 1992) p. 429.
2. Margaret Atwood, 'True Stories', in *Poems 1976–1986* (London: Virago, 1992) p. 58.
3. Margaret Atwood, 'Not the Moon', in ibid., pp. 146–7.

Bibliography

Primary Sources

All references in this text to Margaret Atwood's novels, short stories and poetry* are to Virago Press Ltd editions.

The Edible Woman (1969) (London: Virago, 1980).
Surfacing (1972) (London: Virago, 1979).
Lady Oracle (1976) (London: Virago, 1993).
Life Before Man (1979) (London: Virago, 1992).
Bodily Harm (1981) (London: Virago, 1983).
Murder in the Dark: Short Fictions and Prose Poems (1983) (London: Virago, 1994).
The Handmaid's Tale (1985) (London: Virago, 1987).
Poems: 1976–1986 (1987) (London: Virago, 1992).
Cat's Eye (1988) (London: Virago, 1994).
Wilderness Tips (1991) (London: Virago, 1992).
Good Bones (1992) (London: Virago, 1993).
The Robber Bride (1993) (London: Virago, 1994).

Margaret Atwood: Conversations, ed. Earl E. Ingersoll (London: Virago, 1992)

*Texts from which I quote which are published in Canada and not available in Virago:
The Journals of Susanna Moodie (Toronto: Oxford University Press, 1970).
Survival: A Thematic Guide to Canadian Literature (Toronto: Anansi, 1972).
Second Words: Selected Critical Prose (Toronto: Anansi, 1982).

Secondary Sources

Bartowski, Frances, *Feminist Utopias* (Lincoln and London: University of Nebraska Press, 1989).
Belsey, Catherine and Jane Moore (eds), *The Feminist Reader: Essays in Gender and the Politics of Literary Criticism* (London: Macmillan, 1989).

Berger, John, *Ways of Seeing* (London: British Broadcasting Corporation and Penguin Books, 1972)

Bhabha, Homi K., *The Location of Culture* (London and New York: Routledge, 1994)

Bignell, Jonathan, '*The Handmaid's Tale*: Novel and Film', *British Journal of Canadian Studies*, vol. 8, no. 1 (1993) pp. 71–84

Birkett, J. and E. Harvey (eds), *Determined Women: Studies in the Construction of the Female Subject, 1909–90* (London: Macmillan, 1991)

Bowlby, Rachel, *Shopping with Freud* (London and New York: Routledge, 1993)

Brooks, Peter, *Reading for the Plot: Design and Intention in Narrative* (Oxford: Clarendon Press, 1984)

Brown L. and F. Nussbaum (eds), *The New Eighteenth Century: Theory, Politics, English Literature* (London and New York: Methuen, 1987)

Bryson, Norman, *Word and Image: French Painting of the Ancien Regime* (Cambridge: Cambridge University Press, 1981)

Carrington, Ildiko de Papp, *Margaret Atwood*, Canadian Writers and Their Works: Fiction Series, vol. 9 (Toronto: ECW Press, 1987) pp. 25–119

Cixous, Hélène, 'The Laugh of the Medusa' (1976), repr. in *New French Feminisms: An Anthology*, ed. Elaine Marks and Isabelle de Courtivron (Brighton: Harvester, 1981) pp. 245–64

Cluett, Robert, *Canadian Literary Prose: A Preliminary Stylistic Atlas* (Toronto: ECW, 1990)

Davey, Frank, *Margaret Atwood: A Feminist Poetics* (Vancouver: Talonbooks, 1984)

_____, *Post-National Arguments: The Politics of the Anglophone-Canadian Novel* (Toronto, Buffalo, London: University of Toronto Press, 1993)

Davidson, A. E. and Cathy N. Davidson (eds), *The Art of Margaret Atwood: Essays in Criticism* (Toronto: Anansi, 1981)

Day, W. P., *In the Circles of Fear and Desire: A Study of Gothic Fantasy* (Chicago and London: University of Chicago Press, 1985)

Derrida, Jacques, 'Signature Event Context', in *Margins of Philosophy*, trans. Alan Bass (New York and London: Harvester-Wheatsheaf, 1982) pp. 307–30

Ellis, Kate Ferguson, *The Contested Castle: Gothic Novels and the Subversion of Domestic Ideology* (Urbana and Chicago: University of Illinois Press, 1989)

Fee, Margery, *The Fat Lady Dances: Margaret Atwood's 'Lady Oracle'* (Toronto: ECW, 1993)

Friedan, Betty, *The Feminine Mystique* (1963) (London: Gollancz, 1965)

Frye, Northrop, *The Bush Garden* (Toronto: Anansi, 1971)

Fulford, Margaret (ed.), *The Canadian Women's Movement, 1960–1990: A Guide to Archival Resources/Le Mouvement Canadien des Femmes, 1960–1990: Guide des resources archivistiques* (Toronto: ECW, 1992)

Fullbrook, Kate, *Free Women: Ethics and Aesthetics in Twentieth-century Women's Fictions* (Hemel Hempstead: Harvester-Wheatsheaf, 1990)

Gibson, Graeme, *Eleven Canadian Novelists* (Toronto: Anansi, 1973)

Godard, Barbara, 'My (m)Other, My Self: Strategies for Subversion in Atwood and Hébert', *ECW*, vol. 26 (1982) pp. 13–44

Grace, Sherrill and Lorraine Weir, *Margaret Atwood: Language, Text and System* (Vancouver, UBC, 1983)

Gilligan, Carol, *In a Different Voice: Psychological Theory and Women's Development* (Cambridge, Mass., and London: Harvard University Press, 1982)

Hawking, Stephen, *A Brief History of Time* (London: Bantam, 1988)

Howells, Coral Ann, *Love, Mystery and Misery: Feeling in Gothic Fiction* (London: Athlone Press, 1978).

Howells, Coral Ann, *Private and Fictional Words: Canadian Women Novelists of the 1970s and 80s* (London: Methuen, 1987)

Humm, Maggie, *Border Traffic: Strategies of Contemporary Women Writers* (Manchester and New York: Manchester University Press, 1991)

——(ed.), *Feminisms: A Reader* (New York and London: Harvester-Wheatsheaf, 1992)

Hurley, Michael, *The Borders of Nightmare: The Fiction of John Richardson* (Toronto: University of Toronto Press, 1992)

Hutcheon, Linda, *The Canadian Postmodern: A Study of Contemporary English–Canadian Fiction* (Toronto: Oxford University Press, 1988)

Irigaray, Luce, 'This Sex Which Is Not One' and 'When the Goods Get Together', trans. Claudia Reeder, repr. In *New French Feminisms: An Anthology*, ed. Elaine Marks and Isabelle de Courtivron (Brighton: Harvester, 1981) pp. 99–110

Irvine, Lorna, *Sub/Version* (Toronto: ECW, 1986)

Jackson, Rosemary, *Fantasy: The Literature of Subversion* (London: Methuen, 1981).

Keith, W. J., *Introducing Margaret Atwood's 'The Edible Woman': A Reader's Guide* (Toronto: ECW, 1989)

——, *A Sense of Style* (Toronto: ECW, 1989)

Keohane, N. O., M. Z. Rosaldo and B. G. Gelpi (eds), *Feminist Theory: A Critique of Ideology* (Brighton: Harvester, 1982)

Ketterer, David, *Canadian Science Fiction and Fantasy* (Bloomington and Indianapolis: Indiana University Press, 1992)

Kumar, Krishan, *Utopianism* (Milton Keynes: Open University Press, 1991)

Lecker, Robert (ed.), *Canadian Canons: Essays in Literary Value* (Toronto: University of Toronto Press, 1991)

Light, Alison, 'Returning to Manderley: Romance Fiction, Sexuality, and Class', *Feminist Review*, vol. 16 (1984) pp. 7–25

Lodge, David, *After Bakhtin: Essays on Fiction and Criticism* (London and New York: Routledge, 1990)

Makaryk, Irena, K., 'Ophelia as Poet: Lesje Ukrainka and the Woman as Artist', *Canadian Review of Comparative Literature*, vol. 20, nos 3–4 (1993) pp. 337–54

Man, Paul de, 'Autobiography as Defacement', *Modern Language Notes*, vol. 94 (1979) pp. 931–55

Marks, Elaine and Isabelle de Courtivron (eds), *New French Feminisms: An Anthology* (Brighton: Harvester, 1981)

Massé, Michelle A., *In the Name of Love: Women, Masochism and the Gothic* (Ithaca, N.Y., and London: Cornell University Press, 1992)

McCombs, Judith (ed.), *Critical Essays on Margaret Atwood* (Boston: Mass. G. K. Hall, 1988)

Mendez-Egle, Beatrice (ed.), *Margaret Atwood: Reflection and Reality* (Edinburg, Texas: Pan American University, 1988)

Miles, Robert, *Gothic Writing 1750–1820* (London and New York: Routledge, 1993).

Moi, Toril, *Sexual/Textual Politics* (London: Routledge, 1985)

Mycak, Sonia, 'Divided and Dismembered: the Decentred Subject in M. Atwood's *Bodily Harm*', *Canadian Review of Comparative Literature*, vol. 20, nos 3–4 (1993) pp. 469–78

Neuman, Shirley and Smaro Kamboureli (eds), *A Mazing Space: Writing Canadian Women Writing* (Edmonton: Longspoon/NeWest, 1986)

Nicholson, Colin (ed.), *Critical Approaches to the Fiction of Margaret Laurence* (London: Macmillan, 1990)

——(ed.), *Margaret Atwood: Writing and Subjectivity* (London: Macmillan; New York: St Martin's Press, 1994)

Patton, Marilyn, '*Lady Oracle* and the Politics of the Body', *Ariel*, vol. 22, no. 1 (1991) pp. 29–50

Radway, Janice, *Reading the Romance: Women, Patriarchy and Popular Literature* (Chapel Hill: University of North Carolina Press, 1984)

Rich, Adrienne, *On Lies, Secrets and Silence: Selected Critical Prose 1966–1978* (London: Virago, 1980)

Rigney, Barbara Hill, *Margaret Atwood*, Women Writers Series (London: Macmillan, 1987)

Rooke, Constance, *Fear of the Open Heart: Essays on Contemporary Writing* (Toronto: Coach House, 1989)

Sedgwick, Eve Kosofsky, *The Coherence of Gothic Conventions* (New York and London: Methuen, 1986)

Still, Judith and Michael Worton (eds), *Textuality and Sexuality: Reading Theories and Practices* (Manchester and New York: Manchester University Press, 1993)

Suleiman, Susan Rubin (ed.), *The Female Body in Western Culture: Contemporary Perspectives* (Cambridge, Mass., and London: Harvard University Press, 1985)

Tiffin, Helen, 'Post-colonial Literature and Counter-discourse', *Kunapipi*, vol. 9, no. 3 (1987) pp. 17–34

Van Spanckeren, Kathryn and Jan Garden Castro, *Margaret Atwood: Vision and Forms* (Carbondale: Southern Illinois University Press, 1988)

Weedon, Chris, *Feminist Practice and Poststructuralist Theory* (Oxford: Basil Blackwell, 1987)

White, Hayden, *Tropics of Discourse: Essays in Cultural Criticism* (Baltimore, Md, and London: Johns Hopkins University Press, 1978)

Williams, Linda, *Hard Core: Power, Pleasure, and the 'Frenzy of the Visible'* (London: Pandora, 1990)

Woodcock, George, *Introducing Margaret Atwood's 'Surfacing': A Reader's Guide* (Toronto: ECW, 1990)

Index